iOS Game Development Cookbook

Jonathon Manning and Paris Buttfield-Addison

Beijing · Cambridge · Farnham · Köln · Sebastopol · Tokyo

iOS Game Development Cookbook

by Jonathon Manning and Paris Buttfield-Addison

Printed in the United States of America.

Published by O'Reilly Media, Inc., 1005 Gravenstein Highway North, Sebastopol, CA 95472.

O'Reilly books may be purchased for educational, business, or sales promotional use. Online editions are also available for most titles (*http://my.safaribooksonline.com*). For more information, contact our corporate/institutional sales department: 800-998-9938 or *corporate@oreilly.com*.

Editor: Rachel Roumeliotis	**Indexer:** Ellen Troutman-Zaig
Production Editor: Melanie Yarbrough	**Cover Designer:** Karen Montgomery
Copyeditor: Rachel Head	**Interior Designer:** David Futato
Proofreader: Jasmine Kwityn	**Illustrator:** Rebecca Demarest

April 2014:   First Edition

Revision History for the First Edition:

2014-04-09:   First release

See *http://oreilly.com/catalog/errata.csp?isbn=9781449368760* for release details.

ISBN: 978-1-449-36876-0

[LSI]

Table of Contents

Preface

Games rule mobile devices. The iPhone, iPad, and iPod touch are all phenomenally powerful gaming platforms, and making amazing games that your players can access at a moment's notice has never been easier. The iTunes App Store category with the most apps is Games; it includes games ranging from simple one-minute puzzle games to in-depth, long-form adventures. The time to jump in and make your own games has never been better. We say this having been in iOS game development since the App Store opened: Our first iOS game, in 2008, a little strategy puzzler named *Culture*, led us to working on a hundreds of other awesome projects, ranging from a digital board game for museums to educational children's games, and everything in between! The possibilities for games on this platform are only becoming wider and wider.

This book provides you with simple, direct solutions to common problems found in iOS game programming. If you're stuck figuring out how to give objects physical motion, how to handle Game Center, or just want a refresher on common gaming-related math problems, you'll find simple, straightforward answers, explanations, and sample projects. This book is designed as part-way between a series of tutorials and a reference work: it's something you'll want to keep handy for quick reference, as well as browse through to get new ideas about what's possible.

Audience

We assume that you're a reasonably capable programmer, and assume that you know at least a little bit about developing for iOS: what Xcode is and how to get around in it, how to use the iOS Simulator, and the basics of the Objective-C programming language. We also assume you know how to use an iOS device. We don't assume any existing knowledge of game development on any platform, but we're guessing that you're reading this book with a vague idea about the kind of game you'd like to make.

This book isn't based on any particular genre of games—you'll find the recipes in it applicable to all kinds of games, though some will suit some genres more than others.

Organization of This Book

Each chapter of this book contains *recipes*: short solutions to common problems found in game development. The book is designed to be read in any order; you don't need to read it cover-to-cover, and you don't need to read any chapter from start to finish. (Of course, we encourage doing that, since you'll probably pick up on stuff you didn't realize you wanted to know.)

Each recipe is structured like this: the **problem** being addressed is presented, followed by the **solution**, which explains the technique of solving the problem (or implementing the feature, and so on). Following the solution, the recipe contains a **discussion** that goes into more detail on the solution, which gives you more information about what the solution does, what other things to watch out for, and other useful knowledge.

Here is a concise breakdown of the material each chapter covers:

Chapter 1, Laying Out a Game
> This chapter discusses different ways to design the architecture and code layout of your game, how to work with timers in a variety of different ways, and how blocks work in iOS. You'll also learn how to schedule work to be performed in the future using blocks and operation queues, and how to add unit tests to your project.

Chapter 2, Views and Menus
> This chapter focuses on interface design, and working with UIKit, the built-in system for displaying user interface graphics. In addition to providing common objects like buttons and text fields, UIKit can be customised to suit your needs—for some kinds of games, you might not need to use any more complex graphical tools than it.

Chapter 3, Input
> In this chapter, you'll learn how to get input from the user so that you can apply it to your game. This includes touching the screen, detecting different types of gestures (such as tapping, swiping and pinching), as well as other kinds of input like the user's current position on the planet, or motion information from the variety of built-in sensors in the device.

Chapter 4, Sound
> This chapter discusses how to work with sound effects and music. You'll learn how to load and play audio files, how to work with the user's built-in music library, and how to make your game's sound work well when the user wants to listen to their music while playing your game.

Chapter 5, Data Storage
> This chapter is all about storing information for later use. The information that games need to save ranges from the very small (such as high scores), to medium (saved games), all the way up to very large (collections of game assets). In this

chapter, you'll learn about the many different ways that information can be stored and accessed, and which of these is best suited for what you want to do.

Chapter 6, 2D Graphics and Sprite Kit

This chapter discusses Sprite Kit, the 2D graphics system built into iOS. Sprite Kit is both powerful and very easy to use; in this chapter, you'll learn how to create a scene, how to animate sprites, and how to work with textures and images. This chapter also provides you with info you can use to brush up on your 2D math skills.

Chapter 7, Physics

In this chapter, you'll learn how to use the two-dimensional physics simulation that's provided as part of Sprite Kit. Physics simulation is a great way to make your game's movements feel more realistic, and you can use it to get a lot of great-feeling game for very little programmer effort. You'll learn how to work with physics bodies, joints and forces, as well as how to take user input and make it control your game's physical simulation.

Chapter 8, 3D Graphics

This chapter and the two that follow it provide a tutorial on OpenGL ES 2, the 3D graphics system used on iOS. These three chapters follow a slightly different structure to the rest of the book, because it's not quite as easy to explain parts of OpenGL in isolation. Instead, these chapters follow a more linear approach, and we recommend that you read the recipes in order, so that you can get the best use out of them. Chapter 8 introduces the basics of OpenGL, and shows you how to draw simple shapes on the screen; at the same time, the math behind the graphics is explained.

Chapter 9, Intermediate 3D Graphics

This chapter is designed to follow on from the previous, and discusses more advanced techniques in 3D graphics. You'll learn how to load a 3D object from a file, how to animate objects, and how to make a camera that moves around in 3D space.

Chapter 10, Advanced 3D Graphics

This chapter follows on from the previous two, and focuses on shaders, which give you a tremendous amout of control over how objects in your game look. You'll learn how to write shader code, how to create different shading effects (including diffiuse and specular lighting, cartoon shading, and more), and how to make objects transparent.

Chapter 11, Artificial Intelligence and Behavior

This chapter discusses how to make objects in your game behave on their own, and react to the player. You'll learn how to make an object chase another, make objects flee from something, and how to work out a path from one point to another while avoiding obstacles.

Chapter 12, Networking and Social Media

In this chapter, you'll learn about Game Center, the social network and match-making system built into iOS. You'll learn how to get information about the player's profile, as well as let the player connect to their friends. On top of this, you'll also learn how to connect to nearby devices using Bluetooth. Finally, you'll learn how to share text, pictures and other content to social media sites like Twitter and Facebook.

Chapter 13, Game Controllers and External Screens

This chapter discusses the things that players can connect to their device: external displays, like televisions and monitors, and game controllers that provide additional input methods like thumbsticks and physical buttons. You'll learn how to detect, use and design your game to take advantage of additional hardware where it's present.

Chapter 14, Performance and Debugging

The last chapter of the book looks at improving your game's performance and stability. You'll learn how to take advantage of advanced Xcode debugging features, how to use compressed textures to save memory, and how to make your game load faster.

Additional Resources

You can download, or fork using GitHub, the code samples from this book at *https://github.com/thesecretlab/iOSGameDevCookbook1stEd*.

O'Reilly has a number of other excellent books on game development and software development (both generally, and related to iOS) available that can help you on your iOS game development journey, including:

- *Physics for Game Developers*
- *Learning Cocoa with Objective-C* (by us!)
- *Programming iOS 7*

We strongly recommend that you add Gamasutra (*http://gamasutra.com*) to your regular reading list, due to the high quality of their coverage of game industry news.

Game designer Marc LeBlanc's website (*http://8kindsoffun.com*) is where he collects various presentations, notes, and essays. We've found him to be a tremendous inspiration.

Finally, we'd be remiss if we didn't link to our own blog (*http://secretlab.com.au*).

Conventions Used in This Book

The following typographical conventions are used in this book:

Italic

Indicates new terms, URLs, email addresses, filenames, and file extensions.

`Constant width`

Used for program listings, as well as within paragraphs to refer to program elements such as variable or function names, databases, data types, environment variables, statements, and keywords.

`Constant width bold`

Shows commands or other text that should be typed literally by the user.

`Constant width italic`

Shows text that should be replaced with user-supplied values or by values determined by context.

 This element signifies a tip or suggestion.

 This element signifies a general note.

 This element indicates a warning or caution.

Using Code Examples

Supplemental material (code examples, exercises, etc.) is available for download at *https://github.com/thesecretlab/iOSGameDevCookbook1stEd*.

This book is here to help you get your job done. In general, if example code is offered with this book, you may use it in your programs and documentation. You do not need to contact us for permission unless you're reproducing a significant portion of the code. For example, writing a program that uses several chunks of code from this book does not require permission. Selling or distributing a CD-ROM of examples from O'Reilly books does require permission. Answering a question by citing this book and quoting example code does not require permission. Incorporating a significant amount of example code from this book into your product's documentation does require permission.

We appreciate, but do not require, attribution. An attribution usually includes the title, author, publisher, and ISBN. For example: "*iOS Game Development Cookbook* by Jonathan Manning and Paris Buttfield-Addison (O'Reilly). Copyright 2014 Jonathon Manning and Paris Buttfield-Addison, 978-1-449-36876-0."

If you feel your use of code examples falls outside fair use or the permission given above, feel free to contact us at *permissions@oreilly.com*.

Safari® Books Online

 Safari Books Online is an on-demand digital library that delivers expert content in both book and video form from the world's leading authors in technology and business.

Technology professionals, software developers, web designers, and business and creative professionals use Safari Books Online as their primary resource for research, problem solving, learning, and certification training.

Safari Books Online offers a range of product mixes and pricing programs for organizations, government agencies, and individuals. Subscribers have access to thousands of books, training videos, and prepublication manuscripts in one fully searchable database from publishers like O'Reilly Media, Prentice Hall Professional, Addison-Wesley Professional, Microsoft Press, Sams, Que, Peachpit Press, Focal Press, Cisco Press, John Wiley & Sons, Syngress, Morgan Kaufmann, IBM Redbooks, Packt, Adobe Press, FT Press, Apress, Manning, New Riders, McGraw-Hill, Jones & Bartlett, Course Technology, and dozens more. For more information about Safari Books Online, please visit us online.

How to Contact Us

Please address comments and questions concerning this book to the publisher:

O'Reilly Media, Inc.
1005 Gravenstein Highway North
Sebastopol, CA 95472
800-998-9938 (in the United States or Canada)
707-829-0515 (international or local)
707-829-0104 (fax)

We have a web page for this book, where we list errata, examples, and any additional information. You can access this page at *http://oreil.ly/ios_game_dev_cookbook*.

To comment or ask technical questions about this book, send email to *bookques tions@oreilly.com*.

For more information about our books, courses, conferences, and news, see our website at *http://www.oreilly.com*.

Find us on Facebook: *http://facebook.com/oreilly*

Follow us on Twitter: *http://twitter.com/oreillymedia*

Watch us on YouTube: *http://www.youtube.com/oreillymedia*

Acknowledgement

Jon thanks his mother, father, and the rest of his weirdly extended family for their tremendous support.

Paris thanks his mother, whose credit card bankrolled literally hundreds of mobile devices through his childhood—an addiction that, in all likelihood, created the gadget-obsessed monster he is today. He can't wait to read her upcoming novel.

Thank you to our editor, Rachel Roumeliotis, who kept the book under control and provided a ton of useful advice on content. We know it was a ton because we measured it. Likewise, all the O'Reilly Media staff and contractors we've worked with over the course of writing the book have been absolutely fantastic, and every one of them made this book better for having had them work on it. Thank you also to Brian Jepson, our first editor at O'Reilly.

A huge thank you to Tony Gray and the AUC for the monumental boost they gave us and many others listed on this page. We wouldn't be working in this industry, let alone writing this book, if it wasn't for Tony and the AUC community.

Thanks also to Neal Goldstein, who richly deserves all of the credit and/or blame for getting both of us into the whole book-writing racket.

We'd like to thank the support of the goons at Maclab, who know who they are and continue to stand watch for Admiral Dolphin's inevitable apotheosis, as well as Professor Christopher Lueg, Dr Leonie Ellis, and the rest of the staff at the University of Tasmania for putting up with us.

Additional thanks to Tim N, Nic W, Andrew B, Jess L, and Rex S for a wide variety of reasons. Thanks also to Ash Johnson, for general support.

Finally, very special thanks to Steve Jobs, without whom this book (and many others like it) would not have reason to exist.

CHAPTER 1

Laying Out a Game

Games are software, and the best software has had some thought put into it regarding how it's going to work. When you're writing a game, you need to keep in mind how you're going to handle the individual tasks that the game needs to perform, such as rendering graphics, updating artificial intelligence (AI), handling input, and the hundreds of other small tasks that your game will need to deal with.

In this chapter, you'll learn about ways you can lay out the structure of your game that will make development easier. You'll also learn how to organize the contents of your game so that adding more content and gameplay elements is easier, and find out how to make your game do multiple things at once.

1.1. Laying Out Your Engine

Problem

You want to determine the best way to lay out the architecture of your game.

Solution

The biggest thing to consider when you're thinking about how to best lay out your game is how the game will be updated. There are three main things that can cause the state of the game to change:

Input from the user

> The game may change state when the user provides some input, such as tapping a button or typing some text. Turn-based games are often driven by user input (e.g., in a game of chess, the game state might only be updated when the user finishes moving a piece).

Timers
> The game state may change every time a timer goes off. The delay between timer updates might be very long (some web-based strategy games have turns that update only once a day), or very short (such as going off every time the screen finishes drawing). Most real-time games, like shooters or real-time strategy games, use very short-duration timers.

Input from outside
> The game state may change when information from outside the game arrives. The most common example of this is some information arriving from the network, but it can also include data arriving from built-in sensors, such as the accelerometer.
>
> Sometimes, this kind of updating is actually a specific type of timer-based update, because some networks or sensors need to be periodically checked to see if new information has arrived.

Discussion

None of these methods are mutually exclusive. You can, for example, run your game on a timer to animate content, and await user input to move from one state to the next.

Updating every frame is the least efficient option, but it lets you change state often, which makes the game look smooth.

1.2. Creating an Inheritance-Based Game Layout

Problem

You want to use an inheritance-based (i.e., a hierarchy-based) architecture for your game, which is simpler to implement.

Solution

First, define a class called GameObject:

```
@interface GameObject : NSObject {
}

- (void) update:(float)deltaTime;

@end

@implementation GameObject

- (void) update:(float)deltaTime {
        // Do some updating
}
```

```
@end
```

When you want to create a new *kind* of game object, you create a subclass of the `Game Object` class, which inherits all of the behavior of its parent class and can be customized:

```
@interface Monster : GameObject {
}

@property (assign) float hitPoints; // num of times it can be hit without dying
@property (weak) GameObject* targetObject; // try to kill this object

@end

@implementation Monster

- (void) update:(float)deltaTime {
        [super update:deltaTime];

        // Do some monster-specific updating
}

@end
```

Discussion

In an inheritance-based layout, as seen in Figure 1-1, you define a single base class for your game object (often called `GameObject`), which knows about general tasks like being updated, and then create subclasses for each specific type of game object. This hierarchy of subclasses can be multiple levels deep (e.g., you might subclass the `GameObject` class to make the `Monster` subclass, and then subclass *that* to create the `Goblin` and `Dragon` classes, each of which has its own different kinds of monster-like behavior).

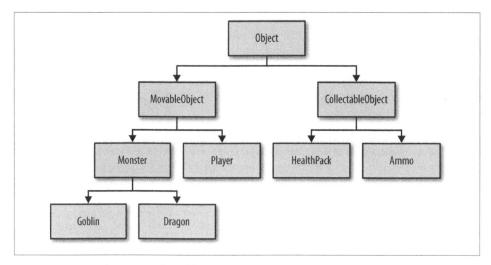

Figure 1-1. An inheritance-based layout

The advantage of a hierarchy-based layout is that each object is able to stand alone: if you have a Dragon object, you know that all of its behavior is contained inside that single object, and it doesn't rely on other objects to work. The downside is that you can often end up with a very deep hierarchy of different game object types, which can be tricky to keep in your head as you program.

1.3. Creating a Component-Based Game Layout

Problem

You want to use a component-based architecture for your game, which allows for greater flexibility.

Solution

First, define a Component class. This class represents components that are attached to game objects—it is a very simple class that, at least initially, only has a single method and a single property:

```
@class GameObject;
@interface Component : NSObject

- (void) update:(float)deltaTime;

@property (weak) GameObject* gameObject;
@end
```

Next, define a GameObject class. This class represents game objects:

```
#import "Component.h"

@interface GameObject : NSObject

@property (strong) NSSet* components;

- (void) addComponent:(Component*)component;
- (void) removeComponent:(Component*)component;

- (void)update:(float)deltaTime;

- (id)componentWithType:(Class)componentType;
- (NSArray*)componentsWithType:(Class)componentType;
@end
```

The implementation for this class looks like this:

```
#import "GameObject.h"

@implementation GameObject {
    NSMutableSet* _components;
}

@synthesize components = _components;

- (id)init {
    self = [super init];

    if (self) {
        _components = [NSMutableSet set];
    }

    return self;
}

- (void)addComponent:(Component *)component {
    [_components addObject:component];
component.gameObject = self;
}

- (void)removeComponent:(Component *)component {
    [_components removeObject:component];
component.gameObject = nil;
}

- (void)update:(float)deltaTime {
    for (Component* component in _components) {
        [component update:deltaTime];
    }
}

- (id)componentWithType:(Class)componentType {
    // Helper function that just returns the first component with a given type
```

```
        return [[self componentsWithType:componentType] firstObject];
    }

    - (NSArray*)componentsWithType:(Class)componentType {
        // Return nil if the class isn't actually a type of component
        if ([componentType isSubclassOfClass:[Component class]] == NO)
            return nil;

        // Work out which components match the component type, and return them all
        return [[_components objectsPassingTest:^BOOL(id obj, BOOL *stop) {
            return [obj isKindOfClass:componentType];
        }] allObjects];
    }
    @end
```

Using these objects looks like this:

```
    // Make a new game object
    GameObject gameObject = [[GameObject alloc] init];

    // Add some components
    Component* component = [[Component alloc] init];
    [gameObject addComponent:component];

    // When the game needs to update, send all game objects the "update" message
    // This makes all components get updated as well
    [gameObject update];
```

Discussion

In a component-based architecture, as seen in Figure 1-2, each game object is made up of multiple components. Compare this to an inheritance-based architecture, where each game object is a subclass of some more general class (see Recipe 1.2).

A component-based layout means you can be more flexible with your design and not worry about inheritance issues. For example, if you've got a bunch of monsters, and you want one specific monster to have some new behavior (such as, say, exploding every five seconds), you just write a new component and add it to that monster. If you later decide that you want other monsters to also have that behavior, you can add that behavior to them too.

In a component-based architecture, each game object has a list of components. In this recipe, we're using an NSMutableSet, which means that if you add the same component more than once, the list will only contain one copy of the component. When something happens to an object—for example, the game updates, or the object is added to or removed from the game—the object goes through each one of its components and notifies them. This gives them the opportunity to respond in their own way.

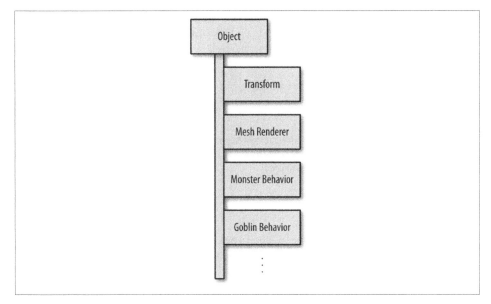

Figure 1-2. A component-based layout

The main problem with component-based architectures is that it's more laborious to create multiple copies of an object, because you have to create and add the same set of components every time you want a new copy.

1.4. Calculating Delta Times

Problem

You want to know how many seconds have elapsed since the last time the game updated.

Solution

First, decide which object should be used to keep track of time. This may be a view controller, an SKScene, a GLKViewController, or something entirely custom.

Create an instance variable inside that object:

```
@interface MyTimeKeepingObject {
        double lastFrameTime;
}
```

Then, each time your game is updated, get the current time in milliseconds, and subtract lastFrameTime from that. This gives you the amount of time that has elapsed since the last update.

When you want to make something happen at a certain rate—for example, moving at 3 meters per second—multiply the rate by the delta time:

```
- (void)update:(double)currentTime {

    double deltaTime = currentTime - lastFrameTime;

    // Move at 3 units per second
    float movementSpeed = 3;
    [someObject moveAtSpeed:movementSpeed * deltaTime];

    lastFrameTime = currentTime;
}
```

Discussion

"Delta time" means "change in time." Delta times are useful to keep track of how much time has elapsed from one point in time to another—in games, this means the time from one frame to the next. Because the game content changes frame by frame, the amount of time between frames becomes important.

Additionally, the amount of time between frames might change a little. You should always be aiming for a constant frame rate of 60 frames per second (i.e., a delta time of 16 milliseconds: $1 \div 60 = 0.0166$); however, this may not always be achievable, depending on how much work needs to be done in each frame. This means that delta time might vary slightly, so calculating the delta time between each frame becomes necessary if you want rates of change to appear constant.

Some engines give you the delta time directly. For example, CADisplayLink gives you a duration property (see Recipe 1.7), and GLKViewController gives you timeSinceLastUpdate (see Recipe 8.6).

Some engines give you just the current time, from which you can calculate the delta time. For example, the SKScene class passes the currentTime parameter to the update: method (discussed further in Recipe 7.15).

In other cases (e.g., if you're doing the main loop yourself), you won't have easy access to either. In these cases, you need to get the current time yourself:

```
double currentTime = [NSDate timeIntervalSinceReferenceDate];
```

1.5. Detecting When the User Enters and Exits Your Game

Problem

You want to detect when the user leaves your game, so that you can pause the game. You also want to know when the user comes back.

Solution

To get notified when the user enters and exits your game, you register to receive notifications from an NSNotificationCenter. The specific notifications that you want to receive are UIApplicationDidBecomeActiveNotification, UIApplicationWillEnterForegroundNotification, UIApplicationWillResignActiveNotification, and UIApplicationDidEnterBackgroundNotification:

```
- (void)viewDidAppear:(BOOL)animated {
    // Called when the application becomes the active one
    // (i.e., when nothing's covering it up)
    [[NSNotificationCenter defaultCenter]
        addObserver:self selector:@selector(applicationDidBecomeActive:)
        name:UIApplicationDidBecomeActiveNotification object:nil];

    // Called when the application will enter the foreground (i.e.,
    // when the user has left another app and entered this one)
    [[NSNotificationCenter defaultCenter]
        addObserver:self selector:@selector(applicationWillEnterForeground:)
        name:UIApplicationWillEnterForegroundNotification object:nil];

    // Called when the application will resign active (i.e., when something's
    // covering it up, like the notification tray or a phone call)
    [[NSNotificationCenter defaultCenter]
        addObserver:self selector:@selector(applicationWillResignActive:)
        name:UIApplicationWillResignActiveNotification object:nil];

    // Called when the application enters the background
    // (i.e., when the user has left it)
    [[NSNotificationCenter defaultCenter]
        addObserver:self selector:@selector(applicationDidEnterBackground:)
        name:UIApplicationDidEnterBackgroundNotification object:nil];

}

- (void)viewDidDisappear:(BOOL)animated {
    [[NSNotificationCenter defaultCenter] removeObserver:self];
}

- (void) applicationDidBecomeActive:(NSNotification*)notification {
    NSLog(@"Application did become active!");
}

- (void) applicationWillResignActive:(NSNotification*)notification {
    NSLog(@"Application will resign active!");
}

- (void) applicationDidEnterBackground:(NSNotification*)notification {
    NSLog(@"Application did enter background!");
}
```

```
- (void) applicationWillEnterForeground:(NSNotification*)notification {
    NSLog(@"Application will enter foreground!");
}
```

Discussion

On iOS, only one app can be the "active" application (i.e., the app that is taking up the screen and that the user is interacting with). This means that apps need to know when they become the active one, and when they stop being active.

When your game is no longer the active application, the player can't interact with it. This means that the game should pause (see Recipe 1.8). When the game resumes being the active application, the player should see a pause screen.

 Pausing, of course, only makes sense in real-time games, such as shooters, driving games, arcade games, and so on. In a turn-based game, like a strategy or puzzle game, you don't really need to worry about the game being paused or not.

In addition to being the active application, an application can be in the *foreground* or the *background*. When an application is in the foreground, it's being shown on the screen. When it's in the background, it isn't visible at all. Apps that are in the background become *suspended* after a short period of time, to save battery power. Apps that enter the background should reduce their memory consumption as much as possible; if your app consumes a large amount of memory while it is in the background, it is more likely to be terminated by iOS.

1.6. Updating Based on a Timer

Problem

You want to update your game after a fixed amount of time.

Solution

Use an NSTimer to receive a message after a certain amount of time, or to receive an update on a fixed schedule.

First, add an instance variable to your view controller:

```
NSTimer* timer;
```

Next, add a method that takes an NSTimer parameter:

```
- (void) updateWithTimer:(NSTimer*) timer {
    // The timer's gone off; update the game
```

```
    NSLog(@"Updated from timer!");
}
```

Finally, when you want to start the timer:

```
timer = [NSTimer scheduledTimerWithTimeInterval:0.5
    target:self selector:@selector(updateWithTimer:) userInfo:nil repeats:YES];
```

To stop the timer:

```
[timer invalidate];
timer = nil;
```

Discussion

An NSTimer waits for a specified number of seconds, and then calls a method on an object that you specify. You can change the number of seconds by changing the time-Interval parameter:

```
// Wait 2 seconds
[NSTimer scheduledTimerWithTimeInterval:2
    target:self selector:@selector(updateWithTimer:) userInfo:nil repeats:YES];

// Wait 0.1 seconds (100 milliseconds)
[NSTimer scheduledTimerWithTimeInterval:0.1
    target:self selector:@selector(updateWithTimer:) userInfo:nil repeats:YES];
```

You can also make a timer either fire only once or repeat forever, by changing the repeats parameter to NO or YES, respectively.

1.7. Updating Based on When the Screen Updates

Problem

You want to update your game every time the screen redraws.

Solution

Use a CADisplayLink, which sends a message every time the screen is redrawn.

First, add an instance variable to your view controller:

```
@interface ViewController () {
    CADisplayLink* displayLink;
}
```

Next, add a method that takes a single parameter (a CADisplayLink):

```
- (void) update:(CADisplayLink*)displayLink {
    // The screen's just updated; update the game
    NSLog(@"Updated from display link!");
}
```

Finally, add this code when you want to begin receiving updates:

```
// Create the CADisplayLink; "self" will receive the updateWithDisplayLink:
// message every time the screen updates
displayLink = [CADisplayLink
    displayLinkWithTarget:self selector:@selector(update:)];

// Add the display link and start receiving updates
[displayLink addToRunLoop:[NSRunLoop mainRunLoop] forMode:NSRunLoopCommonModes];
```

When you want to pause receiving updates, set the paused property of the CADisplay Link to YES:

```
displayLink.paused = YES;
```

When you want to stop receiving updates, call invalidate on the CADisplayLink:

```
[displayLink invalidate];
displayLink = nil;
```

Discussion

When we talk about "real-time" games, what comes to mind is objects like the player, vehicles, and other things moving around the screen, looking like they're in continuous motion. This isn't actually what happens, however—what's really going on is that the screen is redrawing itself every 1/60th of a second, and every time it does this, the locations of some or all of the objects on the screen change slightly. If this is done fast enough, the human eye is fooled into thinking that everything's moving continuously.

In fact, you don't technically *need* to update as quickly as every 1/60th of a second—anything moving faster than 25 frames per second (in other words, one update every 1/25th of a second) will look like motion. However, faster updates yield smoother-looking movement, and you should always aim for 60 frames per second.

You'll get the best results if you update your game at the same rate as the screen. You can achieve this with a CADisplayLink, which uses the Core Animation system to figure out when the screen has updated. Every time this happens, the CADisplayLink sends its target a message, which you specify.

It's worth mentioning that you can have as many CADisplayLink objects as you like, though they'll all update at the same time.

1.8. Pausing a Game

Problem

You want to be able to pause parts of your game, but still have other parts continue to run.

Solution

Keep track of the game's "paused" state in a `BOOL` variable. Then, divide your game objects into two categories—ones that run while paused, and ones that don't run while paused:

```
// This is just pseudocode--your game will likely look slightly different
for (GameObject* gameObject in gameObjects) {
        if (paused == NO || gameObject.shouldPause == NO) {
                [gameObject update];
        }
}
```

Discussion

The simplest possible way to pause the game is to keep track of a pause state; every time the game updates, you check to see if the pause state is set to `YES`, and if it is, you don't update any game objects.

However, you often don't want every single thing in the game to freeze. For example:

- The user interface may need to continue to animate.
- The network may need to keep communicating with other computers, rather than stopping entirely.

In these cases, having special objects that never get paused makes more sense.

1.9. Calculating Time Elapsed Since the Game Start

Problem

You want to find out how much time has elapsed since the game started.

Solution

When the game starts, create an `NSDate` object and store it:

```
// In your class's @interface:
@property (strong) NSDate* gameStartDate;
```

```
// When the game starts:
self.gameStartDate = [NSDate date];
```

When you want to find out how much time has elapsed since the game started, create a second NSDate and use the timeIntervalSinceDate: method to calculate the time:

```
NSDate* now = [NSDate date];

NSTimeInterval timeSinceGameStart =
    [self.gameStartDate timeIntervalSinceDate:self.gameStartDate];

NSLog(@"The game started %.2f seconds ago", timeSinceGameStart);
```

Discussion

NSDate objects represent moments in time. They're the go-to object for representing any instant of time that you want to be able to refer to again later, such as when your game starts. NSDate objects can refer to practically any date in the past or future and are very precise.

When you create an NSDate with the [NSDate date] method, you get back an NSDate object that refers to the current time (i.e., the instant when the NSDate object was created).

To determine the interval between two dates, you use timeIntervalSinceDate:. This method returns an NSTimeInterval, which is actually another term for a floating-point number. These values are represented in seconds, so it's up to your code to do things like determine the number of hours and minutes:

```
NSTimeInterval timeElapsed = ... // an NSTimeInterval from somewhere

float minutes = timeElapsed / 60.0; // 60 seconds per minute
float hours = timeElapsed / 3600.0; // 3600 seconds per hour
float seconds = fmodf(timeElapsed, 60.0); // get the remainder

NSLog(@"Time elapsed:%.0f:%.0f:%.2f", hours, minutes, seconds);
```

1.10. Working with Blocks

Problem

You want to store some code in a variable, for later execution.

Solution

Blocks are ideal for this:

```
void(^onCollision)(void);
```

```
onCollision = ^(void) {
    NSLog(@"Character collided with something!");
};

// Later, when a collision happens:
onCollision();
```

Discussion

Blocks are a language feature in Objective-C that allow you to store chunks of code in variables, which can then be worked with like any other variable.

Here's an example of a simple block:

```
void(^MyBlock)(void); ❶
MyBlock = ^(void) { ❷
    NSLog(@"Hello from the block!");
};
MyBlock(); ❸
```

❶   This is how you define a block. In this case, the block returns void, is named MyBlock, and accepts no parameters.

❷   Just like any other variable, once a block is defined, it needs to be given a value. In this case, we're providing a block that takes no parameters and returns nothing, just like the block variable's definition.

❸   Calling a block works just like calling any other function.

How blocks work

So far, this just seems like a very roundabout way to call a function. However, the real power of blocks comes from two facts:

- Blocks *capture the state* of any other variables their code references.
- Blocks are objects, and they stay around until you need them. If you store a block, you can call it however often you like.

Let's talk about the first point. Say you had a block like this:

```
int i = 1;

void(^MyBlock)(void) = ^(void) {
    NSLog(@"i = %i", i);
};

MyBlock();
```

As you'd expect, running this code would print i = 1 to the console. But watch what happens when you change the value of i *after* creating the block, like this:

```
int i = 1;

void(^MyBlock)(void) = ^(void) {
    NSLog(@"i = %i", i);
};

i = 5;

MyBlock();
```

This code will print the following to the console:

```
i = 1
```

That's right—running this code produces the *same* result as the first version. Even though the i variable has been modified, the console will still print i = 1. This is because i had the value of 1 at the moment the block was created—the fact that i was later changed to 5 doesn't affect the block's copy of that variable.

This is extremely powerful, because it means that your game doesn't need to carefully store values for later use; if a block needs a value, it automatically keeps it.

The syntax for creating blocks is a little messy, with carets (^) and parentheses all over the place. An easier way to do it is to define a *block type*, which is just a simple type definition of a block. For example, here's a block type for the preceding examples:

```
typedef void(^ExampleBlock)(void);
```

This allows you to declare variables with nicer syntax, and with significantly fewer parentheses and carets:

```
ExampleBlock myBlock = ^(void) {
    NSLog(@"i SPILL my DRINK!");
};
```

So far, we've talked entirely about blocks that don't have parameters or return types. These are easy to define, though. For example, here's a block that returns a BOOL and takes two parameters, one NSString and one int:

```
typedef BOOL(^ParameterBlock)(NSString* string, int number);
```

The syntax to create this block is very similar to the earlier examples:

```
ParameterBlock paramBlock = ^(NSString* string, int number) {
    NSLog(@"I received a string %@, and a number %i!", string, number);

    return YES;
};

paramBlock(@"Hello", 1337);
```

If your block doesn't take any parameters, you can actually skip the parameter list entirely:

```
typedef void(^ExampleBlock)(void);

[...]

ExampleBlock aBlock = ^{
    NSLog(@"Whoa!");
};
```

Blocks and other objects

When a block is created, the compiler looks at all of the variables that the block is referencing. If a variable is a simple value, like an int or a float, that value is simply copied. However, if the variable is an Objective-C object, it can't be copied, because it could potentially be very large. Instead, the object is *retained* by the block. When a block is freed, any objects retained by the block are released.

This means that if you have a block that references another object, that block will keep the other object around.

For example, say you have code that looks like this:

```
NSString* aString = [NSString stringWithFormat:@"One = %i", 1];

void(^MyBlock)(void) = ^(void) {
    NSLog(@"The string is %@", aString);
};

aString = nil;

// aString is still in memory, because MyBlock is keeping it around!
```

The block MyBlock, because it references the aString object, will maintain an owning reference to aString. This means that even if all other references to aString go away, the string is kept in memory, and it will only be released when MyBlock goes away. (This example only makes sense if you're using automatic reference counting, or ARC—which you should be.)

This is usually what you want, since it would be annoying to have to remember to keep the variables referenced by blocks in memory. However, sometimes that's not what you want.

One example is when you want a block to run in two seconds' time that causes an enemy object to run an attack animation. However, between the time you schedule the block and the time the block runs, the enemy is removed from the game. If the block has a strong reference to the enemy, the enemy isn't actually removed from memory until the block is scheduled to run, which could have unintended side effects.

To get around this problem, you use *weak references*. A weak reference is a reference that does not keep an object in memory; additionally, if the object that is being referred to is removed (because all owning references to it have gone away), the weak reference will automatically be set to nil.

You create a weak reference by prepending the keyword __weak to a variable declaration, like so:

```
__weak NSString* weakString = aString;
```

This makes weakString into a weak reference to aString. Now, when aString is removed from memory, the weakString reference will automatically point to nil instead.

Using weak references, the previous example code looks like this:

```
NSString* aString = [NSString stringWithFormat:@"One = %i", 1];

__weak NSString* weakString = aString;

void(^MyBlock)(void) = ^(void) {
    NSLog(@"The string is %@", weakString);
};

aString = nil;

// aString is no longer in memory, and calling MyBlock will print
// "The string is (null)"
```

1.11. Writing a Method That Calls a Block

Problem

You want to write a method that, after performing its work, calls a block to indicate that the work is complete.

For example, you want to tell a character to start moving to a destination, and then run a block when the character finishes moving.

Solution

To create a method that takes a block as a parameter, you just do this:

```
- (void) moveToPosition:(CGPoint)position
    completionBlock:(void (^)(void))completion {

    // Do the actual work, which might take place over several frames
    [...]

    // Call the completion block
    if (completion != nil) {
        completion();
```

```
    }
}
```

And to pass the block to the method, you do this:

```
CGPoint destination = ...
[someObject moveToPosition:destination completionBlock:^{
    NSLog(@"Finished moving!");
}];
```

Discussion

Methods that take a block as a parameter are useful for when you're writing code that starts off a long-running process, and you want to run some code at the conclusion of that process but want to keep that conclusion code close to the original call itself.

Before blocks were added to the Objective-C language, the usual technique was to write two methods: one where you started the long-running process, and one that would be called when the process completed. This separates the various parts of the code, which decreases the readability of your code; additionally, passing around variables between these two methods is more complicated (because you need to manually store them in a temporary variable at the start, and retrieve them at the end; with blocks, you just use the variables without any additional work).

1.12. Working with Operation Queues

Problem

You want to put chunks of work in a queue, so that they're run when the operating system has a moment to do them.

Solution

Use an NSOperationQueue to schedule blocks to be run in the background without interfering with more time-critical tasks like rendering or accepting user input:

```
NSOperationQueue* concurrentQueue = [[NSOperationQueue alloc] init];
concurrentQueue.maxConcurrentOperationCount = 10;

[concurrentQueue addOperationWithBlock:^{
    UploadHighScores();
}];

[concurrentQueue addOperationWithBlock:^{
    SaveGame();
}];

[concurrentQueue addOperationWithBlock:^{
```

```
    DownloadMaps();
}];
```

Discussion

An operation queue is a tool for running chunks of work. Every application has an operation queue called the *main queue*. The main queue is the queue that normal application tasks (e.g., handling touches, redrawing the screen, etc.) are run on.

 Many tasks can only be run on the main queue, including updating anything run by UIKit. It's also a good idea to only have a single operation queue that's in charge of sending OpenGL instructions.

The main queue is a specific NSOperationQueue, which you can access using the mainQueue method:

```
NSOperationQueue* mainQueue = [NSOperationQueue mainQueue];

[mainQueue addOperationWithBlock:^{
    ProcessPlayerInput();
}];
```

It's often the case that you want to do something in the background (i.e., on another operation queue), and then alert the user when it's finished. However, as we've already mentioned, you can only do UIKit or OpenGL tasks (e.g., displaying an alert box) on the main queue

To address this, you can put tasks on the main queue from inside a background queue:

```
NSOperationQueue* backgroundQueue = [[NSOperationQueue alloc] init];

[backgroundQueue addOperationWithBlock:^{
    [[NSOperationQueue mainQueue] addOperationWithBlock:^{
        NSLog(@"This is run on the main queue");
    }];
}];
```

An operation queue runs as many operations as it can simultaneously. The number of concurrent operations that can be run depends on a number of conditions, including the number of processor cores available, and the different priorities that other operations may have.

By default, an operation queue determines the number of operations that it can run at the same time on its own. However, you can specify a maximum number of concurrent operations by using the maxConcurrentOperationCount property:

```
NSOperationQueue* aQueue = [[NSOperationQueue alloc] init];
aQueue.maxConcurrentOperationCount = 2;
```

1.13. Performing a Task in the Future

Problem

You want to run some code, but you want it to happen a couple of seconds from now.

Solution

Use `dispatch_after` to schedule a block of code to run in the future:

```
// Place a bomb, but make it explode in 10 seconds
PlaceBomb();

double timeToWait = 10.0;
dispatch_time_t delayTime = dispatch_time(DISPATCH_TIME_NOW,
    (int64_t)(timeToWait * NSEC_PER_SEC));

dispatch_queue_t queue = dispatch_get_main_queue();

dispatch_after(delayTime, queue, ^(void){
    // Time's up. Kaboom.
    ExplodeBomb();
});
```

Discussion

`NSOperationQueue` is actually a higher-level wrapper around the lower-level features provided by the C-based *Grand Central Dispatch* API. Grand Central Dispatch, or GCD, works mostly with objects called "dispatch queues," which are basically `NSOperation` `Queues`. You do work with GCD by putting blocks onto a queue, which runs the blocks. Just as with `NSOperationQueue`, there can be many queues operating at the same time, and they can be serial or concurrent queues.

GCD provides a function called `dispatch_after` that runs a block on an operation queue at a given time. To use the function, you first need to figure out the time when the block should be run. GCD doesn't actually work in seconds, or even in nanoseconds, but rather with time units called `dispatch_time_t`, which Apple's documentation (*http://bit.ly/1fHgXco*) describes as "a somewhat abstract representation of time."

To work with `dispatch_time_t`, you use the function `dispatch_time`, which takes two parameters: a base time and an amount of time to be added on top, measured in nanoseconds.

Therefore, to get a `dispatch_time_t` that represents 1 second in the future, you would use this:

```
double timeToWait = 1.0;
dispatch_time_t delayTime = dispatch_time(DISPATCH_TIME_NOW,
    (int64_t)(timeToWait * NSEC_PER_SEC));
```

Once you have a time for the block to run at, you need to get a reference to a GCD dispatch_queue. You can create your own, but you generally only want the main queue, which you can get using dispatch_get_main_queue:

```
dispatch_queue_t queue = dispatch_get_main_queue();
```

Finally, you instruct GCD to run the block:

```
dispatch_after(delayTime, queue, ^(void){
    NSLog(@"Delayed block");
});
```

1.14. Storing Blocks in Objects

Problem

You want to store a block in an object, so that the object can call it later.

Solution

Blocks can be stored as properties in objects. For example:

```
typedef void(^CallbackBlock)(void);

@interface Monster : NSObject

@property (copy) CallbackBlock onDeathBlock;
@property (copy) CallbackBlock onHitBlock;

@end

[...]

// In the Monster class:
- (void) die {
    self.onDeathBlock();
}

- (void) hit {
    self.onHitBlock();
}

[...]

Monster* monster = ...

monster.onDeathBlock = ^{
```

```
        NSLog(@"Monster died!");
    };

    monster.onHitBlock = ^{
        NSLog(@"Monster hit something")!
    };
```

Note that the property settings for the aBlock copy in this example indicate that the block should be copied. This is important—if you don't do this, then your application will crash when you try to call it.

The reason for this is that when a block is created, it's created on the stack. When the function that it's created in returns, the block is destroyed.

Copying a block moves the block from the stack to the heap, which means that the block stays around after the function that created it returns. It also means that the block needs to be explicitly freed (though ARC handles this for you, either when you set the property that contains the block to nil or when the object is freed).

Discussion

A block stored as a property can be accessed just like any other variable, and called like all blocks are:

```
- (void) doSomething {
    self.aBlock();
}
```

 If you call a block that's set to nil, your app will crash. For example:

```
ExampleBlock aBlock = nil;
aBlock(); // CRASH!
```

You need to do explicit checking if you want to be safe:

```
if (aBlock != nil) {
    aBlock();
}
```

When you store a block as a property of an object, it's important to remember that blocks can retain objects. If an object is retaining a block, and that block is retaining the object as well, you have a *retain cycle*.

Say you have a block that looks like this:

```
void(^MyBlock)(void) = ^(void) {
    NSLog(@"I am %@", self); // block now retains self
};

self.aBlock = MyBlock; // self now retains block; retain cycle!
```

Note how `MyBlock` references the `self` object. The compiler notices this, and will make the block retain the `self` object in memory (because in order for the block to function, it needs to be able to use that variable, which means that the object that that variable points to needs to be kept around). See Figure 1-3.

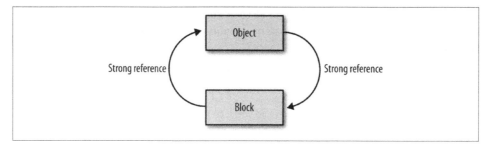

Figure 1-3. Retain cycles

However, if you store that block in a property in `self`, the block and the object will be retaining each other. This prevents the object from being removed from memory when all other strong references to it have gone away, as shown in Figure 1-4.

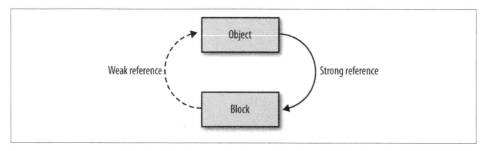

Figure 1-4. A fixed retain cycle

To prevent this from happening, you should always use *weak* references to `self` by declaring the variable with the __weak keyword:

```
__weak id weakSelf = self;

void(^MyBlock)(void) = ^(void) {
    NSLog(@"I am %@", weakSelf); // block does NOT retain self
};

self.aBlock = MyBlock; // self now retains block; no retain cycle
```

1.15. Using a Timer

Problem

You want to create a timer that repeatedly calls a block.

Solution

First, create an instance variable to store the timer:

```
@interface ViewController () {
    dispatch_source_t timer;
}

@end
```

Then, create the timer like so:

```
// Get the queue to run the blocks on
dispatch_queue_t queue = dispatch_get_main_queue();

// Create a dispatch source, and make it into a timer that goes off every second
timer = dispatch_source_create(DISPATCH_SOURCE_TYPE_TIMER, 0, 0, queue);

dispatch_source_set_timer(timer, DISPATCH_TIME_NOW, 1 * NSEC_PER_SEC, 0);

// When the timer goes off, heal the player
dispatch_source_set_event_handler(timer, ^{
    GivePlayerHitPoints();
});

// Dispatch sources start out paused, so start the timer by resuming it
dispatch_resume(timer);
```

To cancel the timer, just set the `timer` variable to `nil`:

```
timer = nil;
```

Discussion

In addition to dispatch queues, GCD has a concept called a *dispatch source*, which is something that triggers work to be done. Dispatch sources can be created for things like file I/O where you can run a block when data is available to be read, and timers, where you run a block at a fixed interval.

To create a dispatch timer, you first create a `dispatch_source_t`, and then configure it to be a timer. As part of setting it up, you also give it a `dispatch_queue_t` for it to run its code on:

```
dispatch_queue_t queue = dispatch_get_main_queue();

timer = dispatch_source_create(DISPATCH_SOURCE_TYPE_TIMER, 0, 0, queue);
```

The next step is to tell the timer how often it should be fired. This is defined in nano-seconds:

```
dispatch_source_set_timer(timer, DISPATCH_TIME_NOW, 1 * NSEC_PER_SEC, 0);
```

Finally, you provide the timer with the block that should be run every time the timer goes off. Dispatch sources start out paused, so you also need to unpause the timer by calling `dispatch_resume`:

```
dispatch_source_set_event_handler(timer, ^{
    GivePlayerHitPoints();
});

dispatch_resume(timer);
```

When you want to stop the timer, you just set it to `nil`. ARC knows about GCD objects, so setting it to `nil` will cause it to be cleaned up properly.

1.16. Making Operations Depend on Each Other

Problem

You want to run some operations, but they need to run only after certain other operations are done.

Solution

To make an operation wait for another operation to complete, store each individual operation in a variable, and then use the `addDependency:` method to indicate which operations need to complete before a given operation begins:

```
NSBlockOperation* firstOperation = [NSBlockOperation blockOperationWithBlock:^{
    NSLog(@"First operation");
}];

NSBlockOperation* secondOperation = [NSBlockOperation blockOperationWithBlock:^{
    NSLog(@"Second operation (depends on third operation and first operation)");
}];

NSBlockOperation* thirdOperation = [NSBlockOperation blockOperationWithBlock:^{
    NSLog(@"Third operation");
}];

[secondOperation addDependency:thirdOperation];
[secondOperation addDependency:firstOperation];
```

```
[[NSOperationQueue mainQueue] addOperations:@[firstOperation, secondOperation,
    thirdOperation] waitUntilFinished:NO];
```

Discussion

You can add an operation to another operation as a *dependency*. This is useful for cases where you want one block to run only after one or more operations have completed.

To add a dependency to an operation, you use the addDependency: method. Doing this doesn't run the operation, but just links the two together.

Once the operation dependencies have been set up, you can add the operations to the queue in any order that you like; operations will not run until all of their dependencies have finished running.

1.17. Filtering an Array with Blocks

Problem

You have an array, and you want to filter it with your own custom logic.

Solution

Use the filteredArrayUsingPredicate method to create an array that only contains objects that meet certain conditions:

```
NSArray* array = @[@"One", @"Two", @"Three", @"Four", @"Five"];

NSLog(@"Original array: %@", array);

array = [array filteredArrayUsingPredicate:
    [NSPredicate predicateWithBlock:^BOOL(id evaluatedObject,
                                          NSDictionary *bindings) {

    NSString* string = evaluatedObject;

    // Search for an "e" in the string
    if ([string rangeOfString:@"e"].location != NSNotFound)
        return YES;
    else
        return NO;

}]];

NSLog(@"Filtered array: %@", array);
```

Discussion

Arrays can be filtered using the `filteredArrayUsingPredicate:` method. This method uses an `NSPredicate` to test each object in the array, and returns a new array; if an object passes the test, it's included in the new array.

`NSPredicate` objects can be set up to run their tests in a variety of ways. One of them is by providing a block, which receives the object to be tested and returns a `BOOL` value: YES means it's included, and NO means it's not.

Note that using `filteredArrayUsingPredicate:` doesn't modify the existing array, but rather creates a new one.

1.18. Loading New Assets During Gameplay

Problem

You want to load new resources without impacting the performance of the game.

Solution

For each resource that needs loading, run a block that does the loading into memory, and run it in the background. Then run a subsequent block when all of the blocks have completed.

You can do this through *dispatch groups*, which are a way to submit multiple units of work to Grand Central Dispatch:

```
NSArray* imagesToLoad = [NSArray array];

dispatch_group_t group = dispatch_group_create();
dispatch_queue_t backgroundQueue = dispatch_get_global_queue(
    DISPATCH_QUEUE_PRIORITY_BACKGROUND, 0);

for (NSString* imageFileName in imagesToLoad) {
    dispatch_group_async(group, backgroundQueue, ^{
        // Load the file
    });
}

dispatch_queue_t mainQueue = dispatch_get_main_queue();

dispatch_group_notify(group, mainQueue, ^{
    // All images are done loading at this point
});
```

Discussion

Using a dispatch group will make GCD spin up as many threads as it needs to load all of the resources.

You can control how much CPU time will be allocated to the loading task by changing the priority of the background queue. Here are the available priorities:

DISPATCH_QUEUE_PRIORITY_HIGH
: Blocks on this queue will be scheduled to run before those on all other lower-priority queues.

DISPATCH_QUEUE_PRIORITY_DEFAULT
: Blocks on this queue will be scheduled to run after those on high-priority queues, but before blocks on low-priority queues.

DISPATCH_QUEUE_PRIORITY_LOW
: Blocks on this queue will be scheduled to run after those on all other higher-priority queues.

DISPATCH_QUEUE_PRIORITY_BACKGROUND
: The same as PRIORITY_LOW, but the system will dedicate even fewer resources to it.

When you create a dispatch group with `dispatch_group_create`, you add one or more blocks to it. You can also add a *notification* block, which is run immediately after all blocks in the dispatch group have finished running. It's generally good practice to put the notification block on the main queue, so that it's easier to coordinate with other parts of your game's engine.

1.19. Adding Unit Tests to Your Game

Problem

You want to test different parts of your game's code in isolation, so that you can ensure that each part is working.

Solution

You can write code that tests different parts of your app in isolation using unit tests. By default, all newly created projects come with an empty set of unit tests, in which you can add isolated testing functions.

If you're working with an existing project, you can create a new set of unit tests by choosing File→New→Target and creating a Cocoa Touch Unit Testing Bundle.

You'll find your unit test files in a group whose name ends with `Tests`. For example, if your Xcode project is called `MyAwesomeGame`, your testing files will be in a group named `MyAwesomeGameTests`, and it will by default come with a file called *MyAwesomeGameTests.m*.

When you want to add a test, open your test file (the *.m* file) and add a method whose name begins with `test`:

```
- (void) testDoingSomethingCool {

    SomeAwesomeObject* object = [[SomeAwesomeObject alloc] init];

    BOOL succeeded = [object doSomethingCool];

    if (succeeded == NO) {
            XCTFail("Failed to do something cool");
    }

}
```

When you want to run the tests, choose Product→Test or press Command-U. All of the methods in your testing classes that begin with `test` will be run, one after the other.

You can also add additional collections of tests, by creating a new *test suite*. You do this by choosing File→New→File and creating a new Objective-C test case class. When you create this new class, don't forget to make it belong to your testing target instead of your game target, or you'll get compile errors.

Discussion

Unit testing is the practice of writing small tests that test specific features of your code. In normal use, your code is used in a variety of ways, and if there's a bug, it can be difficult to track down exactly why your code isn't behaving the way you want it to. By using unit tests, you can run multiple tests of your code and check each time to see if the results are what you expect. If a test fails, then the parts of your game that use your code in that particular way will also fail.

Each test is actually a method in a *test case*. Test cases are subclasses of `XCTestCase` whose names begin with `test`. The `XCTestCase` objects in a testing bundle make up a *test suite*, which is what's run when you tell Xcode to test your application.

When tests run, Xcode performs the following tasks for each test method, in each test case, in each test suite:

- Call the test case's `setUp` method.
- Call the test method itself, and note if the test succeeds or fails.
- Call the test case's `tearDown` method.
- Show a report showing which tests failed.

As you can see, the test case's `setUp` and `tearDown` methods are called for *each* test method. The idea behind this is that you use `setUp` to create whatever conditions you want to run your test under (e.g., if you're testing the behavior of an AI, you could use `setUp` to load the level that the AI needs to operate in). Conversely, the `tearDown` method is used to dismantle whatever resources are set up in `setUp`. This means that each time a test method is run, it's operating under the same conditions.

The contents of each test method are entirely up to you. Typically, you create objects that you want to test, run methods, and then check to see if the outcomes were what you expected. The actual way that you check the outcomes is through a collection of dedicated *assertion methods*, which flag the test as failing if the condition you pass in evaluates to false. The assertion methods also take a string parameter, which is shown to the user if the test fails.

For example:

```
// Fails if X is not nil
XCTAssertNil(X, @"X should be nil");

// Fails if X IS nil
XCTAssertNotNil(X, @"X should not be nil");

// Fails if X is not true
XCTAssertTrue(1 == 1, @"1 really should be equal to 1");

// Fails if X is not false
XCTAssertFalse(2 != 3, @"In this universe, 2 equals 3 apparently");

// Fails if X and Y are not equal (tested by calling [X equals:Y])
XCTAssertEqualObjects(@(2), @(1+1), @"Objects should be equal");

// Fails if X and Y ARE equal (tested by calling [X equals:Y])
XCTAssertNotEqualObjects(@"One", @"1", @"Objects should not be equal");

// Fails, regardless of circumstances
XCTFail("Everything is broken");
```

There are several other assertion methods available for you to use that won't fit in this book; for a comprehensive list, see the file *XCTestAssertions.h* (press Command-Shift-O and type **XCTestAssertions** then press Enter).

1.20. 2D Grids

Problem

You want to store objects in a two-dimensional grid.

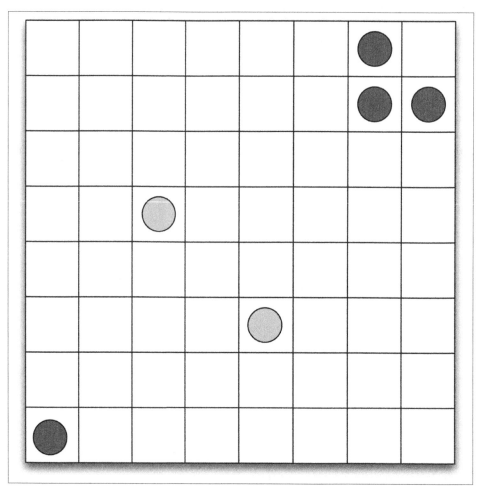

Figure 1-5. The grid: a digital frontier

Solution

Use a Grid class, which lets you store and look up objects.

Create an NSObject subclass called Grid, and put the following code in *Grid.h*:

```
#import <Foundation/Foundation.h>

// Grid points are just integers defining the location of an object
typedef struct {
    int x;
    int y;
} GridPoint;

enum {GridPointNotValid = INT_MAX};

@interface Grid : NSObject

// Returns the list of objects that occupy the given position
- (NSArray*) objectsAtPosition:(GridPoint)position;

// Returns a GridPoint describing the position of an object
- (GridPoint) positionForObject:(id)objectToFind;

// Adds or move the object to a location on the board
- (void) addObject:(id)object atPosition:(GridPoint)position;

// Removes a given object from the board
- (void) removeObjectFromGrid:(id)object;

// Removes all objects at a given point from the board
- (void) removeAllObjectsAtPosition:(GridPoint)position;

// Removes all objects from the board.
- (void) removeAllObjects;

@end
```

Then, put the following code in *Grid.m*:

```
#import "Grid.h"

@implementation Grid {
    NSMutableDictionary* _grid;
}

- (id)init
{
    if((self = [super init]))
    {
        // Create the dictionary that maps all objects to locations
        _grid = [[NSMutableDictionary alloc] init];
    }
```

```
        return self;
}

// Returns an NSString given a point. For example, the location (1,2)
// is turned into "1-2".
- (NSString*) keyForGridPoint:(GridPoint)position {
    return [NSString stringWithFormat:@"%i-%i", position.x, position.y];
}

// Returns a GridPoint given a key. The string "1-2" is turned into (1,2).
- (GridPoint) gridPointForKey:(NSString*)key {

    // Split the string into two
    NSArray* components = [key componentsSeparatedByString:@"-"];

    // Check to see if there are exactly two components; if not, it's not
    // a valid grid point and so return (GridPointNotValid,GridPointNotValid).
    if (components.count != 2)
        return (GridPoint){GridPointNotValid,GridPointNotValid};

    // Construct and return the grid point
    return (GridPoint){[components[0] intValue], [components[1] intValue]};
}

// Returns the array containing all objects at a given position
- (NSArray*) objectsAtPosition:(GridPoint)position {
    NSString* key = [self keyForGridPoint:position];

    return [_grid objectForKey:key];
}

// Returns the array containing a specific object
- (NSMutableArray*) arrayContainingObject:(id)object {
    for (NSMutableArray* array in _grid) {
        if ([array containsObject:object])
            return array;
    }

    return nil;
}

// Returns the GridPoint for an object on the board
- (GridPoint) positionForObject:(id)objectToFind {

    // Find the array containing this object
    NSArray* arrayWithObject = [self arrayContainingObject:objectToFind];

    // Find the key associated with this array
    NSString* key = [[_grid allKeysForObject:arrayWithObject] lastObject];

    // Convert the key into a grid point and return it
    return [self gridPointForKey:key];
```

```
}

// Adds an object to the board. It's moved from its previous location
// if necessary.
- (void) addObject:(id)object atPosition:(GridPoint)position {

    // First, remove the object from its current location
    [self removeObjectFromGrid:object];

    // Next, work out which array it should go in. If no suitable array exists,
    // create a new one.
    NSString* key = [self keyForGridPoint:position];

    NSMutableArray* foundArray = [_grid objectForKey:key];

    if (foundArray == nil) {
        foundArray = [NSMutableArray array];
        [_grid setObject:foundArray forKey:key];
    }

    // Finally, add the object if it doesn't already exist.
    if ([foundArray containsObject:object] == NO) {
        [foundArray addObject:object];
    }
}

// Removes an object from the board.
- (void) removeObjectFromGrid:(id)object {
    NSMutableArray* arrayContainingObject = [self arrayContainingObject:object];
    [arrayContainingObject removeObject:object];
}

// Removes all objects from a position on the board.
- (void) removeAllObjectsAtPosition:(GridPoint)position {
    [_grid removeObjectForKey:[self keyForGridPoint:position]];
}

// Removes all objects.
- (void) removeAllObjects {

    // Blow away the existing dictionary and replace it with an empty one.
    _grid = [NSMutableDictionary dictionary];
}

@end
```

Discussion

When working with 2D grids, you usually have two main tasks that you want to perform with it:

- You have a game object on the board, and want to work out *where* on the board it is.

- You have a location on the board, and you want to work out *what* object (or objects) are at that point on the board.

This `Grid` class doesn't require that you limit the board to a pre-defined size. Any location works, as long the number doesn't exceeed the integer limit (that is, −2,147,483,648 to 2,147,483,647).

This class implements grids by using an `NSDictionary` to map locations to mutable arrays of objects. When you add a piece to the board, the class works out which array should contain the object (and creates one if necessary) and inserts it. Later, when you want to get the objects at a given location, it simply looks up the location in the dictionary.

 For small boards (for example, those with a size of about 14×14), you can get away with a simple implementation. However, this implementation will slow down when you start having larger boards (especially with many objects on the board). In those cases, you'd be better off creating multiple dictionaries for different areas of the board (for example, one for the upper-left corner, one for the top-right, and so on). This improves the lookup speed of getting objects at a location, though it complicates your implementation.

CHAPTER 2

Views and Menus

When you fire up a game, you don't often get immediately dropped into the action. In most games, there's a lot of "non-game" stuff that your game will need to deal with first, such as showing a settings screen to let your player change volume levels and the like, or a way to let the player pick a chapter in your game to play.

While it's definitely possible to use your game's graphics systems to show this kind of user interface, there's often no reason to re-create the built-in interface libraries that already exist on iOS.

UIKit is the framework that provides the code that handles controls like buttons, sliders, image views, and checkboxes. Additionally, UIKit has tools that let you divide up your game's screens into separate, easier-to-work-with units called *view controllers*. These view controllers can in turn be linked up together using *storyboards*, which let you see how each screen's worth of content connects to the others.

The controls available to you in UIKit can also be customized to suit the look and feel of your game, which means that UIKit can fit right into your game's visual design. In addition to simply tinting the standard iOS controls with a color, you can use images and other material to theme your controls. This means that you don't have to reimplement standard stuff like sliders and buttons, which saves you a lot of time in programming your game.

To work with menus, it's useful to know how to work with storyboards. So, before we get into the meat of this chapter, we'll first talk about how to set up a storyboard with the screens you want.

2.1. Working with Storyboards

Problem

You need a way to organize the different screens of your game, defining how each screen links to other screens and what content is shown on each screen.

Solution

You can use storyboards to organize your screens:

1. Create a new single-view application. Call it whatever you like.

2. Open the *Main.storyboard* file. You're now looking at an empty screen.

3. Open the Utilities pane, if it isn't already open, by clicking on the Utilities pane button at the far right of the toolbar.

   At the bottom of the pane, the objects library should be visible, showing a list of objects you can add to the storyboard (see Figure 2-1). If it isn't visible, click the "Show or hide object library" button. Alternatively, press Control-Option-Command-3.

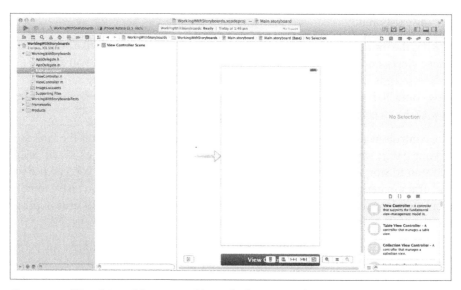

Figure 2-1. The objects library, visible at the bottom-right

4. Scroll down in the objects library until you find the button, as shown in Figure 2-2. You can also type "button" into the search field at the bottom of the objects library.

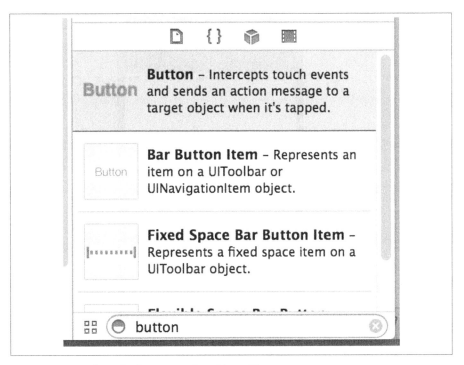

Figure 2-2. Finding the button in the objects library

5. Drag a button into the window.

6. Run the application. A button will appear on the screen, as shown in Figure 2-3. You can tap it, but it won't do anything yet.

Figure 2-3. A button shown on the iPhone's screen

Next, we'll set up the application so that tapping on the button displays a new screen.

7. Find the navigation controller in the objects library, and drag one into the story-board.

   Navigation controllers come with an attached Table View. We don't want this—select it and delete it.

8. The original screen currently has a small arrow attached to it. This indicates that it's the screen that will appear when the application begins. Drag this arrow from where it is right now to the navigation controller.

9. Hold down the Control key, and drag from the navigation controller to the first screen.

10. A window containing a list of possible "segues" will appear, as shown in Figure 2-5. Choose the "root view controller" option.

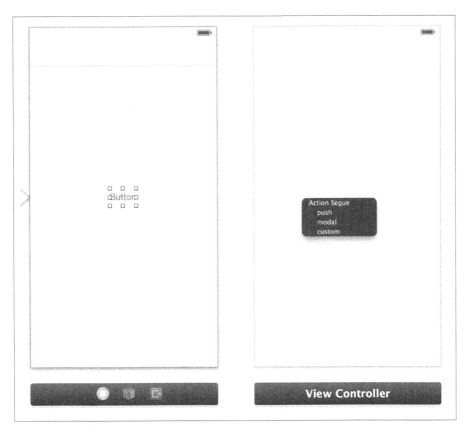

Figure 2-4. Selecting a segue

When the application starts up, the navigation controller will appear, and inside it, you'll see the screen you designed. Next, we'll make it so that the button shows an additional screen when it's tapped.

11. Drag a new view controller into the storyboard.

    A new, empty screen will appear.

12. Hold down the Control key, and drag from the button to the new screen.

    Another list of possible segues will appear. Choose "push."

13. The two screens will appear linked with a line, as shown in Figure 2-4, which indicates that it's possible to go from one screen to the next.

Figure 2-5. The linked view controllers

14. Run the application.

    When you tap the button, a new screen will appear. A Back button will also appear in the navigation bar at the top of the screen.

When you create a new project, it will come with a storyboard file. *Storyboards* are files that define what *view controllers* are used in your application, and how those view controllers are linked together via *segues*.

A view controller is an Objective-C object that contains the logic that controls an individual screen. Typically, you have one view controller per screen. For each type of screen that the user will see, you create a subclass of the UIViewController class, and you instruct the storyboard to use that subclass for specific screens. (For information on how to do this, see Recipe 2.2.)

In a storyboard, screens can be linked together using segues. A segue is generally a transition from one screen to the next (e.g., a *push* segue tells the system that, when the segue is activated, the next screen should be *pushed* into the current navigation controller, assuming one exists).

Segues are also used to indicate relationships between different view controllers. For example, navigation controllers need to know which screen they should display when they're first shown; this is done by creating a *root view controller* segue.

2.2. Creating View Controllers

Problem

You have a project that has a storyboard, and you want to keep all of the logic for your screens in separate, easily maintainable objects. For example, you want to keep your main menu code separate from the high scores screen.

Solution

Follow these steps to create a new view controller:

1. Create a subclass of UIViewController.

   Choose New→File from the File menu. Select the Cocoa Touch category, and choose to make an Objective-C subclass, as shown in Figure 2-6.

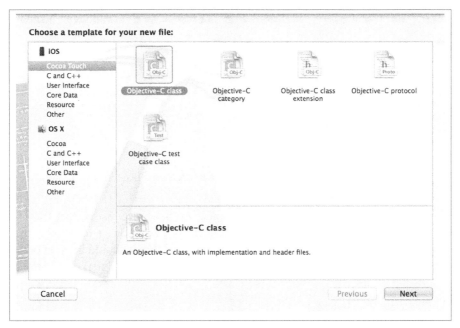

Figure 2-6. Creating a new Objective-C subclass

2. Create the new UIViewController subclass.

   Name the class "MainMenuViewController," and set "Subclass of" to "UIView-Controller."

Make sure that both "Targeted for iPad" and "With XIB for user interface" are "unchecked," as shown in Figure 2-7.

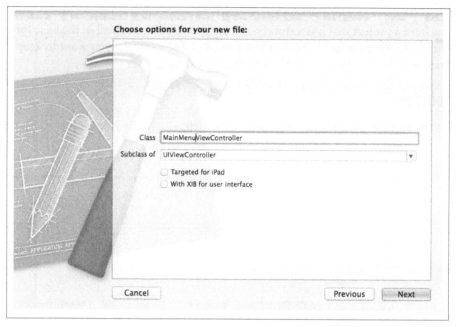

Figure 2-7. Setting up the new file

3. Create the files.

   Xcode will ask you where to put the newly created files. Choose somewhere that suits your particular purpose.

   Once this is done, two new files will appear in the Project Navigator: *MainMenu-ViewController.m* and *MainMenuViewController.h*. In order to actually use this new class, you need to indicate to the storyboard that it should be used on one of the screens. In this example, there's only one screen, so we'll make it use the newly created `MainMenuViewController` class.

4. Open the storyboard.

   Find *Main.storyboard* in the Project Navigator, and click it.

5. Open the outline view.

   The outline view lists all of the parts making up your user interface. You can open it either by choosing Show Document Outline from the Editor menu, or by clicking on the Show Outline button at the bottom left of the Interface Builder.

6. Select the view controller.

You'll find it at the top of the outline view.

7. Open the Identity inspector.

You can do this by choosing View→Utilities→Identity Inspector, or by pressing Command-Option-3. (There's also a toolbar at the top of the Utilities pane, which you can use to open the Identity inspector.)

8. Change the class of the selected view controller to `MainMenuViewController`.

At the top of the Identity inspector, you'll find the class of the currently selected view controller. Change it to "MainMenuViewController," as shown in Figure 2-8. Doing this means that the `MainMenuViewController` class will be the one used for this particular screen.

Figure 2-8. Changing the class of the view controller

Now that this is done, we'll add a text field to the screen and make the view controller class able to access its contents (on its own, a text field can't communicate with the view controller—you need an outlet for that). We'll also add a button to the screen, and make some code run when the user taps it.

9. Add a text field.

The objects library should be at the bottom of the Utilities pane, on the righthand side of the Xcode window. If it isn't visible, choose View→Utilities→Objects Library, or press Command-Control-Option-3.

Scroll down until you find the Text Field control. Alternatively, type "text field" into the search bar at the bottom of the objects library.

Drag and drop a text field into the screen, as shown in Figure 2-9.

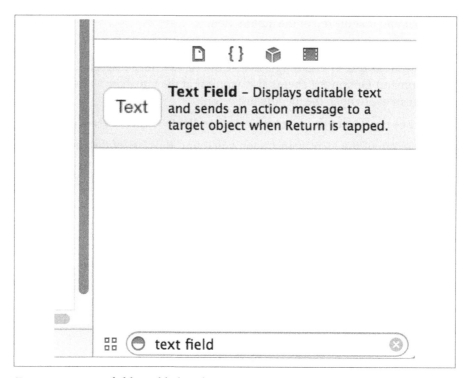

Figure 2-9. A text field is added to the screen

On its own, a text field can't communicate with the view controller—you need an *outlet* for that.

10. Open the view controller's code in the Assistant editor.

Open the Assistant editor, by clicking on the Assistant button at the top right of the Xcode window or by choosing View→Assistant Editor→Show Assistant Editor.

Once you've opened it, *MainMenuViewController.m* should be visible in the editor. If it isn't, choose Automatic→*MainMenuViewController.h* from the jump bar at the top of the Assistant editor (Figure 2-10).

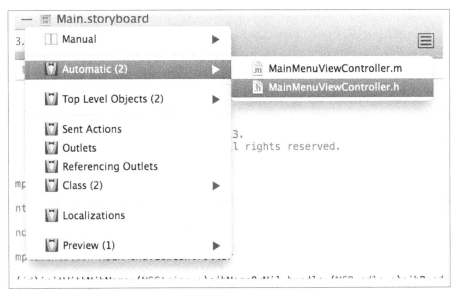

Figure 2-10. Selecting MainMenuViewController.h in the Assistant

11. Add the outlet for the text field.

    Hold down the Control key, and drag from the text field into the @interface of MainMenuViewController. When you finish dragging, a dialog box will appear, a new property will appear (see Figure 2-11) asking you what to name the variable.

    Type "textField," and click the Connect button.

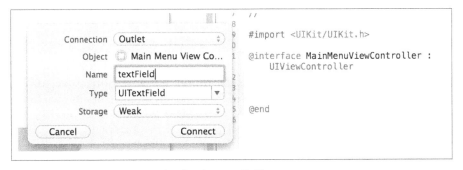

Figure 2-11. Creating an outlet for the text field

Finally, we'll add a button, which will run code when the button is tapped.

12. Add a button to the screen.

    Follow the same instructions for adding a text field, but this time, add a button.

13. Add the action.

Hold down the Control key, and drag from the button into the `@implementation` part of `MainMenuViewController`'s code.

Another dialog will appear, as seen in Figure 2-12, asking you what to name the action. Name it "buttonPressed," and click Connect. A new method will be added to `MainMenuViewController`.

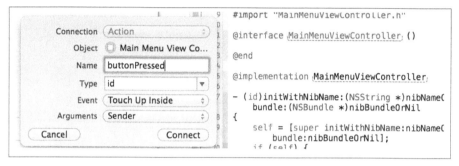

Figure 2-12. Creating an action

14. Add some code to the newly created method.

    We'll use the following code:

    ```
    UIAlertView* alertView = [[UIAlertView alloc] init];
    alertView.title = @"Button tapped";
    alertView.message = @"The button was tapped!";
    [alertView addButtonWithTitle:@"OK"];
    [alertView show];
    ```

Discussion

In almost every single case, different screens perform different tasks. A "main menu" screen, for example, has the task of showing the game's logo, and probably a couple of buttons to send the player off to a new game, to continue an existing game, to view the high scores screen, and so on. Each one of these screens, in turn, has its own functionality.

The easiest way to create an app that contains multiple screens is via a storyboard. However, a storyboard won't let you define the behavior of the screens—that's the code's job. So, how do you tell the application what code should be run for different screens?

Every view controller that's managed by a storyboard is an instance of the `UIView Controller` class. `UIViewControllers` know how to be presented to the user, how to show whatever views have been placed inside them in the interface builder, and how to do a few other things, like managing their life cycle (i.e., they know when they're about to appear on the screen, when they're about to go away, and when other important events are about to occur, like the device running low on memory).

However, a `UIViewController` doesn't have any knowledge of what its role is—they're designed to be empty templates, and it's your job to create subclasses that perform the work of being a main menu, or of being a high scores screen, and so on.

When you subclass `UIViewController`, you override some important methods:

- `viewDidLoad` is called when the view has completed loading and all of the controls are present.

- `viewWillAppear` is called when the view is about to appear on the screen, but is not yet visible.

- `viewDidAppear` is called when the view has finished appearing on the screen and is now visible.

- `viewWillDisappear` is called when the view is about to disappear from the screen, but is currently still visible.

- `viewDidDisappear` is called when the view is no longer visible.

- `applicationReceivedMemoryWarning` is called when the application has received a memory warning and will be force quit by iOS if memory is not freed up. Your `UIViewController` subclass should free any objects that can be re-created when needed.

Additionally, your `UIViewController` is able to respond to events that come from the controls it's showing, and to manipulate those controls and change what they're doing.

This is done through outlets and actions. An *outlet* is a property on the `UIView Controller` that is connected to a view; once `viewDidLoad` has been called, each outlet property has been connected to a view object. You can then access these properties as normal.

To define an outlet, you create a property that uses the special keyword `IBOutlet`, like so:

```
@property (strong) IBOutlet UITextField* aTextField;
```

Actions are methods that are called as a result of the user doing something with a control on the screen. For example, if you want to know when a button has been tapped, you create an action method and connect the button to that method. You create similar action methods for events such as the text in a text field changing, or a slider changing position.

Action methods are defined in the `@interface` of a class, like this:

```
- (IBAction) anActionMethod:(id)sender;
```

Note that IBAction isn't really a return type—it's actually another name for void. However, Xcode uses the IBAction keyword to identify methods that can be connected to views in the interface builder.

In the preceding example, the action method takes a single parameter: an id (i.e., an object of any type) called sender. This object will be the object that triggered the action: the button that was tapped, the text field that was edited, and so on.

If you don't care about the sender of the action, you can just define the method with no parameters, like so:

```
- (IBAction) anActionMethod;
```

2.3. Using Segues to Move Between Screens

Problem

You want to use segues to transition between different screens.

Solution

We'll step through the creation of two view controllers, and show how to create and use segues to move between them:

1. Create a new single-view project.
2. Open *Main.storyboard*.
3. Add a new view controller.

   You can do this by searching for "view controller" in the objects library.

4. Add a button to the first view controller.

   Label it "Automatic Segue."

5. Add a segue from the button to the second view controller.

   Hold down the Control key, and drag from the button to the second view controller. A menu will appear when you finish dragging, which shows the possible types of segues you can use. Choose "modal."

6. Run the application.

   When you tap the button, the second (empty) view controller will appear.

Currently, there's no way to return to the first one. We'll now address this:

1. Open *ViewController.m*.

   This is the class that powers the first screen.

2. Add an exit method.

Add the following method to ViewController's @implementation section:

```
- (IBAction)closePopup:(UIStoryboardSegue*)segue {
    NSLog(@"Second view controller was closed!");
}
```

3. Add an exit button to the second view controller.

Add a button to the second view controller, and label it "Exit."

Then, hold down the Control key, and drag from the button to the Exit icon underneath the screen. It looks like a little green box.

A menu will appear, listing the possible actions that can be run. Choose "closePopup:."

4. Run the application.

Open the pop-up screen, and then tap the Exit button. The screen will disappear, and the console will show the "Second view controller was closed!" text.

Finally, we'll demonstrate how to manually trigger a segue from code. To do this, we'll first need a named segue in order to trigger it. One already exists—you created it when you linked the button to the second view controller:

1. Give the segue an identifier.

In order to be triggered, a segue must have a name. Click on the segue you created when you linked the button to the second view controller (i.e., the line connecting the first view controller to the second).

In the Attributes inspector (choose View→Utilities→Show Attributes Inspector, or press Command-Option-4), set the identifier of the segue to "ShowPopup," as seen in Figure 2-13.

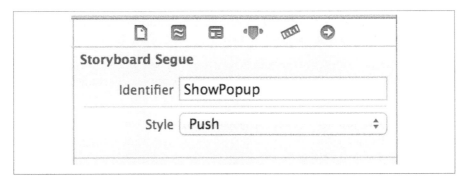

Figure 2-13. Naming the segue

Make sure you use the same capitalization as we've used here. "ShowPopup" isn't the same as "showpopup" or even "Show-PopUp."

2. Add a button that manually triggers the segue.

   Add a new button to the first view controller. Label it "Manual Segue."

   Open *ViewController.m* in the Assistant editor.

   Hold down the Control key, and drag from the new button into ViewController's @implementation section. Create a new method called "showPopup"—note the capitalization.

   Add the following code to this new method:

   ```
   [self performSegueWithIdentifier:@"ShowPopup" sender:self];
   ```

3. Run the application.

   Now, tapping on the Manual Segue button shows the second screen.

Discussion

A segue is an object that describes a transition from one view controller to the next.

When you run a segue, the segue takes care of presenting the new view controller for you. For example, if you create a push segue, the segue will handle creating the view controller and pushing the new view controller onto the navigation controller's stack.

A segue performs its work of transitioning between view controllers when it's *triggered*. There are two ways you can trigger a segue: you can connect it to a button in the interface builder, or you can trigger it from code.

When you hold down the Control key and drag from a button to a different screen, you create a segue. This new segue is set up to be triggered when the button is tapped.

Triggering a segue from code is easy. First, you need to give the segue an *identifier*, which is a string that uniquely identifies the segue. In our example, we set the identifier of the segue to "ShowPopup."

Once that's done, you use the performSegueWithIdentifier:sender: method. This method takes two parameters—the name of the segue you want to trigger, and the object that was responsible for triggering it:

```
[self performSegueWithIdentifier:@"ShowPopup" sender:self];
```

You can trigger any segue from code, as long as it has an identifier. You don't need to create multiple segues from one view controller to the next.

When a view controller is about to segue to another, the view controller that's about to disappear is sent the `prepareForSegue:sender:` message. When you want to know about the next screen that's about to be shown to the user, you implement this method, like so:

```
- (void)prepareForSegue:(UIStoryboardSegue *)segue sender:(id)sender {
    NSLog(@"About to perform the %@ segue", segue.identifier);
}
```

The method has two parameters: the segue that's about to run, and the object that triggered the segue. The segue object itself contains two particularly useful properties: the `identifier` of the segue, which allows you to differentiate between different segues; and the `destinationViewController`, which is the view controller that's about to be displayed by the segue. This gives you an opportunity to send information to the screen that's about to appear.

Finally, *exit segues* are segues that allow you to return to a previously viewed view controller. You don't create these segues yourself; rather, you define an action method in the view controller that you'd like to return *to*, and then connect a control to the "exit" segue in the interface builder.

2.4. Using Constraints to Lay Out Views

Problem

You have a screen with another view (such as a button) inside it. You want the views to stay in the correct places when the screen rotates.

Solution

You use *constraints* to position views, as illustrated here:

1. Drag the view into the place you'd like to put it.
2. Add the constraint.

   Select the view, and open the Pin menu. This is the second button in the second group of buttons at the bottom right of the interface builder canvas (Figure 2-14).

Figure 2-14. The Constraints menu buttons (the Pin button is the second one from the left)

3. Apply the values you want to use for the new constraints.

Let's assume that you want the view to always be 20 pixels from the top edge of the screen and 20 pixels from the left edge of the screen, as shown in Figure 2-15.

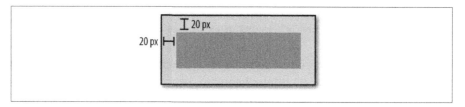

Figure 2-15. The view should always be 20 pixels from the top and left edges

Type "20" into the top field, and "20" into the left field.

Set "Update Frames" to "Items of New Constraints." This will reposition the view when the constraints are added (Figure 2-16).

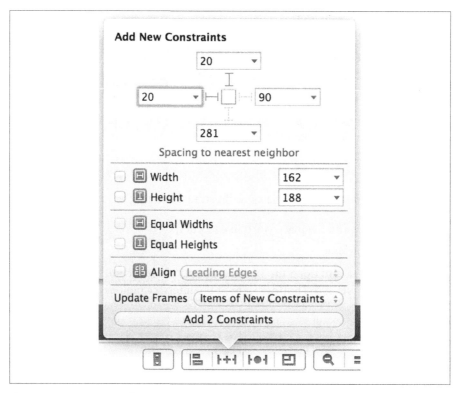

Figure 2-16. Creating the constraints

4. Add the constraints.

The button at the bottom of the menu should now read "Add 2 Constraints." Click it, and the button will be locked to the upper-right corner.

Discussion

To control the positioning and sizing of views, you use constraints. Constraints are rules that are imposed on views, along the lines of "Keep the top edge 10 pixels beneath the top edge of the container," or "Always be half the width of the screen." Without constraints, views don't change position when the size and shape of their superview changes shape (such as when the screen rotates).

Constraints can modify both the position and the size of a view, and will change these in order to make the view fit the rules.

2.5. Adding Images to Your Project

Problem

You want to add images to your game's project in Xcode, so that they can be used in your menu interface.

Solution

When you create a new project in Xcode, an *asset catalog* is created, which contains your images. Your code can then get images from the catalog, or you can use them in your interface.

If your project doesn't have one, or if you want a new one, choose File → New → File, choose Resource, and choose Asset Catalog.

Select the asset catalog in the Project Navigator, and then drag and drop your image into the catalog.

You can rename individual images by double-clicking on the name of the image in the left pane of the asset catalog.

The easiest way to display an image is through a `UIImageView`. To add an image view, search for "image view" in the objects library, and add one to your screen. Then, select the new image view, open the Attributes inspector, and change the Image property to the name of the image you added (Figure 2-17).

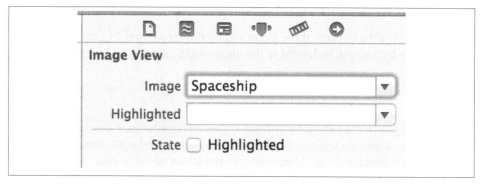

Figure 2-17. Setting the image for a UIImageView

You can also use images in your code. For example, if you've added an image called "Spaceship" to an asset catalog, you can use it in your code as follows:

```
UIImage* image = [UIImage imageNamed:@"Spaceship"];
```

Once you have this image, you can display it in a `UIImageView`, display it as a sprite, or load it as a texture.

Discussion

It's often the case that you'll need to use different versions of an image under different circumstances. The most common example of this is when working with devices that have a retina display, as such devices have a screen resolution that's double the density of non-retina-display devices.

In these cases, you need to provide two different copies of each image you want to use: one at regular size, and one at double the size.

Fortunately, asset catalogs make this rather straightforward. When you add an image to the catalog, you can add alternative representations of the same image, making available both 1x (non-retina) and 2x (retina) versions of the image. You can also add specific versions of an image for the iPhone and iPad; when you get the image by name, the correct version of the image is returned to you, which saves you having to write code that checks to see which platform your game is running on.

2.6. Slicing Images for Use in Buttons

Problem

You want to customize a button with images. Additionally, you want the image to not get distorted when the button changes size.

Solution

To customize your button, perform the following steps:

1. Add the image you want to use to an asset catalog.

   See Recipe 2.5 to learn how to do this.

2. Select the newly added image, and click Show Slicing.

   The button is at the bottom right of the asset catalog's view.

3. Click Start Slicing.

   Choose one of the slicing options. You can slice the image horizontally, vertically, or both horizontally and vertically, as seen in Figure 2-18.

Figure 2-18. The available slicing options are, from left to right, horizontal, both horizontal and vertical, and vertical

4. Open your storyboard, and select the button you want to theme.

5. Open the Attributes inspector, and set the background.

   Select the name of the image that you added to the Xcode catalog. The button will change to use the new background image. You can also resize the image, and the background image will scale appropriately.

Discussion

One of the most effective ways to customize the look and feel of your game's user interface is to use custom images for buttons and other controls, which you can do by setting the "Background" property of your buttons.

However, if you want to use background images, you need to take into account the size of the controls you're theming: if you create an image that's 200 pixels wide and try to use it on a button that's only 150 pixels wide, your image will be squashed. Do the reverse, and you'll end up with a repeating background, which may look worse.

To solve this issue, you can *slice* your images. Slicing divides your image into multiple regions, of which only some are allowed to squash and stretch or repeat.

In this solution, we looked at customizing a button; however, the same principles apply to other other controls as well.

2.7. Using UI Dynamics to Make Animated Views

Problem

You want to make the views on your screen move around the screen realistically.

Solution

You can add physical behaviors to any view inside a view controller, using UIDynamicAnimator. In these examples, we'll assume that you've got a view called animatedView. It can be of any type—button, image, or anything else you like.

First, create a UIDynamicAnimator object in your view controller. Add this property to your view controller's @interface section:

```
@property (strong) UIDynamicAnimator* animator;
```

Then, in your view controller's viewDidLoad method, add the following code:

```
self.animator = [[UIDynamicAnimator alloc] initWithReferenceView:self.view];
```

We'll now talk about how you can add different kinds of physical behaviors to your views. Because these behaviors interact with each other, we'll go through each one and, in each case, assume that the previous behaviors have been added.

Adding gravity to views

Add the following code to your viewDidLoad method:

```
UIGravityBehavior* gravity =
[[UIGravityBehavior alloc] initWithItems:@[animatedView]];

[self.animator addBehavior:gravity];
```

Run the application. The view will move down the screen (and eventually fall off!).

Adding collision

Add the following code to your viewDidLoad method:

```
UICollisionBehavior* collision =
[[UICollisionBehavior alloc] initWithItems:@[animatedView]];

[collision setTranslatesReferenceBoundsIntoBoundary:YES];

[self.animator addBehavior:collision];
```

Run the application. The button will fall to the bottom of the screen.

 By default, the collision boundaries will be the same as the boundaries of the container view. This is what's set when `setTranslatesRe ferenceBoundsIntoBoundary:` is called. If you would prefer to create boundaries that are inset from the container view, use `setTrans latesReferenceBoundsIntoBoundaryWithInsets:` instead:

```
// Inset the collision bounds by 10 points on all sides
[collision setTranslatesReferenceBoundsIntoBoundaryWithInsets:
    UIEdgeInsetsMake(10, 10, 10, 10)];
```

Adding collision

Add the following code to your `viewDidLoad` method:

```
UIAttachmentBehavior* attachment =
    [[UIAttachmentBehavior alloc] initWithItem:animatedView
    attachedToAnchor:CGPointZero];

[self.animator addBehavior:attachment];
```

Run the application. The button will swing down and hit the side of the screen.

When you create a `UIAttachmentBehavior`, you can attach your views to specific points, or to other views. If you want to attach your view to a point, you should use `initWithI tem:attachedToAnchor:`, as seen in the previous example. If you want to attach a view to another view, you use `initWithItem:attachedToItem::`

```
[[UIAttachmentBehavior alloc] initWithItem:animatedButton
    attachedToItem:anotherView];
```

Discussion

UIKit has a physics engine in it, which you can use to create a complex set of physically realistic behaviors.

The dynamic animation system is designed for user interfaces, rather than games—if you're interested in using physics simulation for games, use Sprite Kit (see Chapter 6).

Keep in mind that controls that move around too much may end up being disorienting for users, who are used to buttons generally remaining in one place. Additionally, if you're displaying your UI content on top of your game, you may end up with performance problems if you have lots of controls that use the dynamic animation system.

2.8. Moving an Image with Core Animation

Problem

You want an image to move around the screen, and smoothly change its position over time.

Solution

To animate your image, follow these steps:

1. Create a new single-view application for iPhone, named "ImageAnimation."

2. Add an image of a ball to the project (one has been provided as part of the sample code):

    - Open *ViewController.xib*.

    - Add an image view to the screen. Set it to display the image you dragged in.

    - Open the Assistant editor by clicking on the middle button in the Editor selector, at the top right of the Xcode window. The code for *ViewController.h* will appear.

    - Hold down the Control key, and drag from the image view into *View-Controller.h*, between the @interface and @end lines.

      A small window will pop up, prompting you to provide information. Use the following settings:

      — Connection: Outlet

      — Name: ball

      — Type: UIImageView

      — Storage: Strong

    - Click Connect. The following line will appear in your code:

        ```
        @property (strong, nonatomic) IBOutlet UIImageView *ball;
        ```

    - Close the Assistant editor, and open *ViewController.m*.

    - Add the following method to the code:

        ```
        - (void)viewDidAppear:(BOOL)animated {
            [UIView animateWithDuration:2.0 animations:^{
                self.ball.center = CGPointMake(0, 0);
            }];
        }
        ```

3. Run the application.

When the app starts up, the ball will slowly move up to the upper-left corner of the screen.

Discussion

This application instructs a UIImageView to change its position over the course of two seconds.

Image views, being completely passive displays of images, have no means (nor any reason) to move around on their own, which means that something else needs to do it for them. That "something else" is the view controller, which is responsible for managing each view that's displayed on the screen.

In order for the view controller to be able to tell the image view to move, it first needs an outlet to that image view. An outlet is a variable in an object that connects to a view. When you hold the Control key and drag and drop from the image view into the code, Xcode recognizes that you want to add a connection and displays the "add connection" dialog.

When the application launches, the first thing that happens is that all connections that were created in the interface builder are set up. This means that all of your code is able to refer to properties like self.ball without having to actually do any of the work involved in setting them up.

Once the connection is established, the real work of moving the ball around on the screen is done in the viewWillAppear: method. This method is called, as you can probably tell from the name, when the view (i.e., the screen) is about to appear to the user. This snippet of code is where the actual work is done:

```
[UIView animateWithDuration:2.0 animations:^{
    self.ball.center = CGPointMake(0, 0);
}];
```

The animateWithDuration:animations method takes two parameters: the duration of the animation, and a block that performs the changes that should be seen during the animation.

In this case, the animation being run takes two seconds to complete, and a single change is made: the center property of whatever view self.ball refers to is changed to the point (0,0). Additional changes can be included as well. For example, try adding the following line of code between the two curly braces ({}):

```
self.ball.alpha = 0;
```

This change causes the view's alpha setting (its opacity) to change from whatever value it currently is to zero, which renders it fully transparent. Because this change is run at the same time as the change to the view's position, it will fade out while moving.

2.9. Rotating an Image

Problem

You want to rotate an image on the screen.

Solution

To rotate an image view, use the `transform` property:

```
self.rotatedView.transform = CGAffineTransformMakeRotation(M_PI_2);
```

In this example, `self.rotatedView` is a `UIImageView`. Any view can be rotated, though, not just image views.

Discussion

The `transform` property allows you to modify a view's presentation without affecting its contents. This allows you to rotate, shift, squash, and stretch a view however you want.

The value of `transform` is a `CGAffineTransform`, which is a 4-by-4 matrix of numbers. This matrix is multiplied against the four vertices that define the four corners of the view. The default transform is the identity transform, `CGAffineTransformIdenti ty`, which makes no changes to the presentation of the view.

To create a transform matrix that rotates a view, you use the `CGAffineTransform MakeRotation` method. This method takes a single parameter: the amount to rotate by, measured in radians. There are 2π radians in a circle; therefore, a rotation of one-quarter of a circle is $2\pi/4 = \pi/2$. This value is available via the built-in shorthand `M_PI_2`.

In our example, we have created a transform matrix using the `CGAffineTransform MakeRotation` function. Other functions you can use include:

CGAffineTransformMakeTranslation
    Adjusts the position of the view

CGAffineTransformMakeScale
    Scales the view, on the horizontal or vertical axis

Once you've created a transform matrix, you can modify it by scaling, translating (moving), or rotating it. You can do this using the `CGAffineTransformScale`, `CGAffine TransformTranslate`, and `CGAffineTransformRotate` functions, which each take an existing transform and modify it. Once you're done making changes to the transform, you can then apply it.

For example:

```
CGAffineTransform transform = CGAffineTransformIdentity; ❶
transform = CGAffineTransformTranslate(transform, 50, 0); ❷
transform = CGAffineTransformRotate(transform, M_PI_2); ❸
transform = CGAffineTransformScale(transform, 0.5, 2); ❹

self.myTransformedView.transform = transform; ❺
```

This code does the following:

❶   Start with the default identity transform.

❷   Translate the transform 50 pixels to the right.

❸   Rotate the transform one quarter-circle clockwise.

❹   Scale the transform by 50% on the horizontal axis and 200% on the vertical axis.

❺   Apply the transform to a view.

The `transform` property of a view can be animated, just like its opacity and position. This lets you create animations where views rotate or squash and stretch.

2.10. Animating a Popping Effect on a View

Problem

You want the main menu of your game to feature buttons that appear with a visually appealing "pop" animation, which draws the player's eye (the object starts small, expands to a large size, and then shrinks back down to its normal size, as shown in Figure 2-19).

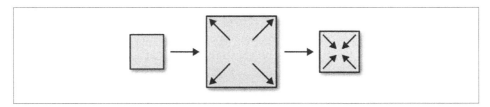

Figure 2-19. A "pop" animation

Solution

The solution to this problem makes use of features available in the Quartz Core framework, which allows access to animation features in UIKit. To use it, you'll need to add the Quartz Core framework to your project. For instructions on doing this, see Recipe 4.6. Then, add the following line to the top of your source code:

```
#import <QuartzCore/QuartzCore.h>
```

Finally, add the following code at the point where you want the popping animation to happen:

```
CAKeyframeAnimation* keyframeAnimation =
    [CAKeyframeAnimation animationWithKeyPath:@"transform.scale"];

keyframeAnimation.values = @[@0.0, @1.2, @1.0];

keyframeAnimation.keyTimes = @[@0.0, @0.7, @1.0];

keyframeAnimation.duration = 0.4;

keyframeAnimation.timingFunction =
    [CAMediaTimingFunction functionWithName:kCAMediaTimingFunctionEaseOut];

[self.poppingButton.layer addAnimation:keyframeAnimation forKey:@"pop"];
```

 In this example, self.poppingButton is a UIView, but any view can be animated in this way.

Discussion

Every single view on the screen can be animated using Core Animation. These animations can be very simple, such as moving an item from one location to another, or they can be more complex, such as a multiple-stage "pop" animation.

This can be achieved using a CAKeyframeAnimation. CAKeyframeAnimations allow you to change a visual property of any view over time, and through multiple stages. You do this by creating a CAKeyframeAnimation, providing it with the values that the property should animate through, and providing corresponding timing information for each value. Finally, you give the animation object to the view's CALayer, and the view will perform the animation.

Every animation object must have a "key path" that indicates what value should change when the animation runs. The key path used for this animation is transform.scale, which indicates that the animation should be modifying the scale of the view.

The values property is an NSArray that contains the values that the animation should move through. In this animation, there are three values: 0, 1.2, and 1.0. These will be used as the scale values: the animation will start with a scale of zero (i.e., scaled down to nothing), then expand to 1.2 times the normal size, and then back down to the normal size.

The keyTimes property is another NSArray that must contain the same number of NSNumbers as there are values in the values array. Each number in the keyTimes array indicates at which point the corresponding value in the `values` array will be reached. Each key time is given as a value from 0 to 1, with 0 being the start of the animation and 1 being the end.

In this case, the second value (1.2) will be reached at 70% of the way through the animation, because its corresponding key time is 0.7. This is done to make the first phase of the animation, in which the button expands from nothing, take a good amount of time, which will look more natural.

The duration of the animation is set to 0.4 seconds, and the timing function is set to "ease out." This means that the "speed" of the animation will slow down toward the end. Again, this makes the animation feel more organic and less mechanical.

Lastly, the animation is given to the view's layer using the `addAnimation:forKey:` method. The "key" in this method is any string you want—it's an identifier to let you access the animation at a later time.

2.11. Theming UI Elements with UIAppearance

Problem

You want to change the color of views, or use background images to customize their look and feel.

Solution

You can set the color of a view by changing its tint color or by giving it a background image:

```
UIButton* myButton = ... // a UIButton

[myButton setTintColor:[UIColor redColor]];

UIImage* backgroundImage = ... // a UIImage
[myButton setBackgroundImage:backgroundImage forState:UIControlStateNormal];
```

Discussion

Most (though not all) controls can be themed. There are two main ways you can change a control's appearance:

- Set a *tint color*, which sets the overall color of the control.
- Set a *background image*, which sets a background image.

To set a tint color for a specific control, you call one of the `setTintColor:` family of methods. Some controls have a single tint color, which you set with `setTintColor:`, while other controls can have multiple tint colors, which you set independently. For example, to tint a `UIProgressView`, do the following:

```
// self.progressView is a UIProgressView
[self.progressView setProgressTintColor:[UIColor orangeColor]];
```

You can also set the tint color for *all* controls of a given type, like this:

```
[[UIProgressView appearance] setProgressTintColor:[UIColor orangeColor]];
```

Background images work similarly:

```
UIImage* backgroundImage = [UIImage imageNamed:@"NavigationBarBackground.png"];
[[UIProgressView appearance] setBackgroundImage:backgroundImage
    forBarMetrics:UIBarMetricsDefault];
```

You'll notice that the specific method used to customize different controls varies, because different controls have different visual elements that need theming in different ways. There isn't room in this book to list all of the different ways each control can be customized, but if you Command-click on the name of a class, such as `UIButton`, you'll be taken to the header file for that class. In the header file, any property that has `UI_AP PEARANCE_SELECTOR` is one that can be used for theming—that is, you can use [`UIButton appearance`] to change that property for all `UIButtons`.

You can customize the appearance of individual controls by using the appearance methods. If you want to customize every control of a given class, you first get that class's *appearance proxy*. The appearance proxy is a special object that stores all changes submitted to it; all views consult it when they're appearing on-screen and update their appearance based on it.

To get the appearance proxy for a class, you use the `appearance` method, like so:

```
[UIProgressView appearance];
```

You then send the appearance customization messages to it, as if it were a specific instance of that class. All instances of that class will update their appearance to reflect what you provide:

```
// Set ALL UIProgressViews to have an orange tint
[[UIProgressView appearance] setProgressTintColor:[UIColor orangeColor]];
```

2.12. Rotating a UIView in 3D

Problem

You want to make a view rotate in 3D, and have a perspective effect as it does so (i.e., as parts of the view move away from the user, they get smaller, and as they get closer, they get larger).

Solution

To implement this functionality, you'll need to add the Quartz Core framework to your project and import the *QuartzCore/QuartzCore.h* header file (see Recipes 2.10 and 4.6).

Then, when you want the animation to begin, you do this:

```
CABasicAnimation* animation =
    [CABasicAnimation animationWithKeyPath:@"transform.rotation.y"];
animation.fromValue = @(0);
animation.toValue = @(2 * M_PI);
animation.repeatCount = INFINITY;
animation.duration = 5.0;

[self.rotatingView.layer addAnimation:animation forKey:@"rotation"];

CATransform3D transform = CATransform3DIdentity;
transform.m34 = 1.0 / 500.0;
self.rotatingView.layer.transform = transform;
```

To stop the animation, you do this:

```
[self.rotatingView.layer removeAnimationForKey:@"rotation"];
```

 In this example code, `self.rotatingView` is a `UIView` that's on the screen. This technique can be applied to any view, though—buttons, image views, and so on.

Discussion

`CABasicAnimation` allows you to animate a property of a view from one value to another. In the case of rotating a view, the property that we want to animate is its rotation, and the values we want to animate from and to are angles.

When you use `[CABasicAnimation animationWithKeyPath:]` to create the animation, you specify the property you want to animate. In this case, the one we want is the rotation around the y-axis:

```
CABasicAnimation* animation =
    [CABasicAnimation animationWithKeyPath:@"transform.rotation.y"];
```

The animation is then configured. In this example, we made the rotation start from zero, and proceed through to a full circle. In Core Animation, angles are measured in radians, and there are 2π radians in a full circle. So, the `fromValue` and `toValue` are set thusly:

```
animation.fromValue = @(0);
animation.toValue = @(2 * M_PI);
```

Next, the animation is told that it should repeat an infinite number of times, and that the full rotation should take five seconds:

```
animation.repeatCount = INFINITY;
animation.duration = 5.0;
```

The animation is started by adding it to the view's layer, using the addAnimation:forK ey: method. This method takes two parameters, the animation object that you want to use and a key (or name) to use to refer to the animation:

```
[self.rotatingView.layer addAnimation:animation forKey:@"rotation"];
```

Don't be confused by the similarity between the "key" that you use when you add the animation and the "key path" you use when creating the animation. The former is just a name you give the animation, and can be anything; the key path describes exactly what the animation modifies.

The last step is to give the rotating view a little perspective. If you run the code while omitting the last few lines, you'll end up with a view that appears to horizontally squash and stretch. What you want is for the edge that's approaching the user's eye to appear to get bigger, while the edge that's moving away from the user's eye appears to get smaller.

This is done by modifying the view's 3D transform. By default, all views have a transform matrix applied to them that makes them all lie flat over each other. When you want something to have perspective, though, this doesn't apply, and you need to override it:

```
CATransform3D transform = CATransform3DIdentity;
transform.m34 = 1.0 / 500.0;
self.rotatingView.layer.transform = transform;
```

The key to this part of the code is the second line: the one where the m34 field of the transform is updated. This part of the transform controls the sharpness of the perspective. (It's basically how much the z coordinate gets scaled toward or away from the vanishing point as it moves closer to or further from the "camera.")

2.13. Overlaying Menus on Top of Game Content

Problem

You want to overlay controls and views on top of your existing game content. For example, you want to overlay a pause menu, or put UIButtons on top of sprites.

Solution

You can overlay any UIView you like on top of any other UIView. Additionally, both OpenGL views and Sprite Kit views are actually UIViews, which means anything can be overlaid on them.

To create a view that you can show, you can use *nibs*. A nib is like a storyboard, but only contains a single view.

To make a nib, choose File→New→File from the menu, choose User Interface, and choose View. Save the new file wherever you like. You can then edit the file and design your interface.

To instantiate the nib and use the interface you've designed, you first create a `UINib` object by loading it from disk, and then ask the nib to instantiate itself:

```
UINib* nib = [UINib nibWithNibName:@"MyNibFile" bundle:nil];

NSArray* nibObjects = [nib instantiateWithOwner:self options:nil];
```

The `instantiateWithOwner:options:` method returns an `NSArray` that contains the objects that you've designed. If you've followed these instructions and created a nib with a single view, this array will contain a single object—the `UIView` object that you designed:

```
UIView* overlayView = [nibObjects firstObject];
```

Once you have this, you can add this view to your view controller using the `addSub view:` method:

```
// In your view controller code:
[self.view addSubview:overlayView];
```

Discussion

Keep in mind that if you overlay a view on top of Sprite Kit or OpenGL, you'll see a performance decrease. This is because the Core Animation system, which is responsible for compositing views together, has to do extra work to combine UIKit views with raw OpenGL.

That's not to say that you shouldn't ever do it, but be mindful of the possible performance penalty.

2.14. Designing Effective Game Menus

Problem

You want to build a game that uses menus effectively.

Solution

You should make your menus as simple and easy to navigate as possible. There's nothing worse than an iOS game that has an overly complicated menu structure, or tries to present too many options to the player. Menus should be simple and have the minimum amount of options required to make your game work.

Including only the minimum required set of options will make players feel more confident and in control of the game—ideally they'll be able to play through your entire game without ever using any menus beyond those necessary to start and end the game. And those menus should be super simple too!

Discussion

It's important to keep your game menus as simple as possible. When your game is the app running on a device, a simple and clear menu will ensure that the user is more likely to be playing the game than trying to configure it. You're building a game, not an elaborate set of menus!

CHAPTER 3

Input

Without a way to collect input from the user, your game is nothing but a pretty graphics demo. In this chapter, we'll look at common tasks that games often need to perform in order to get input from their players. The only way that a game can know about what the user wants to do is via the input that it collects, and the main way that the player provides that input is through the device's built-in touchscreen.

Behind the scenes, a touchscreen is a very complex piece of technology. However, the information that it provides to your game is rather simple: you get told when a touch lands on the screen, when a touch moves, and when a touch is lifted from the screen. This might not sound like much—everyone knows you can detect taps, for example—but the touch system built in to iOS is able to use this information to determine when the user is dragging, pinching, rotating, and flicking, all of which can be used to interpret the user's will.

In addition to the touch system, iOS devices have a number of built-in sensors that detect the current state of the hardware. These include an accelerometer (which detects force and movement), a gyroscope (which detects rotation), a magnetometer (which detects magnetic fields), and a receiver for the Global Positioning System, or GPS (which can calculate where on the planet the device is).

All of this information can be combined to learn a great deal about what the user's doing with the device, which can be used as input to your game. For example, it's possible to determine the user's speed by observing the distance traveled over time, which can give you an idea of whether the player is in a vehicle—which you can then use as part of your game's input.

3.1. Detecting When a View Is Touched

Problem

You want to know when the user touches a view.

Solution

You can override certain UIView methods that get called when a touch begins, moves, ends, and is cancelled.

Put this code in your view controller, or in your UIView subclasses:

```
- (void)touchesBegan:(NSSet *)touches withEvent:(UIEvent *)event {
    for (UITouch* touch in touches) {
        NSLog(@"A touch landed at %@", NSStringFromCGPoint([touch
            locationInView:touch.view]));
    }
}

- (void)touchesMoved:(NSSet *)touches withEvent:(UIEvent *)event {
    for (UITouch* touch in touches) {
        NSLog(@"A touch was moved at %@", NSStringFromCGPoint([touch
            locationInView:touch.view]));
    }
}

- (void)touchesEnded:(NSSet *)touches withEvent:(UIEvent *)event {
    for (UITouch* touch in touches) {
        NSLog(@"A touch ended at %@", NSStringFromCGPoint([touch
            locationInView:touch.view]));
    }
}

- (void)touchesCancelled:(NSSet *)touches withEvent:(UIEvent *)event {
    for (UITouch* touch in touches) {
        NSLog(@"A touch was cancelled at %@", NSStringFromCGPoint([touch
            locationInView:touch.view]));
    }
}
```

Discussion

A touch can be in one of four states:

Began
: The touch just landed on the screen.

Moved
> The touch moved from one location to another. (The related method is often called multiple times over the life of a touch.)

Ended
> The touch was lifted from the screen.

Cancelled
> The touch was interrupted by something happening on the iPhone, such as a phone call coming in.

When a touch lands on the screen, iOS first determines which view should be responsible for handling that touch. It does this by first determining where the touch landed on the screen, and which view happens to contain that point; second, it determines if this view, or any of its subviews, is capable of handling the touch. This is determined by checking to see if the view (or any of its subviews) has implemented any of the touches Began, touchesMoved, touchesEnded, or touchesCancelled methods.

Each of these methods is called when a touch that belongs to the view changes state; because several touches can change state at the same time (e.g., two fingers being moved simultaneously over a view), each of the methods takes an NSSet that contains each of the UITouch objects that recently changed state.

3.2. Responding to Tap Gestures

Problem

You want to detect when the user taps on a view.

Solution

A tap is when a finger lands on a view, and then lifts back up without having moved.

Use a UIGestureRecognizer (specifically, UITapGestureRecognizer):

```
    UITapGestureRecognizer* tap = [[UITapGestureRecognizer alloc]
                            initWithTarget:self action:@selector(tapped:)];

    [self.tapView addGestureRecognizer:tap];
}

- (void) tapped:(UITapGestureRecognizer*)tap {
    if (tap.state == UIGestureRecognizerStateRecognized) {
        self.tapCount++;

        self.tapCountLabel.text = [NSString stringWithFormat:@"It's been tapped
                            %i times!", self.tapCount];
    }
```

```
    }

    @end
```

Discussion

Gesture recognizers are objects that you can attach to views that look for specific patterns of touches, such as pinches, taps, and drags.

`UITapGestureRecognizer` is a gesture recognizer that looks for taps—that is, a touch landing and then being lifted up quickly, without moving. Taps are the most common gesture performed on the iPhone or iPad.

When the gesture recognizer detects that the user has performed the gesture that it's looking for, it sends a message to a target object. You specify the message and the target object when you create the recognizer, as follows:

```
UITapGestureRecognizer* tap = [[UITapGestureRecognizer alloc] initWithTarget:self
                                 action:@selector(tapped:)];
```

In this example, the message that's sent is `tapped:`. This method needs to be implemented on the target object (in this example, `self`). The method takes one parameter, which is the gesture recognizer itself:

```
- (void) tapped:(UITapGestureRecognizer*)tap
```

By default, a tap gesture recognizer looks for a single finger that taps one time. However, you can configure the recognizer so that it looks for multiple taps (such as double taps, triple taps, or even the fabled quadruple tap), or taps with more than one finger at the same time (e.g., two-finger taps). These can also be combined to create, for example, double-fingered double-taps:

```
tap.numberOfTapsRequired = 2; // double tap
tap.numberOfTouchesRequired = 2; // with two fingers
```

3.3. Dragging an Image Around the Screen

Problem

You want to let the user directly manipulate the position of an image on the screen, by dragging it around.

Solution

In this example, `self.draggedView` is a property that connects to a `UIView`. It can be any type of view that you like, but image views work particularly well:

```
- (void) viewWillAppear:(BOOL)animated {
    self.draggedView.userInteractionEnabled = YES;
```

```
    UIPanGestureRecognizer* drag = [[UIPanGestureRecognizer alloc]
                                    initWithTarget:self action:@selector(drag:)];
    [self.draggedView addGestureRecognizer:drag];
}

- (void) drag:(UIPanGestureRecognizer*)pan {

    if (pan.state == UIGestureRecognizerStateBegan ||
        pan.state == UIGestureRecognizerStateChanged) {

        CGPoint newPosition = [pan translationInView:pan.view];
        newPosition.x += pan.view.center.x;
        newPosition.y += pan.view.center.y;

        pan.view.center = newPosition;

        [pan setTranslation:CGPointZero inView:pan.view];
    }

}
```

Discussion

This code uses a gesture recognizer to detect and handle the user dragging a finger over the screen (a drag is when the user places a single finger on the screen within the bounds of the view, and then begins moving that finger).

The first thing that happens in this code is this:

```
    self.draggedView.userInteractionEnabled = YES;
```

It's possible that the view may have interaction disabled by default. Some views do this, including UIImageViews. So, to be sure that it's going to work correctly, the view is set to allow user interaction.

The next two lines create and add the gesture recognizer:

```
    UIPanGestureRecognizer* drag = [[UIPanGestureRecognizer alloc]
                                    initWithTarget:self action:@selector(drag:)];
    [self.draggedView addGestureRecognizer:drag];
```

The drag: method is called when the recognizer changes state. For dragging, there are two states that we want to know about: when the drag begins, and when the drag changes. In both cases, we need to do the following:

1. Determine how much the drag has moved by.

2. Figure out where the view is on the screen.

3. Decide where it should now be, by adding the movement to the current position.

4. Make the view's position be this new position.

Pan gesture recognizers expose a value called "translation," which is the amount of movement that they've seen. This value allows your code to work out a new position for the view:

```
- (void) drag:(UIPanGestureRecognizer*)pan {

    if (pan.state == UIGestureRecognizerStateBegan ||
        pan.state == UIGestureRecognizerStateChanged) {

        CGPoint newPosition = [pan translationInView:pan.view];
        newPosition.x += pan.view.center.x;
        newPosition.y += pan.view.center.y;

        pan.view.center = newPosition;

        [pan setTranslation:CGPointZero inView:pan.view];
    }

}
```

The translation value needs to be manually reset once you've done this, because when the gesture recognizer next updates, you want to update the view's position from its current position rather than its starting position.

3.4. Detecting Rotation Gestures

Problem

You want to let the user use two fingers to rotate something on the screen.

Solution

Use a UIRotationGestureRecognizer:

```
@interface ViewController ()
@property (strong, nonatomic) IBOutlet UIView *rotationView;
@property (strong, nonatomic) IBOutlet UILabel *rotationStatusLabel;
@property (assign) float angle;

@end

@implementation ViewController

- (void)viewDidLoad
{
    [super viewDidLoad];

    UIRotationGestureRecognizer* rotation = [[UIRotationGestureRecognizer alloc]
```

```
                              initWithTarget:self action:@selector(rotated:)];

      [self.rotationView addGestureRecognizer:rotation];

}

- (void) rotated:(UIRotationGestureRecognizer*)rotation {
    if (rotation.state == UIGestureRecognizerStateBegan) {
        self.rotationStatusLabel.text = @"Rotation started";
    }
    if (rotation.state == UIGestureRecognizerStateChanged) {
        self.angle += [rotation rotation];
        rotation.rotation = 0.0;
        self.rotationView.transform = CGAffineTransformMakeRotation(self.angle);
        self.rotationStatusLabel.text = [NSString stringWithFormat:@"Rotation:
                                          %.2f radians", self.angle];
    }
    if (rotation.state == UIGestureRecognizerStateEnded) {
        self.rotationStatusLabel.text = @"Rotation ended";
    }
    if (rotation.state == UIGestureRecognizerStateCancelled) {
        self.rotationStatusLabel.text = @"Rotation cancelled";
    }
}

@end
```

Discussion

The UIRotationGestureRecognizer is a *continuous* gesture recognizer (in other words, unlike a tap, rotation starts, changes over time, and then ends).

When a rotation gesture recognizer realizes that the user has begun a rotation—that is, when the user has placed two fingers on the view and begun to rotate them around a central point—it sends its target the message that it was configured with when it was created.

This method then checks the current state of the recognizer, and reacts accordingly. Recognizers can be in several different states. The states relevant to the rotation gesture recognizer are the following:

UIGestureRecognizerStateBegan

   The recognizer enters this state when it determines that a rotation gesture is in progress.

UIGestureRecognizerStateChanged

   This state is entered when the angle of the rotation that the user is performing changes.

`UIGestureRecognizerStateEnded`
> This state is entered when the fingers are lifted from the screen, ending the rotation gesture.

`UIGestureRecognizerStateCancelled`
> This state is entered when the gesture is interrupted by a system-wide event, such as a phone call or an alert box appearing.

The `UIRotationGestureRecognizer`'s key property is `rotation`, which is a measure of how far the rotation has changed since it was last reset, in radians.

In the example code, whenever the gesture changes, the rotation is measured and used to update an angle. Once that's done, the `rotation` property of the gesture recognizer is reset to zero.

3.5. Detecting Pinching Gestures

Problem

You want to track when the user pinches or spreads her fingers on the screen.

Solution

Use a `UIPinchGestureRecognizer` to detect when the user is pinching her fingers together, or spreading them apart:

```
@interface ViewController ()
@property (strong, nonatomic) IBOutlet UIView *scalingView;
@property (strong, nonatomic) IBOutlet UILabel *scalingStatusLabel;
@property (assign) float scale;

@end

@implementation ViewController

- (void)viewDidLoad
{
    [super viewDidLoad];

    self.scale = 1;

    UIPinchGestureRecognizer* pinch = [[UIPinchGestureRecognizer alloc]
                      initWithTarget:self action:@selector(pinched:)];

    [self.scalingView addGestureRecognizer:pinch];

}

- (void) pinched:(UIPinchGestureRecognizer*)pinch {
```

```
        if (pinch.state == UIGestureRecognizerStateBegan) {
            self.scalingStatusLabel.text = @"Pinch started";
        }
        if (pinch.state == UIGestureRecognizerStateChanged) {
            self.scale *= pinch.scale;
            pinch.scale = 1.0;
            self.scalingView.transform = CGAffineTransformMakeScale(self.scale,
                                                                    self.scale);
            self.scalingStatusLabel.text = [NSString stringWithFormat:@"Scale:
                                     %.2f%%", self.scale*100];
        }
        if (pinch.state == UIGestureRecognizerStateEnded) {
            self.scalingStatusLabel.text = @"Pinch ended";
        }
        if (pinch.state == UIGestureRecognizerStateCancelled) {
            self.scalingStatusLabel.text = @"Pinch cancelled";
        }
    }

    @end
```

Discussion

`UIPinchGestureRecognizer` is your friend in this situation. A pinch gesture recognizer looks for fingers moving away from each other, or closer to each other.

The key property for `UIPinchGestureRecognizer` is `scale`. This starts at 1 when the gesture begins, and moves toward 0 when the fingers get closer together, or toward infinity when the fingers move away from each other. This value is always relative to the *initial* scale—so, for example, if the user spreads her fingers so that the scale becomes 2, and then pinches *again*, the scale will reset to 1 when the pinch begins.

To see this in action, comment out the following line of code:

```
    pinch.scale = 1.0;
```

3.6. Creating Custom Gestures

Problem

You want to create a gesture recognizer that looks for a gesture that you define.

Solution

Creating a new gesture recognizer means subclassing `UIGestureRecognizer`. To get started, create a new Objective-C class that's a subclass of `UIGestureRecognizer`.

In this example, we'll create a new gesture recognizer that looks for a gesture in which the finger starts moving down, moves back up, and then lifts from the screen

(Figure 3-1). However, there's nothing stopping you from creating simpler or more complex gestures of your own.

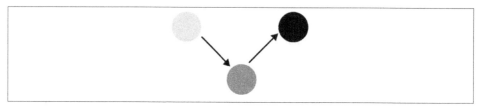

Figure 3-1. The gesture first goes down, then up again

This example shows a new `UIGestureRecognizer` called `DownUpGestureRecognizer`. Create a file called *DownUpGestureRecognizer.h* with the following contents:

```
#import <UIKit/UIKit.h>

typedef enum {
    DownUpGestureMovingDown = 0,
    DownUpGestureMovingUp
} UpDownGesturePhase;

@interface DownUpGestureRecognizer : UIGestureRecognizer

@property (assign) UpDownGesturePhase phase;

@end
```

Next, put the following contents in *DownUpGestureRecognizer.m*:

```
#import "DownUpGestureRecognizer.h"
#import <UIKit/UIGestureRecognizerSubclass.h>

@interface DownUpGestureRecognizer ()

@end

@implementation DownUpGestureRecognizer

- (void)touchesBegan:(NSSet *)touches withEvent:(UIEvent *)event {
    self.phase = DownUpGestureMovingDown;
    self.state = UIGestureRecognizerStatePossible;

    // If there's more than one touch, this is not the type of gesture
    // we're looking for, so fail immediately
    if (self.numberOfTouches > 1) {
        self.state = UIGestureRecognizerStateFailed;
    }
}
```

```objc
- (void)touchesMoved:(NSSet *)touches withEvent:(UIEvent *)event {
    // We know we only have one touch, beacuse touchesBegan will stop
    // recognizing when more than one touch is detected
    UITouch* touch = [touches anyObject];

    // Get the current and previous position of the touch
    CGPoint position = [touch locationInView:touch.view];
    CGPoint lastPosition = [touch previousLocationInView:touch.view];

    // If the state is Possible, and the touch has moved down, the
    // gesture has Begun
    if (self.state == UIGestureRecognizerStatePossible) {
        if (position.y > lastPosition.y) {
            self.state = UIGestureRecognizerStateBegan;
        }
    }

    // If the state is Began or Changed, and the touch has moved, the
    // gesture will change state
    if (self.state == UIGestureRecognizerStateBegan ||
        self.state == UIGestureRecognizerStateChanged) {

        // If the phase of the gesture is MovingDown, and the touch moved
        // down, the gesture has Changed
        if (self.phase == DownUpGestureMovingDown && position.y >
            lastPosition.y) {
            self.state = UIGestureRecognizerStateChanged;
        }
        // If the phase of the gesture is MovingDown, and the touch moved
        // up, the gesture has Changed; also, change the phase to MovingUp
        if (self.phase == DownUpGestureMovingDown && position.y <
            lastPosition.y) {
            self.phase = DownUpGestureMovingUp;
            self.state = UIGestureRecognizerStateChanged;
        }
        // If the phase of the gesture is MovingUp, and the touch moved
        // down, then the gesture has Cancelled
        if (self.phase == DownUpGestureMovingUp && position.y >
            lastPosition.y) {
            self.state = UIGestureRecognizerStateCancelled;
        }

    }
}

- (void)touchesEnded:(NSSet *)touches withEvent:(UIEvent *)event {
    // We know that there's only one touch.

    // If the touch ends while the phase is MovingUp, the gesture has
    // Ended. If the touch ends while the phase is MovingDown, the gesture
    // has Failed.
```

```
        if (self.phase == DownUpGestureMovingDown) {
            self.state = UIGestureRecognizerStateFailed;
        } else if (self.phase == DownUpGestureMovingUp) {
            self.state = UIGestureRecognizerStateEnded;
        }
    }
}

@end
```

Finally, in *ViewController.m*:

```
#import "ViewController.h"
#import "DownUpGestureRecognizer.h"

@interface ViewController ()
@property (strong, nonatomic) IBOutlet UIView *customGestureView;
@property (strong, nonatomic) IBOutlet UILabel *customGestureStatusLabel;

@end

@implementation ViewController

- (void)viewDidLoad
{
    [super viewDidLoad];

    DownUpGestureRecognizer* downUpGesture = [[DownUpGestureRecognizer alloc]
                            initWithTarget:self action:@selector(downUp:)];

    [self.customGestureView addGestureRecognizer:downUpGesture];
}

- (void) downUp:(DownUpGestureRecognizer*)downUp {

    if (downUp.state == UIGestureRecognizerStateBegan) {
        self.customGestureStatusLabel.text = @"Gesture began";
    }

    if (downUp.state == UIGestureRecognizerStateChanged) {
        NSString* phaseString;
        if (downUp.phase == DownUpGestureMovingDown)
            phaseString = @"Down";

        if (downUp.phase == DownUpGestureMovingUp)
            phaseString = @"Up";

        self.customGestureStatusLabel.text = [NSString
            stringWithFormat:@"Gesture changed, phase = %@", phaseString];
    }

    if (downUp.state == UIGestureRecognizerStateEnded) {
        self.customGestureStatusLabel.text = @"Gesture ended";
    }
```

```
    if (downUp.state == UIGestureRecognizerStateCancelled) {
        self.customGestureStatusLabel.text = @"Gesture cancelled";
    }

    if (downUp.state == UIGestureRecognizerStateFailed) {
        self.customGestureStatusLabel.text = @"Gesture failed";
    }

}

- (void)didReceiveMemoryWarning
{
    [super didReceiveMemoryWarning];
    // Dispose of any resources that can be re-created.
}

@end
```

Discussion

The first step in creating a new UIGestureRecognizer is to import the *UIKit/UIGestureRecognizerSubclass.h*. This header file redefines the state property as readwrite, which lets you set the state of the recognizer. Everything else is simply watching touches, and changing state based on that.

A gesture recognizer works by receiving touches, via the touchesBegan, touchesMoved, touchesEnded, and touchesCancelled methods (much like a UIView) does. A recognizer is responsible for keeping track of whatever information it needs in order to determine the state of the gesture.

Recognizers don't communicate directly with their targets; instead, they change the value of the state property, which controls whether they're in the Began, Changed, Ended, Cancelled, or other states.

When your recognizer decides that it's seen a gesture, it changes its state to UIGestureRecognizerStateBegan. This causes the gesture recognition system to send the recognizer's target object its action message. Similarly, your recognizer changes the state property to UIGestureRecognizerStateChanged when it decides that the gesture has changed.

An important state that you can set your recognizer to is Failed. For complex gestures, it's possible that the sequences of touches that the recognizer has been observing won't turn out to actually constitute the kind of gesture you're looking for. For example, if a drag gesture recognizer sees a touch land on the screen, it's possible that it's the start of a drag gesture, but it can't be sure—it's not a drag until the touch starts moving. If the touch immediately lifts up, the drag gesture recognizer changes to the Failed state. This allows other gesture recognizers to step in, if applicable.

3.7. Receiving Touches in Custom Areas of a View

Problem

By default, a UIView detects all touches that fall within its bounds. You want a view to receive touches in a different region.

Solution

To tell iOS that a point should be considered to be within the bounds of a view, you override the pointInside:withEvent: method.

In a UIView subclass:

```
- (BOOL)pointInside:(CGPoint)point withEvent:(UIEvent *)event {
    // A point is inside this view if it falls inside a rectangle
    // that's 40 pt larger than the bounds of the view

    return CGRectContainsPoint(CGRectInset(self.bounds, -40, -40), point);
}
```

Discussion

When a touch lands on the screen, iOS starts checking all views to find out which view was touched. It does this by calling pointInside:withEvent: on the top-level view, and finding out whether the touch is considered "inside" that view. It then begins asking each of the subviews inside that view whether the touch should be considered inside it, proceeding until the lowest-level view is reached.

By default, a point is considered "inside" the view if it's within the view's bounds rectangle. However, you can override this by providing your own implementation of pointInside:withEvent:.

pointInside:withEvent: takes a CGPoint in the coordinate space of the view, and returns YES if the point should be considered inside the view and NO if the point is outside of the view.

3.8. Detecting Shakes

Problem

You want to detect when the user's device is shaking.

Solution

Add this code to a view controller:

```
- (BOOL)canBecomeFirstResponder {
    return YES;
}

- (void)motionBegan:(UIEventSubtype)motion withEvent:(UIEvent *)event {
    self.shakingLabel.hidden = NO;
}

- (void)motionEnded:(UIEventSubtype)motion withEvent:(UIEvent *)event {
    double delayInSeconds = 1.0;
    dispatch_time_t popTime = dispatch_time(DISPATCH_TIME_NOW, (int64_t)
                                    (delayInSeconds * NSEC_PER_SEC));
    dispatch_after(popTime, dispatch_get_main_queue(), ^(void){
        self.shakingLabel.hidden = YES;
    });

}
```

Discussion

Shaking is a kind of gesture that views and view controllers can detect. If you want a view controller to detect it, you first need to indicate to the system that your view controller is capable of becoming the "first responder"—that is, that it's able to receive motion gestures like shaking:

```
- (BOOL)canBecomeFirstResponder {
    return YES;
}
```

When shaking begins, the view controller receives the `motionBegan:withEvent:` message. When shaking ends, the `motionEnded:withEvent:` message is sent:

```
- (void)motionBegan:(UIEventSubtype)motion withEvent:(UIEvent *)event {
    // Shaking started, do something
}

- (void)motionEnded:(UIEventSubtype)motion withEvent:(UIEvent *)event {
    // Shaking stopped, do something else
}
```

In the case of the example code, all we're doing is making a label become visible when shaking begins, and making it invisible two seconds after shaking ends.

3.9. Detecting Device Tilt

Problem

You want to detect how the device has been tilted. For example, if you're making a driving game, you want to know how far the device is being turned, so that you can figure out how the user's car is being steered.

Solution

You get information about how the device is being moved and rotated by using the Core Motion framework. Select the project at the top of the Project Navigator and scroll down to "Linked Frameworks and Libraries." Click the + button, search for "CoreMotion," and double-click "CoreMotion.framework." Then, in your view controller, import the Core Motion header file and create a motion manager that will give you information about how the device is being manipulated. To use it, you'll first need to add *CoreMotion.framework* to your project:

```objc
#import "ViewController.h"
#import <CoreMotion/CoreMotion.h>

@interface ViewController () {
    CMMotionManager* motionManager;
}

@property (strong, nonatomic) IBOutlet UILabel *pitchLabel;
@property (strong, nonatomic) IBOutlet UILabel *yawLabel;
@property (strong, nonatomic) IBOutlet UILabel *rollLabel;
@end

@implementation ViewController

- (void)viewDidLoad
{
    [super viewDidLoad];

    motionManager = [[CMMotionManager alloc] init];

    NSOperationQueue* mainQueue = [NSOperationQueue mainQueue];

    [motionManager startDeviceMotionUpdatesToQueue:mainQueue
        withHandler:^(CMDeviceMotion *motion, NSError *error) {

        float roll = motion.attitude.roll;
        float rollDegrees = roll * 180 / M_PI;

        float yaw = motion.attitude.yaw;
        float yawDegrees = yaw * 180 / M_PI;

        float pitch = motion.attitude.pitch;
        float pitchDegrees = pitch * 180 / M_PI;


        self.rollLabel.text = [NSString stringWithFormat:@"Roll: %.2f°",
                                rollDegrees];
        self.yawLabel.text = [NSString stringWithFormat:@"Yaw: %.2f°",
                                yawDegrees];
        self.pitchLabel.text = [NSString stringWithFormat:@"Pitch: %.2f°",
                                pitchDegrees];
```

```
    }];
}
```

@end

Discussion

Objects can be tilted in three different ways. As illustrated in Figure 3-2, they can *pitch*, *yaw*, and *roll*: that is, rotate around three different imaginary lines. When an object pitches, it rotates around a line drawn from its left edge to its right edge. When it yaws, it rotates around a line drawn from the top edge to the bottom edge. When it rolls, it rotates around a line drawn from the middle of its front face to the middle of the back face.

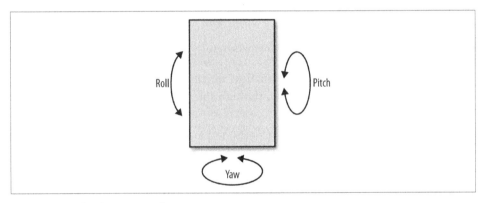

Figure 3-2. The three axes of rotation

Your app can get information regarding how the device is angled through the Core Motion framework. The main class in this framework is `CMMotionManager`, which allows you to sign up to be notified when the device is moved or tilted. So, to get started, you first need to create a `CMMotionManager`.

 It's important to keep a reference to your `CMMotionManager` around. Without one, the automatic reference counting system will notice that there's no reason to keep the `CMMotionManager` in memory, and it'll be deallocated. This won't lead to a crash, but it will mean that you won't get any information from it when the device is rotated or moved.

That's why, in the example, we store the `CMMotionManager` in an instance variable. Doing this means that the view controller has a strong reference to the `CMMotionManager`, which will keep it in memory.

Once you've created your motion manager, you can start receiving information about the device's movement. To receive this information, you need to call `startDeviceMo tionUpdatesToQueue:withHandler:` on your `CMMotionManager`:

```
[motionManager startDeviceMotionUpdatesToQueue:mainQueue
    withHandler:^(CMDeviceMotion *motion, NSError *error) {
        // Do something with the motion info here
    }
```

This method takes two parameters: an `NSOperationQueue` and a block. Every time the device moves, the motion manager will call the block, using the operation queue you provide. In our example, we're using the main queue (i.e., `[NSOperationQueue main Queue]`), so that the block is able to update the user interface.

Every time the block is called, it receives two parameters: a `CMMotion` object, and an `NSError` object. The `CMMotion` object contains information about how the device is currently moving, and the `NSError` object either is `nil` if nothing's gone wrong, or contains information about what's gone wrong and why.

A `CMMotion` object contains a *lot* of information for you to work with:

- You can access accelerometer information, which tells you how the device is moving and in which direction gravity is, through the `userAcceleration` and `gravity` properties.

- You can access calibrated gyroscope information, which tells you how the device is oriented and how fast it's currently rotating, through the `attitude` and `rotation Rate` properties.

- You can access calibrated magnetic field information, which tells you about the total magnetic field that the device is in (minus device bias), through the `magnetic Field` property.

 The `magneticField` property is really cool. It's not too tricky to write an app that watches the magnetic field—once you've made that, wave your device near something made of iron or steel. Congratulations, you've just turned your phone into a metal detector! See Recipe 3.18.

In this particular example, we care most about the device's *attitude*. The attitude of an object means how it's oriented in space. The attitude of a device is represented by three angles, *pitch*, *yaw*, and *roll*, measured in radians—if you remember your high school math, there are 2π radians in a circle.

To convert from radians to degrees, and vice versa, use these formulas:

```
degrees = radians / n * 180

radians = degrees * n / 180
```

This recipe talks about how you can access tilt across all axes; to use this information for steering, take a look at Recipe 3.18.

3.10. Getting the Compass Heading

Problem

You want to know which direction the user is facing, relative to north.

Solution

First, add the Core Motion framework to your project and set up a `CMMotionManager`, as per Recipe 3.9.

Then, when you ask the system to start delivering device motion information to your application, use the `startDeviceMotionUpdatesUsingReferenceFrame:to Queue:withHandler:` method and pass in `CMAttitudeReferenceFrameXTrueNorthZ Vertical` as the first parameter:

```
[motionManager startDeviceMotionUpdatesUsingReferenceFrame:
    CMAttitudeReferenceFrameXTrueNorthZVertical toQueue:mainQueue
    withHandler:^(CMDeviceMotion *motion, NSError *error) {

    float yaw = motion.attitude.yaw;

    float yawDegrees = yaw * 180 / M_PI;

    self.directionLabel.text = [NSString stringWithFormat:@"Direction: %.0f°",
                                yawDegrees];

}];
```

Discussion

When you begin receiving device motion information, all attitude information is relative to a *reference frame*. The reference frame is your "zero point" for orientation.

By default, the zero point is set when you activate the device motion system. That is, the first attitude information you receive will indicate that the device is oriented at the zero point. As you rotate the device, the attitude information will change relative to the zero point.

The default reference frame is able to determine the device's pitch and roll, by measuring the direction of gravity. That is, it's always possible to know what direction "down" is. However, it isn't possible for a gyroscope and accelerometer to measure the *yaw*, for the same reason that you don't have a constant, innate knowledge of which direction is north.

To get this information, a magnetometer is needed. Magnetometers sense magnetic fields, which allows you to figure out where the north pole of the strongest magnet near you is. In other words, a magnetometer is able to function as a compass.

Magnetometers require additional power to use, as well as additional CPU resources necessary to integrate the magnetic field data with the accelerometer and gyroscope data. By default, therefore, the magnetometer is turned off. However, if you need to know where north is, you can indicate to the Core Motion system that you need this information.

When you call the `startDeviceMotionUpdatesUsingReferenceFrame:toQueue:with Handler:` method, you have a choice regarding what reference frame you can use. The options available are as follows:

`CMAttitudeReferenceFrameXArbitraryZVertical`
Yaw is set to zero when the device motion system is turned on.

`CMAttitudeReferenceFrameXArbitraryCorrectedZVertical`
Yaw is set to zero when the device motion system is turned on, and the magnetometer is used to keep this stable over time (i.e., the zero point won't drift as much).

`CMAttitudeReferenceFrameXMagneticNorthZVertical`
The zero yaw point is magnetic north.

`CMAttitudeReferenceFrameXTrueNorthZVertical`
The zero yaw point is true north. The system needs to use the location system to figure this out.

If you need the most accuracy, `CMAttitudeReferenceFrameXTrueNorthZVertical` should be used. This uses the most battery power, and takes the longest time to get a fix. If you don't really care about which direction north is, go with `CMAttitudeRefer enceFrameXArbitraryZVertical` or `CMAttitudeReferenceFrameXArbitraryCorrec tedZVertical`.

3.11. Accessing the User's Location

Problem

You want to determine where on the planet the user currently is.

Solution

To get the user's location, you first need to add the Core Location framework to your application. Refer to Recipe 3.9 for instructions on doing this; choose the file *Core-Location.framework*.

When you want to work with user location data, you need to explain to the user for what purpose the location data is going to be used:

- Go to the project's information screen by clicking on the project at the top of the Project Navigator (at the left of the Xcode window).

- Go to the Info tab.

- Add a new entry in the list of settings that appears: "Privacy - Location Usage Description." In the Value column, add some text that explains what the user location will be used for. (In this example, it can be something like "the app will display your coordinates.")

 Adding this information is mandatory. If you don't explain why you need access to the user's location, Apple will likely reject your app from the App Store.

The reason for this is that the user's location is private information, and your app needs to have a good reason for using it. That's not to say that you shouldn't make games that ask for the user's location—far from it! But don't get the user's location just so that you can gather statistics about where your users live.

To actually get the user's location and work with it, you use a `CLLocationManager`:

```objc
#import "ViewController.h"
#import <CoreLocation/CoreLocation.h>

@interface ViewController () <CLLocationManagerDelegate> {
    CLLocationManager* locationManager;
}

@property (strong, nonatomic) IBOutlet UILabel *latitudeLabel;
@property (strong, nonatomic) IBOutlet UILabel *longitudeLabel;
@property (strong, nonatomic) IBOutlet UILabel *locationErrorLabel;
@end

@implementation ViewController

- (void)viewDidLoad
{
    [super viewDidLoad];
```

```
        locationManager = [[CLLocationManager alloc] init];
        locationManager.delegate = self;

        [locationManager startUpdatingLocation];

        self.locationErrorLabel.hidden = YES;
    }

    - (void)locationManager:(CLLocationManager *)manager
        didUpdateLocations:(NSArray *)locations {

        self.locationErrorLabel.hidden = YES;

        CLLocation* location = [locations lastObject];

        float latitude = location.coordinate.latitude;
        float longitude = location.coordinate.longitude;

        self.latitudeLabel.text = [NSString stringWithFormat:@"Latitude: %.4f",
                                    latitude];
        self.longitudeLabel.text = [NSString stringWithFormat:@"Longitude: %.4f",
                                     longitude];

    }

    - (void)locationManager:(CLLocationManager *)manager
        didFailWithError:(NSError *)error {
            self.locationErrorLabel.hidden = NO;
    }

    @end
```

Discussion

A CLLocationManager, once set up and configured, sends messages to a delegate object, notifying it of the user's location.

To receive messages from a CLLocationManager, an object needs to conform to the CLLocationManagerDelegate protocol:

```
@interface ViewController () <CLLocationManagerDelegate>
```

To set up a CLLocationManager, you create an instance of the class. You'll also need to create and keep a strong reference to the CLLocationManager object, to keep it from being freed from memory, and indicate to it what object should receive location updates. Finally, you need to tell the CLLocationManager that it should activate the GPS system and begin telling the delegate object about the user's location:

```
locationManager = [[CLLocationManager alloc] init];
locationManager.delegate = self;
```

```
[locationManager startUpdatingLocation];
```

Once you've told the location manager that you want to start receiving location information, you then need to implement one of the methods in the CLLocationManager Delegate protocol: locationManager:didUpdateLocations:. This method is called every time the location manager decides that the user has changed location. It receives two parameters: the CLLocationManager itself, and an NSArray containing one or more CLLocation objects.

There can be more than one CLLocation object in the array. This can happen when, for some reason, your application hasn't been able to receive location updates (e.g., it may have been in the background). In these cases, you'll receive a bunch of CLLocations, which are delivered in the order that they occurred. The last object in the array is always the most recent location the device was observed at. You can access it through NSArray's lastObject method:

```
CLLocation* location = [locations lastObject];
```

A CLLocation object represents the user's current location on the planet. It contains, among other information, the user's latitude, longitude, and altitude.

The user's latitude and longitude, which are almost always the only things you want to know about, can be accessed through the CLLocation's coordinate property, which is a CLLocationCoordinate2D. A CLLocationCoordinate2D contains two things:

```
float latitude = location.coordinate.latitude;
float longitude = location.coordinate.longitude;
```

 The user's location is not guaranteed to be precise—the GPS system is good, but it's not accurate enough to pinpoint the location down to the nearest centimeter (unless you're in the U.S. military, in which case, greetings!).

Therefore, each CLLocation object contains a horizontalAccuracy property, which represents the "radius of uncertainty" of the location, measured in meters.

For example, if the horizontalAccuracy of a CLLocation is 5, this means that the user is within 5 meters of the location indicated by the latitude and longitude.

3.12. Calculating the User's Speed

Problem

You want to determine how fast the user is moving.

Solution

This information can be gained through the Core Location framework.

First, set up a `CLLocationManager`, as discussed in the previous recipe, and start receiving updates to the user's location:

```
- (void)locationManager:(CLLocationManager *)manager
    didUpdateLocations:(NSArray *)locations {

    CLLocation* lastLocation = [locations lastObject];

    if (lastLocation.speed > 0) {
        self.speedLabel.text = [NSString stringWithFormat:@"Currently
                                moving at %.0fm/s", lastLocation.speed];
    }

}
```

Discussion

`CLLocation` objects contain a `speed` property, which contains the speed at which the device is traveling. This is measured in meters per second.

 If you want to convert this to kilometers per hour, you can do this:

```
float kPH = location.speed * 3.6;
```

If you want to convert meters per second to miles per hour, you can do this:

```
float mPH =  location.speed * 2.236936;
```

3.13. Pinpointing the User's Proximity to Landmarks

Problem

You want to calculate how far away the user is from a location.

Solution

We'll assume that you already know the user's location, represented by a `CLLocation` object. If you don't already have this information, see Recipe 3.11.

We'll also assume that you have the latitude and longitude coordinates of the location from which you want to measure the distance. You can use this information to determine the proximity:

```
CLLocation* userLocation = ... // get the user's location from CoreLocation
float latitude = ... // latitude of the other location
```

```
float longitude = ... // longitude of the other location

CLLocation* otherLocation = [CLLocation locationWithLatitude:latitude
                                longitude:longitude];

float distance = [userLocation distanceFromLocation:otherLocation];
```

Discussion

The distanceFromLocation: method returns the distance from the other location, measured in meters.

It's important to note that the distance is not a direct straight-line distance, but rather takes into account the curvature of the earth. Also keep in mind that the distance traveled doesn't take into account any mountains or hills between the user's location and the other location.

3.14. Receiving Notifications When the User Changes Location

Problem

You want to be notified when the user enters a specific region, or exits it.

Solution

This code requires adding the Core Location framework to your application (see Recipe 3.9 for instructions on adding a framework). Additionally, it requires using iOS 7.

Your application can receive updates to the user's location even when it's not running. To enable this, follow these steps:

1. After adding *CoreLocation.framework* to your application, go to your project's Info screen, by clicking on the project at the top of the Project Navigator (at the left of the Xcode window, see Figure 3-3).

2. Click on the Capabilities tab.

3. Turn on "Background Modes."

4. Check the "Location updates" checkbox, as shown in Figure 3-4.

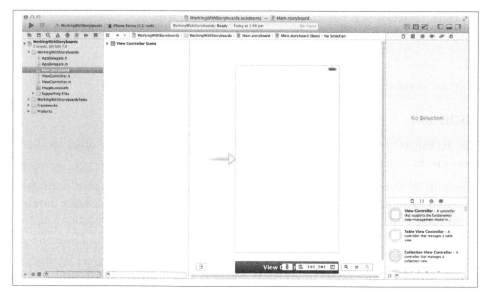

Figure 3-3. An empty screen

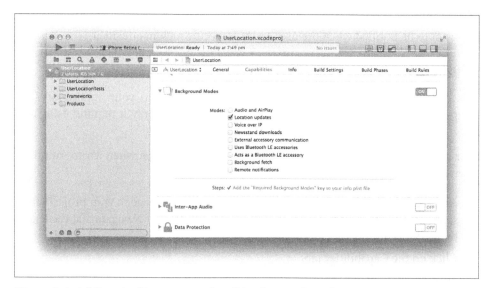

Figure 3-4. Adding the "Location updates" background mode

Make *ViewController.m* look like the following code:

```
#import "ViewController.h"
#import <CoreLocation/CoreLocation.h>

@interface ViewController () <CLLocationManagerDelegate> {
```

```objc
    CLLocationManager* locationManager;
    CLCircularRegion* regionToMonitor;
}

@end

@implementation ViewController

- (void)viewDidLoad
{
    [super viewDidLoad];

    locationManager = [[CLLocationManager alloc] init];
    locationManager.delegate = self;
    [locationManager startUpdatingLocation];

}

- (void)locationManager:(CLLocationManager *)manager
    didUpdateLocations:(NSArray *)locations {

        if (regionToMonitor == nil) {

            CLLocation* location = [locations lastObject];

            regionToMonitor = [[CLCircularRegion alloc]
                initWithCenter:location.coordinate radius:20
                identifier:@"StartingPoint"];

            [locationManager startMonitoringForRegion:regionToMonitor];

            NSLog(@"Now monitoring region %@", regionToMonitor);

        }
}

- (void) locationManager:(CLLocationManager *)manager
    didEnterRegion:(CLRegion *)region {
        NSLog(@"Entering region!");
}

- (void)locationManager:(CLLocationManager *)manager
    didExitRegion:(CLRegion *)region {
        NSLog(@"Exiting region!");
}

@end
```

Discussion

Your application can be notified when the user enters or exits a region. A region is defined by a central point, and a radius—that is to say, regions are always circular.

You register a region by creating a `CLRegion` object and giving it a center point (latitude and longitude) and radius, as well as a name (a string that you will use to refer to the region):

```
float latitude  = ...          // latitude
float longitude = ...          // longitude
float radius    = ...          // radius
NSString* name  = @"My Region"; // something to call the region

CLCoordinate2D coordinate = CLCoordinate2DMake(latitude, longitude);

CLRegion* region = [[CLCircularRegion alloc] initWithCenter:coordinate
                    radius:radius identifier:name];
```

 The maximum allowed radius for a region might vary from device to device. You can check what the maximum allowed radius is by asking the `CLLocationManager` class for its `maximumRegionMonitoringDistance` property:

```
CLLocationDistance maximumRegionRadius = locationManager.maximumRegion
                                         MonitoringDistance;
```

Once the region has been created, you indicate to your `CLLocationManager` that you want to be notified when the user enters and exits the region:

```
[locationManager startMonitoringForRegion:regionToMonitor];
```

Once this is done, the `CLLocationManager`'s delegate will receive a `locationManager:didEnterRegion:` message when the user enters the region, and a `locationManager:didExitRegion:` message when the user exits.

You can only register 20 regions at a time. You can ask the location manager to give you an `NSArray` of all of the `CLRegions` you've registered via the `monitoredRegions` method:

```
NSArray* monitoredRegions = locationManager.monitoredRegions;
```

When you no longer want to receive notifications regarding a region, you send the `CLLocationManager` the `stopMonitoringForRegion:` message:

```
[locationManager stopMonitoringForRegion:regionToMonitor];
```

Finally, a word about how precise regions can be. Later devices tend to be more precise, which means that on devices earlier than the iPhone 4S, you shouldn't create regions with a radius of less than 400 meters. Additionally, when the user enters or exits a region, it generally takes about 3 to 5 minutes for the device to notice it and send a notification to your application. This means that using smaller regions may mean that your app receives notifications well after the user has left the area. In order to report region changes in a timely manner, the region monitoring service requires network connectivity.

3.15. Looking Up GPS Coordinates for a Street Address

Problem

You have a street address, and you want to get latitude and longitude coordinates for it. For example, you have a game that involves players moving from one named location to another, and you want to get the coordinates so you can monitor when they get close.

Solution

iOS has a built-in system that lets you convert between coordinates and street addresses. *Geocoding* is the process of converting a human-readable address (like "1 Infinite Loop, Cupertino, California") into latitude and longitude coordinates, which you can then use with the location system.

First, add the Core Location framework to your project (see Recipe 3.9).

Next, create a CLGeocoder instance variable (in this example, we've named it geocoder):

```
NSString* addressString = @"1 Infinite Loop, Cupertino, California";

geocoder = [[CLGeocoder alloc] init];

[geocoder geocodeAddressString:addressString completionHandler:^(NSArray
    *placemarks, NSError *error) {
        CLPlacemark* placemark = [placemarks lastObject];

        float latitude = placemark.location.coordinate.latitude;
        float longitude = placemark.location.coordinate.longitude;
}];
```

Discussion

To use geocoding, you create a CLGeocoder object. A geocoder object communicates with Apple's geocoding server, and runs the completion handler block that you provide when the geocoding request returns. This means that your device needs to be on the network in order to use geocoding.

When the geocoding request returns, you'll either receive an NSArray that contains CLPlacemark objects, or an NSError that describes what went wrong. You might get more than one CLPlacemark object; for example, if the geocoding server is unsure about the exact location you meant, it may return a few different options.

CLPlacemark objects describe a location, and they contain quite a lot of information for you to use. The specific contents available for each placemark vary, but they include things like the name of the location, the street name, the town or city, country, and so on.

Additionally, every CLPlacemark contains a property called location, which is a CLLo cation object that you can use to get the latitude and longitude.

3.16. Looking Up Street Addresses from the User's Location

Problem

You know the user's location, and you want to find the street address using their coordinates.

Solution

First, add the Core Location framework to your project (see Recipe 3.9).

Next, create a CLGeocoder instance variable (in this example, we've named it geocoder):

```
geocoder = [[CLGeocoder alloc] init];

CLLocation* location = ... // a CLLocation

[geocoder reverseGeocodeLocation:location completionHandler:^(NSArray
    *placemarks, NSError *error) {

        NSString* addressString = [placemarks lastObject]

        self.labelTextView.text = addressString;

}];
```

Discussion

A CLGeocoder object is able to perform both geocoding and *reverse* geocoding. Whereas geocoding involves taking a street address and returning coordinates, reverse geocoding means taking coordinates and providing a street address.

Reverse geocoding works in a very similar manner to geocoding: you create a CLGeo coder, provide it with input data and a block that you want to run when the work is complete, and set it off.

Also like with normal geocoding, reverse geocoding returns an NSArray of CLPlace mark objects. However, there's no built-in method for converting a CLPlacemark into a string (not counting description, which includes all kinds of information that the user doesn't care about). It's therefore up to you to pull the information out of the CLPlace mark object and format it into an NSString for the user to see.

3.17. Using the Device as a Steering Wheel

Problem

You want to let the user use the device as a steering wheel, and get information on how far he's steering.

Solution

You can get information about how far the user is steering by deciding which axis you want to define as the "steering" axis, and using Core Motion to work out the rotation around that axis.

In most cases, games that involve steering are played in landscape mode. To make sure your game only appears in landscape, select the project at the top of the Project Navigator, and scroll down to Device Orientation. Make sure that only Landscape Left and Landscape Right are selected.

Next, import the Core Motion framework (see Recipe 3.9). Finally, add the following code to your project:

```
motionManager = [[CMMotionManager alloc] init];

[motionManager startDeviceMotionUpdatesToQueue:[NSOperationQueue mainQueue]
    withHandler:^(CMDeviceMotion *motion, NSError *error) {

        // Maximum steering left is -50 degrees,
        // maximum steering right is 50 degrees
        float maximumSteerAngle = 50;

        // When in landscape,
        float rotationAngle = motion.attitude.pitch * 180.0f / M_PI;

        // -1.0 = hard left, 1.0 = hard right
        float steering = 0.0;

        UIInterfaceOrientation orientation = [UIApplication
                                        sharedApplication]
                                        .statusBarOrientation;

        if (orientation == UIInterfaceOrientationLandscapeLeft) {
            steering = rotationAngle / -maximumSteerAngle;
        } else if (orientation == UIInterfaceOrientationLandscapeRight) {
            steering = rotationAngle / maximumSteerAngle;
        }

        // Limit the steering to between -1.0 and 1.0
        steering = fminf(steering, 1.0);
        steering = fmaxf(steering, -1.0);
```

```
    NSLog(@"Steering: %.2f", steering);

}];
```

Discussion

In this solution, the code figures out how the device is being held and generates a number to represent how the user is "steering" the device. –1.0 means the device is being steered hard left, and 1.0 means hard right.

In landscape mode, "steering" the device means changing its pitch—that is, changing the angle of the line that extends from the left of the screen to the right of the screen. However, "landscape" can mean that the device is being held in two different ways: "landscape left" means that the home button is to the left of the screen, and "landscape right" means that the home button is to the right. In other words, landscape right is an upside-down version of landscape left.

This means that if we want –1.0 to always mean left, we have to know which orientation the device is being held in. You can check this by asking the shared UIApplication object for the current statusBarOrientation.

3.18. Detecting Magnets

Problem

You want your game to detect when the device is near a magnet or other ferrous material.

Solution

First, you need to import *CoreMotion.framework*. See Recipe 3.9 for instructions. Use the CMMotionManager class's startMagnetometerUpdatesToQueue:withHandler: method to register to receive information from the device's built-in magnetometer:

```
motionManager = [[CMMotionManager alloc] init];

[motionManager startMagnetometerUpdatesToQueue:[NSOperationQueue mainQueue]
    withHandler:^(CMMagnetometerData *magnetometerData, NSError *error) {

        CMMagneticField magneticField = magnetometerData.magneticField;

        NSString* xValue = [NSString stringWithFormat:@"%.2f", magneticField.x];
        NSString* yValue = [NSString stringWithFormat:@"%.2f", magneticField.y];
        NSString* zValue = [NSString stringWithFormat:@"%.2f", magneticField.z];

        double average = (magneticField.x + magneticField.y +
                        magneticField.z) / 3.0;

        NSString* averageValue = [NSString stringWithFormat:@"%.2f", average];
```

```
    NSLog(@"Magnetic field:\nAverage: %@\tX: %@\tY: %@\tZ: %@",
        averageValue, xValue, yValue, zValue);
}];
```

Discussion

The built-in magnetometer in all devices shipped since the iPhone 3GS is used to find the heading of the device (i.e., the direction in which it's pointing). By getting a reading on the magnetic fields surrounding the device, the iPhone can determine which direction is north.

However, this isn't the only reason why magnetometers are cool. The magnetometer can be accessed directly, which gives you information on the presence of magnets (as well as ferromagnetic metals, like steel and iron) near the device.

When you want to start getting information about nearby magnetic fields, you use the CMDeviceMotion class's startMagnetometerUpdatesToQueue:withHandler: method. This method works in a manner very similar to when you want to get overall device motion (see Recipe 3.9); however, instead of receiving a CMDeviceMotion object, you instead get a CMMagnetometerData object.

The CMMagnetometerData object contains two properties: an NSTimeInterval that represents when the information was sampled, and a CMMagneticField structure that contains the data itself.

The information stored in the CMMagneticField is represented in microteslas, which are a measurement of magnetic flux density—that is, the strength of the magnetic field currently affecting the device.

When the device is near a planet—which, at the time of writing, is very likely to be the case—it will be subjected to that planet's magnetic field. Earth has a particularly strong magnetic field, which means that the measurements that come from the magnetometer will never be zero. Additionally, some components in the device itself are slightly magnetic, which contributes to the readings. Finally, the readings that you'll get from the magnetometer will be stronger when the sensor is *moving* through a magnetic field, as opposed to remaining stationary within one.

This means that you can't treat the information that comes from the magnetometer as absolute "near magnet"/"not near magnet" data. Instead, you need to interpret the information over time: if the values you're getting from the magnetometer are rising or falling quickly, the device is near something magnetic.

Magnetometers haven't seen much use in games to date, which means that there's a huge potential area for new kinds of gameplay. This is left as an exercise for the reader—what kind of gameplay can you create that's based on detecting metal?

3.19. Utilizing Inputs to Improve Game Design

Problem

You want to effectively utilize the inputs (some of them unique) that are available on iOS to make a better game.

Solution

When considering how your game is controlled, it pays to consider the environment in which iOS games are frequently played. The iPhone and iPad are, obviously, inherently mobile devices—they are used by people who are often out and about, or at work, lying in front of the television, or commuting to work on a loud train.

Because of this, iOS games should be simple and easy to control, and if possible should use as much direct manipulation—dragging, touching, gestures—as possible. People are distracted, and they don't want to think about the myriad ways in which they could control something. If the obvious doesn't work, they'll go and play a different game—it's hard enough trying to play a game on the train anyway!

If a player can directly drag her character around, rather than using an on-screen directional control, then you should enable that. If your game requires the player to shake loose enemy boarders from a spacecraft, why not let him shake the device instead of tapping a button marked "shake"?

Discussion

Give users direct control and your game will feel more responsive, be more entertaining, and end up getting played a whole lot more often.

CHAPTER 4

Sound

Sound is a frequently overlooked part of games. Even in big-name titles, sound design and programming frequently is left until late in the game development process. This is especially true on mobile devices—the user might be playing the game in a crowded, noisy environment and might not even hear the sounds and music you've put into it, so why bother putting in much effort?

However, sound is an incredibly important part of games. When a game sounds great, and makes noises in response to the visible parts of the game, the player gets drawn in to the world that the game's creating.

In this chapter, you'll learn how to use iOS's built-in support for playing both sound effects and music. You'll also learn how to take advantage of the speech synthesis features, which are new in iOS 7.

Sound good?[1]

4.1. Playing Sound with AVAudioPlayer

Problem

You want to play back an audio file, as simply as possible and with a minimum of work.

Solution

The simplest way to play a sound file is using AVAudioPlayer, which is a class available in the AVFoundation framework. To use this feature, you first need to add the AVFoundation framework to your project. Select the project at the top of the Project Nav-

---

1. We apologize for the pun and have fired Jon, who wrote it.

igator and scroll down to "Linked Frameworks and Libraries." Click the + button and double-click on "AVFoundation.framework."

You'll also need to import the *AVFoundation/AVFoundation.h* file in each file that uses the AVFoundation files:

```
#import <AVFoundation/AVFoundation.h>
```

You create an AVAudioPlayer by providing it with the location of the file you want it to play. This should generally be done ahead of time, before the sound needs to be played, in order to avoid playback delays.

In this example, audioPlayer is an AVAudioPlayer instance variable:

```
NSURL* soundFileURL = [[NSBundle mainBundle] URLForResource:@"TestSound"
                        withExtension:@"wav"];
NSError* error = nil;

audioPlayer = [[AVAudioPlayer alloc] initWithContentsOfURL:soundFileURL
              error:&error];

if (error != nil) {
    NSLog(@"Failed to load the sound: %@", [error localizedDescription]);
}

[audioPlayer prepareToPlay];
```

To begin playback, you use the play method:

```
[audioPlayer play];
```

To make playback loop, you change the audio player's numberOfLoops property. To make an AVAudioPlayer play one time and then stop:

```
player.numberOfLoops = 0;
```

To make an AVAudioPlayer play twice and then stop:

```
player.numberOfLoops = 1;
```

To make an AVAudioPlayer play forever, until manually stopped:

```
player.numberOfLoops = -1;
```

By default, an AVAudioPlayer will play its sound one time only. After it's finished playing, a second call to play will rewind it and play it again. By changing the numberOfLoops property, you can make an AVAudioPlayer play its file a single time, a fixed number of times, or continuously until it's sent a pause or stop message.

To stop playback, you use the pause or stop methods (the pause method just stops playback, and lets you resume from where you left off later; the stop method stops playback completely, and unloads the sound from memory):

```
[audioPlayer pause];
[audioPlayer stop];
```

To rewind an audio player, you change the `currentTime` property. This property stores how far playback has progressed, measured in seconds. If you set it to zero, playback will jump back to the start:

```
audioPlayer.currentTime = 0;
```

You can also set this property to other values, in order to jump to a specific point in the audio.

Discussion

If you use an `AVAudioPlayer`, you need to keep a strong reference to it (using an instance variable) to avoid it being released from memory. If that happens, the sound will stop.

If you have multiple sounds that you want to play at the same time, you need to keep references to each (or use an `NSArray` to contain them all). This can get cumbersome, so it's often better to use a dedicated sound engine instead of managing each player yourself.

Preparing an `AVAudioPlayer` takes a little bit of preparation. You need to either know the location of a file that contains the audio you want the player to play, or have an `NSData` object that contains the audio data.

`AVAudioPlayer` supports a number of popular audio formats. The specific formats vary slightly from device to device; the iPhone 5 supports the following formats:

- AAC (8 to 320 Kbps)
- Protected AAC (from the iTunes Store)
- HE-AAC
- MP3 (8 to 320 Kbps)
- MP3 VBR
- Audible (formats 2, 3, 4, Audible Enhanced Audio, AAX, and AAX+)
- Apple Lossless
- AIFF
- WAV

You shouldn't generally have problems with file compatibility across devices, but it's generally best to go with AAC, MP3, AIFF, or WAV.

In this example, it's assumed that there's a file called *TestSound.wav* in the project. You'll want to use a different name for your game, of course.

Use the NSBundle's URLForResource:withExtension method to get the location of a resource on disk:

```
NSURL* soundFileURL = [[NSBundle mainBundle] URLForResource:@"TestSound"
                       withExtension:@"wav"];
```

This returns an NSURL object that contains the location of the file, which you can give to your AVAudioPlayer to tell it where to find the sound file.

The initializer method for AVAudioPlayer is initWithContentsOfURL:error:. The first parameter is an NSURL that indicates where to find a sound file, and the second is a pointer to an NSError reference that allows the method to return an error object if something goes wrong.

Let's take a closer look at how this works. First, you create an NSError variable and set it to nil:

```
NSError* error = nil;
```

Then you call initWithContentsOfURL:error: and provide the NSURL and a *pointer* to the NSError variable:

```
audioPlayer = [[AVAudioPlayer alloc] initWithContentsOfURL:soundFileURL
              error:&error];
```

When this method returns, audioPlayer is either a ready-to-use AVAudioPlayer object, or nil. If it's nil, then the NSError variable will have changed to be a reference to an NSError object, which you can use to find out what went wrong:

```
if (error != nil) {
    NSLog(@"Failed to load the sound: %@", [error localizedDescription]);
}
```

Finally, the AVAudioPlayer can be told to preload the audio file before playback. If you don't do this, it's no big deal—when you tell it to play, it loads the file and then begins playing back. However, for large files, this can lead to a short pause before audio actually starts playing, so it's often best to preload the sound as soon as you can. Note, however, that if you have many large sounds, preloading everything can lead to all of your available memory being consumed, so use this feature with care.

4.2. Recording Sound with AVAudioRecorder

Problem

You want to record sound made by the player, using the built-in microphone.

Solution

AVAudioRecorder is your friend here. Like its sibling AVAudioPlayer (see Recipe 4.1), AVAudioRecorder lives in the AVFoundation framework, so you'll need to add that framework to your project and import the *AVFoundation/AVFoundation.h* header in any files where you want to use it. You can then create an AVAudioRecorder as follows:

```
NSURL* documentsURL = [[[NSFileManager defaultManager]
                        URLsForDirectory:NSDocumentDirectory
                        inDomains:NSUserDomainMask] lastObject];

NSURL* destinationURL = [documentsURL
    URLByAppendingPathComponent:@"RecordedSound.wav"];

NSURL* destinationURL = [self audioRecordingURL];
    NSError* error;

audioRecorder = [[AVAudioRecorder alloc] initWithURL:destinationURL
                settings:nil error:&error];

if (error != nil) {
    NSLog(@"Couldn't create a recorder: %@", [error localizedDescription]);
}

[audioRecorder prepareToRecord];
```

To begin recording, use the record method:

```
[audioRecorder record];
```

To stop recording, use the stop method:

```
[audioRecorder stop];
```

When recording has ended, the file pointed at by the URL you used to create the AVAudioRecorder contains a sound file, which you can play using AVAudioPlayer or any other audio system.

Discussion

Like an AVAudioPlayer, an AVAudioRecorder needs to have at least one strong reference made to it in order to keep it in memory.

In order to record audio, you first need to have the location of the file where the recorded audio will end up. The AVAudioRecorder will create the file if it doesn't already exist; if it does, the recorder will erase the file and overwrite it. So, if you want to avoid losing recorded audio, either never record to the same place twice, or move the recorded audio somewhere else when you're done recording.

The recorded audio file needs to be stored in a location where your game is allowed to put files. A good place to use is your game's *Documents* directory; any files placed in this folder will be backed up when the user's device is synced.

To get the location of your game's *Documents* folder, you can use the `NSFileManager` class:

```
NSURL* documentsURL = [[[NSFileManager defaultManager]
                        URLsForDirectory:NSDocumentDirectory
                        inDomains:NSUserDomainMask] lastObject];
```

Once you have the location of the directory, you can create a URL relative to it. Remember, the URL doesn't have to point to a real file yet; one will be created when recording begins:

```
NSURL* destinationURL = [documentsURL
    URLByAppendingPathComponent:@"RecordedSound.wav"];
```

4.3. Working with Multiple Audio Players

Problem

You want to use multiple audio players, but reuse players when possible.

Solution

Create a manager object that manages a collection of `AVAudioPlayers`. When you want to play a sound, you ask this object to give you an `AVAudioPlayer`. The manager object will try to give you an `AVAudioPlayer` that's not currently doing anything, but if it can't find one, it will create one.

To create your manager object, create a file called *AVAudioPlayerPool.h* with the following contents:

```
#import <Foundation/Foundation.h>
#import <AVFoundation/AVFoundation.h>

@interface AVAudioPlayerPool : NSObject

+ (AVAudioPlayer*) playerWithURL:(NSURL*)url;

@end
```

and a file called *AVAudioPlayerPool.m* with these contents:

```
#import "AVAudioPlayerPool.h"

NSMutableArray* _players = nil;

@implementation AVAudioPlayerPool
```

```objc
+ (NSMutableArray*) players {
    if (_players == nil)
        _players = [[NSMutableArray alloc] init];

    return _players;
}

+ (AVAudioPlayer *)playerWithURL:(NSURL *)url {
    NSMutableArray* availablePlayers = [[self players] mutableCopy];

    // Try and find a player that can be reused and is not playing
    [availablePlayers filterUsingPredicate:[NSPredicate
        predicateWithBlock:^BOOL(AVAudioPlayer* evaluatedObject,
        NSDictionary *bindings) {
            return evaluatedObject.playing == NO && [evaluatedObject.url
                                                isEqual:url];
    }]];

    // If we found one, return it
    if (availablePlayers.count > 0) {
        return [availablePlayers firstObject];
    }

    // Didn't find one? Create a new one
    NSError* error = nil;
    AVAudioPlayer* newPlayer = [[AVAudioPlayer alloc] initWithContentsOfURL:url
                                error:&error];

    if (newPlayer == nil) {
        NSLog(@"Couldn't load %@: %@", url, error);
        return nil;
    }

    [[self players] addObject:newPlayer];

    return newPlayer;

}

@end
```

You can then use it as follows:

```objc
NSURL* url = [[NSBundle mainBundle] URLForResource:@"TestSound"
            withExtension:@"wav"];
AVAudioPlayer* player = [AVAudioPlayerPool playerWithURL:url];
[player play];
```

Discussion

`AVAudioPlayer`s are allowed to be played multiple times, but aren't allowed to change the file that they're playing. This means that if you want to reuse a single player, you have to use the same file; if you want to use a different file, you'll need a new player.

This means that the `AVAudioPlayerPool` object shown in this recipe needs to know which file you want to play.

Our `AVAudioPlayerPool` object does the following things:

1. It keeps a list of `AVAudioPlayer` objects in an `NSMutableArray`.
2. When a player is requested, it checks to see if it has an available player with the right URL; if it does, it returns that.
3. If there's no `AVAudioPlayer` that it can use—either because all of the suitable `AVAudioPlayer`s are playing, or because there's no `AVAudioPlayer` with the right URL—then it creates one, prepares it with the URL provided, and adds it to the list of `AVAudioPlayer`s. This means that when this new `AVAudioPlayer` is done playing, it will be able to be reused.

4.4. Cross-Fading Between Tracks

Problem

You want to blend multiple sounds by smoothly fading one out and another in.

Solution

This method slowly fades an `AVAudioPlayer` from a starting volume to an end volume, over a set duration:

```
- (void) fadePlayer:(AVAudioPlayer*)player fromVolume:(float)startVolume
    toVolume:(float)endVolume overTime:(float)time {

    // Update the volume every 1/100 of a second
    float fadeSteps = time * 100.0;

    self.audioPlayer.volume = startVolume;

    for (int step = 0; step < fadeSteps; step++) {
        double delayInSeconds = step * (time / fadeSteps);

        dispatch_time_t popTime = dispatch_time(DISPATCH_TIME_NOW,
            (int64_t)(delayInSeconds * NSEC_PER_SEC));
        dispatch_after(popTime, dispatch_get_main_queue(), ^(void){
```

```
                    float fraction = ((float)step / fadeSteps);

                    self.audioPlayer.volume = startVolume + (endVolume - startVolume)
                                                  * fraction;

            });
        }
    }
```

To use this method to fade in an AVAudioPlayer, use a startVolume of 0.0 and an endVolume of 1.0:

```
[self fadePlayer:self.audioPlayer fromVolume:0.0 toVolume:1.0 overTime:1.0];
```

To fade out, use a startVolume of 1.0 and an endVolume of 0.0:

```
[self fadePlayer:self.audioPlayer fromVolume:1.0 toVolume:0.0 overTime:1.0];
```

To make the fade take longer, increase the overTime parameter.

Discussion

When you want the volume of an AVAudioPlayer to slowly fade out, what you really want is for the volume to change very slightly but very often. In this recipe, we've created a method that uses Grand Central Dispatch to schedule the repeated, gradual adjustment of the volume of a player over time.

To determine how many individual volume changes are needed, the first step is to decide how many times per second the volume should change. In this example, we've chosen 100 times per second—that is, the volume will be changed 100 times for every second the fade should last:

```
float fadeSteps = time * 100.0;
```

 Feel free to experiment with this number. Bigger numbers will lead to smoother fades, while smaller numbers will be more efficient but might sound worse.

The next step is to ensure that the player's current volume is set to be the start volume:

```
self.audioPlayer.volume = startVolume;
```

We then repeatedly schedule volume changes. We're actually scheduling these changes all at once; however, each change is scheduled to take place slightly after the previous one.

To know exactly when a change should take place, all we need to know is how many steps into the fade we are, and how long the total fade should take. From there, we can calculate how far in the future a specific step should take place:

```
for (int step = 0; step < fadeSteps; step++) {
    double delayInSeconds = step * (time / fadeSteps);
```

Once this duration is known, we can get Grand Central Dispatch to schedule it:

```
dispatch_time_t popTime = dispatch_time(DISPATCH_TIME_NOW,
    (int64_t)(delayInSeconds * NSEC_PER_SEC));
dispatch_after(popTime, dispatch_get_main_queue(), ^(void){
```

The next few lines of code are executed when the step is ready to happen. At this point, we need to know exactly what the volume of the audio player should be:

```
float fraction = ((float)step / fadeSteps);
self.audioPlayer.volume = startVolume + (endVolume - startVolume) *
                          fraction;
```

When the code runs, the for loop creates and schedules multiple blocks that set the volume, with each block reducing the volume a little. The end result is that the user hears a gradual lessening in volume—in other words, a fade out!

4.5. Synthesizing Speech

Problem

You want to make your app speak.

Solution

First, add *AVFoundation.framework* to your project (see Recipe 4.1).

Then, create an instance of AVSpeechSynthesizer:

```
self.speechSynthesizer = [[AVSpeechSynthesizer alloc] init];
```

When you have text you want to speak, create an AVSpeechUtterance:

```
AVSpeechUtterance* utterance = [AVSpeechUtterance
    speechUtteranceWithString:@"Hello, I'm an iPhone!"];
```

You then give the utterance to your AVSpeechSynthesizer:

```
[self.speechSynthesizer speakUtterance:utterance];
```

Discussion

The voices you use with AVSpeechSynthesizer are the same ones seen in the Siri personal assistant that's built in to all devices released since the iPhone 4S, and in the VoiceOver accessibility feature.

You can send more than one AVSpeechUtterance to an AVSpeechSynthesizer at the same time. If you call speakUtterance: while the synthesizer is already speaking, it will wait until the current utterance has finished before moving on to the next.

 Don't call speakUtterance: with the same AVSpeechUtterance twice —you'll cause an exception.

Once you start speaking, you can instruct the AVSpeechSynthesizer to pause speaking, either immediately or at the next word:

```
// Stop speaking immediately
[self.speechSynthesizer pauseSpeakingAtBoundary:AVSpeechBoundaryImmediate];

// Stop speaking after the current word
[self.speechSynthesizer pauseSpeakingAtBoundary:AVSpeechBoundaryWord];
```

Once you've paused speaking, you can resume it at any time:

```
[self continueSpeaking];
```

If you're done with speaking, you can clear the AVSpeechSynthesizer of the current and pending AVSpeechUtterances by calling stopSpeakingAtBoundary:. This method works in the same way as pauseSpeakingAtBoundary:, but once you call it, anything the synthesizer was about to say is forgotten.

4.6. Getting Information About What the iPod Is Playing

Problem

You want to find out information about whatever song the Music application is playing.

Solution

To do this, you'll need to add the Media Player framework to your project. Do this selecting the project at the top of the Project Navigator, scrolling down to "Linked Frameworks and Libraries," clicking the + button, and double-clicking on "Media-Player.framework."

First, get an `MPMusicPlayerController` from the system, which contains information about the built-in iPod. Next, get the currently playing `MPMediaItem`, which represents a piece of media that the iPod is currently playing. Finally, call `valueForProperty:` to get specific information about that media item:

```
MPMusicPlayerController* musicPlayer = [MPMusicPlayerController iPodMusicPlayer];

MPMediaItem* currentTrack = musicPlayer.nowPlayingItem;

NSString* title = [currentTrack valueForProperty:MPMediaItemPropertyTitle];
NSString* artist = [currentTrack valueForProperty:MPMediaItemPropertyArtist];
NSString* album = [currentTrack valueForProperty:MPMediaItemPropertyAlbumTitle];
```

Once you've got this information, you can do whatever you like with it, including displaying it in a label, showing it in-game, and more.

Discussion

An `MPMusicPlayerController` represents the music playback system that's built in to every iOS device. Using this object, you can get information about the currently playing track, set the currently playing queue of music, and control the playback (such as by pausing and skipping backward and forward in the queue).

There are actually *two* `MPMusicPlayerController`s available to your app. The first is the *iPod music player*, which represents the state of the built-in Music application. The iPod music player is shared across all applications, so they all have control over the same thing.

The second music player controller that's available is the *application music player*. The application music player is functionally identical to the iPod music player, with a single difference: each application has its own application music player. This means that they each have their own playlist.

Only one piece of media can be playing at a single time. If an application starts using its own application music player, the iPod music player will pause and let the application take over. If you're using an app that's playing music out of the application music player, and you then exit that app, the music will stop.

To get information about the currently playing track, you use the `nowPlayingItem` property of the `MPMusicPlayerController`. This property returns an `MPMediaItem`, which is an object that represents a piece of media. Media means music, videos, audiobooks, podcasts, and more—not just music!

To get information about an `MPMediaItem`, you use the `valueForProperty:` method. This method takes one of several possible property names. Here are some examples:

`MPMediaItemPropertyAlbumTitle`
　　The name of the album

`MPMediaItemPropertyArtist`
  The name of the artist

`MPMediaItemPropertyAlbumArtist`
  The name of the album's main artist (for albums with multiple artists)

`MPMediaItemPropertyGenre`
  The genre of the music

`MPMediaItemPropertyComposer`
  The composer of the music

`MPMediaItemPropertyPlaybackDuration`
  The length of the music, in seconds

> The media library is only available on iOS devices—it's not available on the iOS simulator. If you try to use these features on the simulator, it just plain won't work.

4.7. Detecting When the Currently Playing Track Changes

Problem

You want to detect when the currently playing media item changes.

Solution

First, use `NSNotificationCenter` to subscribe to the `MPMusicPlayerControllerNow PlayingItemDidChangeNotification` notification:

```
[[NSNotificationCenter defaultCenter] addObserver:self
    selector:@selector(nowPlayingChanged:)
    name:MPMusicPlayerControllerNowPlayingItemDidChangeNotification
    object:nil];
```

Next, get a reference to the `MPMusicPlayerController` that you want to get notifications for, and call `beginGeneratingPlaybackNotifications` on it:

```
MPMusicPlayerController* musicPlayer = [MPMusicPlayerController iPodMusicPlayer];

[musicPlayer beginGeneratingPlaybackNotifications];
```

Finally, implement the method that receives the notifications. In this example, we've called it `nowPlayingChanged:`, but you can call it anything you like:

```
- (void) nowPlayingChanged:(NSNotification*)notification {
    // Now playing item changed, do something about it
}
```

Discussion

Notifications regarding the current item won't be sent unless `beginGeneratingPlay` `backNotifications` is called. If you stop being interested in the currently playing item, call `endGeneratingPlaybackNotifications`.

Note that you might not receive these notifications if your application is in the background. It's generally a good idea to manually update your interface whenever your game comes back from the background, instead of just relying on the notifications to arrive.

4.8. Controlling iPod Playback

Problem

You want to control the track that the Music application is playing.

Solution

Use the `MPMusicPlayerController` to control the state of the music player:

```
MPMusicPlayerController* musicPlayer = [MPMusicPlayerController iPodMusicPlayer];

// Start playing
[musicPlayer play];

// Stop playing, but remember the current playback position
[musicPlayer pause];

// Stop playing
[musicPlayer stop];

// Go back to the start of the current item
[musicPlayer skipToBeginning];

// Go to the start of the next item
[musicPlayer skipToNextItem];

// Go to the start of the previous item
[musicPlayer skipToPreviousItem];

// Start playing in fast-forward (use "play" to resume playback)
[musicPlayer beginSeekingForward];
```

```
// Start playing in fast-reverse.
[musicPlayer beginSeekingBackward];
```

Discussion

Don't forget that if you're using the shared iPod music player controller, any changes you make to the playback state apply to all applications. This means that the playback state of your application might get changed by *other* applications—usually the Music application, but possibly by other apps.

You can query the current state of the music player by asking it for the `playback State`, which is one of the following values:

`MPMusicPlaybackStateStopped`
> The music player isn't playing anything.

`MPMusicPlaybackStatePlaying`
> The music player is currently playing.

`MPMusicPlaybackStatePaused`
> The music player is playing, but is paused.

`MPMusicPlaybackStateInterrupted`
> The music player is playing, but has been interrupted (e.g., by a phone call).

`MPMusicPlaybackStateSeekingForward`
> The music player is fast-forwarding.

`MPMusicPlaybackStateSeekingBackward`
> The music player is fast-reversing.

You can get notified about changes in the playback state by registering for the `MPMusic PlayerControllerPlaybackStateDidChangeNotification` notification, in the same way `MPMusicPlayerControllerNowPlayingItemDidChangeNotification` allows you to get notified about changes in the currently playing item.

4.9. Allowing the User to Select Music

Problem

You want to allow the user to choose some music to play.

Solution

You can display an `MPMediaPickerController` to let the user select music.

First, make your view controller conform to the `MPMediaPickerControllerDelegate`:

```
@interface ViewController () <MPMediaPickerControllerDelegate>
```

Next, add the following code at the point where you want to display the media picker:

```
MPMediaPickerController* picker = [[MPMediaPickerController alloc]
                                   initWithMediaTypes:MPMediaTypeAnyAudio];

picker.allowsPickingMultipleItems = YES;
picker.showsCloudItems = NO;

picker.delegate = self;

[self presentViewController:picker animated:NO completion:nil];
```

Then, add the following two methods to your view controller:

```
- (void)mediaPicker:(MPMediaPickerController *)mediaPicker
    didPickMediaItems:(MPMediaItemCollection *)mediaItemCollection {

        for (MPMediaItem* item in mediaItemCollection.items) {
            NSString* itemName = [item valueForProperty:MPMediaItemPropertyTitle];
            NSLog(@"Picked item: %@", itemName);
        }

        MPMusicPlayerController* musicPlayer = [MPMusicPlayerController
            iPodMusicPlayer];

        [musicPlayer setQueueWithItemCollection:mediaItemCollection];

        [musicPlayer play];

        [self dismissViewControllerAnimated:NO completion:nil];
}
- (void)mediaPickerDidCancel:(MPMediaPickerController *)mediaPicker {
    [self dismissViewControllerAnimated:NO completion:nil];
}
```

Discussion

An MPMediaPickerController uses the exact same user interface as the one you see in the built-in Music application. This means that your player doesn't have to waste time learning how to navigate a different interface.

When you create an MPMediaPickerController, you can choose what kinds of media you want the user to pick. In this recipe, we've gone with MPMediaTypeAnyAudio, which, as the name suggests, means the user can pick any audio: music, audiobooks, podcasts, and so on. Other options include:

- MPMediaTypeMusic
- MPMediaTypePodcast

- MPMediaTypeAudioBook
- MPMediaTypeAudioITunesU
- MPMediaTypeMovie
- MPMediaTypeTVShow
- MPMediaTypeVideoPodcast
- MPMediaTypeMusicVideo
- MPMediaTypeVideoITunesU
- MPMediaTypeHomeVideo
- MPMediaTypeAnyVideo
- MPMediaTypeAny

In addition to setting what kind of content you want the user to pick, you can also set whether you want the user to be able to pick multiple items or just one:

```
picker.allowsPickingMultipleItems = YES;
```

Finally, you can decide whether you want to present media that the user has purchased from iTunes, but isn't currently downloaded onto the device. Apple refers to this feature as "iTunes in the Cloud," and you can turn it on or off through the showsCloudItems property:

```
picker.showsCloudItems = NO;
```

When the user finishes picking media, the delegate of the MPMediaPickerController receives the mediaPicker:didPickMediaItems: message. The media items that were chosen are contained in an MPMediaItemCollection object, which is basically an array of MPMediaItems.

In addition to getting information about the media items that were selected, you can also give the MPMediaItemCollection directly to an MPMusicPlayerController, and tell it to start playing:

```
MPMusicPlayerController* musicPlayer = [MPMusicPlayerController iPodMusicPlayer];

[musicPlayer setQueueWithItemCollection:mediaItemCollection];

[musicPlayer play];
```

Once you're done getting content out of the media picker, you need to dismiss it, by using the dismissViewControllerAnimated:completion: method. This also applies if the user taps the Cancel button in the media picker: in this case, your delegate receives the mediaPickerDidCancel: message, and your application should dismiss the view controller in the same way.

4.10. Cooperating with Other Applications' Audio

Problem

You want to play background music only when the user isn't already listening to something.

Solution

You can find out if another application is currently playing audio by using the AVAudio Session class:

```
AVAudioSession* session = [AVAudioSession sharedInstance];

if (session.otherAudioPlaying) {
    // Another application is playing audio. Don't play any sound that might
    // conflict with music, such as your own background music.
} else {
    // No other app is playing audio - crank the tunes!
}
```

Discussion

The AVAudioSession class lets you control how audio is currently being handled on the device, and gives you considerable flexibility in terms of how the device should handle things like the ringer switch (the switch on the side of the device) and what happens when the user locks the screen.

By default, if you begin playing back audio using AVAudioPlayer and another application (such as the built-in Music app) is playing audio, the other application will stop all sound, and the audio played by your game will be the only thing audible.

However, you might want the player to be able to listen to her own music while playing your game—the background music might not be a very important part of your game, for example.

To change the default behavior of muting other applications, you need to set the audio session's *category*. For example, to indicate to the system that your application should not cause other apps to mute their audio, you need to set the audio session's category to AVAudioSessionCategoryAmbient:

```
NSError* error = nil;
[[AVAudioSession sharedInstance] setCategory:AVAudioSessionCategoryAmbient
  error:&error];

if (error != nil) {
    NSLog(@"Problem setting audio session: %@", error);
}
```

There are several categories of audio session available. The most important to games are the following:

AVAudioSessionCategoryAmbient
> Audio isn't the most important part of your game, and other apps should be able to play audio alongside yours. When the ringer switch is set to *mute*, your audio is silenced, and when the screen locks, your audio stops.

AVAudioSessionCategorySoloAmbient
> Audio is reasonably important to your game. If other apps are playing audio, they'll stop. However, the audio session will continue to respect the ringer switch and the screen locking.

AVAudioSessionCategoryPlayback
> Audio is very important to your game. Other apps are silenced, and your app *ignores* the ringer switch and the screen locking.

 When using AVAudioSessionCategoryPlayback, your app will still be stopped when the screen locks. To make it keep running, you need to mark your app as one that plays audio in the background. To do this, follow these steps:

1. Open your project's information page, by clicking on the project at the top of the Project Navigator.

2. Go to the Capabilities tab.

3. Turn on "Background Modes," and then turn on "Audio and AirPlay."

Your app will now play audio in the background, as long as the audio session's category is set to AVAudioSessionCategoryPlayback.

4.11. Determining How to Best Use Sound in Your Game Design

Problem

You want to make optimal use of sound and music in your game design.

Solution

It's really hard to make an iOS game that relies on sound. For one, you can't count on the user wearing headphones, and sounds in games (and everything else, really) don't sound their best coming from the tiny speakers found in iOS devices.

Many games "get around" this by prompting users to put on their headphones as the game launches, or suggesting that they are "best experienced via headphones" in the sound and music options menu, if it has one. We think this is a suboptimal solution.

The best iOS games understand and acknowledge the environment in which the games are likely to be played: typically a busy, distraction-filled environment, where your beautiful audio might not be appreciated due to background noise or the fact that the user has the volume turned all the way down.

The solution is to make sure your game works with, or without, sound. Don't count on the fact the user can hear anything at all, in fact.

Discussion

Unless you're building a game that is based around music or sound, you should make it completely playable without sound. Your users will thank you for it, even if they never actually thank you for it!

CHAPTER 5

Data Storage

Games are apps, and apps run on data. Whether it's just resources that your game loads or saved-game files that you need to store, your game will eventually need to work with data stored on the flash chips that make up the storage subsystems present on all iOS devices.

In this chapter, you'll learn how to convert objects into saveable data, how to work with iCloud, how to load resources without freezing up the rest of the game, and more.

5.1. Saving the State of Your Game

Problem

You want game objects to be able to store their state, so that it can be loaded from disk.

Solution

Make your objects conform to the NSCoding protocol, and then implement encode WithCoder: and initWithCoder:, like so:

```
- (void) encodeWithCoder:(NSCoder*) coder {
    [coder encodeObject:self.objectName forKey:@"name"];
    [coder encodeInt:self.hitPoints forKey:@"hitpoints"];
}

- (id) initWithCoder:(NSCoder*)coder {

    // note: not [super initWithCoder:coder]!
    self = [super init];

    if (self) {
        self.objectName = [coder decodeObjectForKey:@"name"];
        self.hitPoints = [coder decodeIntForKey:@"hitpoints"];
```

```
        }

    }
```

When you want to store this information into an NSData object, for saving to disk or somewhere else, you use the NSKeyedArchiver:

```
GameObject* gameObject = ... // an object that conforms to NSCoder

NSData* archivedData = [NSKeyedArchiver archivedDataWithRootObject:gameObject];

// Save archivedData somewhere
```

If you have an NSData object that contains information encoded by NSKeyedArchiver, you can convert it back into a regular object with NSKeyedUnarchiver:

```
NSData* loadedData = ... // an NSData that contains archived data
GameObject* object = [NSKeyedUnarchiver unarchiveObjectWithData:loadedData];
```

Discussion

When you're making objects able to save their state on disk, the first step is to figure out exactly what you *need* to save, and what can be safely thrown away. For example, a monster may need to save the amount of hit-points it has left, but may not need to save the direction in which its eyes are pointing. The less data you store, the better.

The NSKeyedArchiver class lets you store specific data in an archive. When you use it, you pass in an object that you want to be archived. This object can be any object that conforms to the NSCoding protocol, which many built-in objects in Cocoa Touch already do (such as NSString, NSArray, NSDictionary, NSNumber, NSDate, and so on). If you want to archive a collection object, such as an NSArray or NSDictionary, it must only include objects that conform to NSCoding.

NSKeyedArchiver gives you an NSData object, which you can write to disk, upload to another computer, or otherwise keep around. If you load this data from disk, you can *un-archive* the data and get back the original object. To do this, you use NSKeyed Unarchiver, which works in a very similar way to NSKeyedArchiver.

The encodeWithCoder: method is used by the archiving system to gather the actual information that should be stored in the final archive. This method receives an NSCoder object, which you provide information to. For each piece of info you want to save, you use one of the following methods:

- encodeInt:forKey:
- encodeObject:forKey:
- encodeFloat:forKey:
- encodeDouble:forKey:

- encodeBool:forKey:

These encoding methods are only the most popular ones. Others exist, and you can find the complete list in the Xcode documentation for the NSCoder class (*https://developer.apple.com/library/mac/documen tation/cocoa/reference/foundation/classes/NSCoder_Class/Reference/ NSCoder.html*).

When you want to encode, for example, an integer named "hitpoints," you call enco deInt:forKey: like so:

```
[coder encodeInt:self.hitpoints forKey:@"hitpoints"];
```

When you use encodeObject:forKey:, the object that you provide *must* be one that conforms to NSCoding. This is because the encoding system will send it an encodeWith Coder: method of its own.

The encoding system will detect if an object is encoded more than one time and remove duplicates. If, for example, both object A and object B use encodeObject:forKey: to encode object C, that object will be encoded only once.

Decoding is the process of getting back information from the archive. This happens when you use NSKeyedUnarchiver, which reads the NSData object you give it and creates all of the objects that were encoded. Each object that's been unarchived is sent the initWithCoder: method, which allows it to pull information out of the decoder.

You get information from the decoder using methods that are very similar to those present in the encoder (again, this is just a sampling of the available methods):

- decodeObjectForKey:
- decodeIntForKey:
- decodeFloatForKey:
- decodeDoubleForKey:
- decodeBoolForKey:

5.2. Storing High Scores Locally

Problem

You want to store high scores in a file, on disk.

Solution

First, put your high scores in NSDictionary objects, and then put those dictionaries in an NSArray:

```
NSDictionary* scoreDictionary = @{@"score": @(1000), @"date":[NSDate date],
                                  @"playerName": playerName};

// you would probably have more than one of these
NSArray* highScores = @[scoreDictionary];
```

Next, determine the location on disk where these scores can be placed:

```
NSURL* documentsURL = [[[NSFileManager defaultManager]
    URLsForDirectory:NSDocumentDirectory inDomains:NSUserDomainMask]
    lastObject];

NSURL* highScoreURL = [documentsURL URLByAppendingPathComponent:
    @"HighScores.plist"];
```

Finally, write out the high scores array to this location:

```
[highScores writeToURL:highScoreURL atomically:YES];
```

You can load the high scores array by reading from the location:

```
NSError* error = nil;
highScores = [NSArray arrayWithContentsOfURL:highScoreURL error:&error];

if (highScores == nil) {
    NSLog(@"Error loading high scores: %@", error);
} else {
    NSLog(@"Loaded scores: %@", highScores);
}
```

Discussion

When you're saving high scores, it's important to know exactly what information you want to save. This will vary from game to game, but common things include the score, the time when the score was earned, and any additional context needed for that score to make sense.

A very easy way to save information to disk is to put each score in an NSDictionary, and put each NSDictionary in an NSArray. You can then write that array to disk, or load it back.

An application in iOS is only allowed to read and write files that are inside the app's *sandbox*. Each app is limited to its own sandbox and is generally not allowed to access any files that lie outside of it. To get the location of an app's *Documents* folder, which is located inside the sandbox, you use the `NSFileManger` class to give you the `NSURL`. You can then construct an `NSURL` based on that, and give *that* URL to the array, using it to write to the disk.

You can then do the reverse to load the data from disk.

If you want to store your high scores online, you can use Game Center (see Recipe 12.4).

5.3. Using iCloud to Save Games

Problem

You want to save the player's game in iCloud.

Solution

To work with iCloud, you'll need to have an active iOS Developer Program membership.

First, activate iCloud support in your app. To do this, select the project at the top of the Project Navigator, and switch to the Capabilities tab. Turn on the "iCloud" switch.

Saving the player's game in iCloud really means saving game data. This means that we'll assume that you've saved your file somewhere. In these examples, `saveGameURL` is an `NSURL` that points to the location of your saved game file, which you've already written out to disk.

First, you need to check to see if iCloud is available. It may not be; for example, if the user hasn't signed in to an Apple ID or has deliberately disabled iCloud on the device. You can check to see if iCloud is available by doing the following:

```
if ([[NSFileManager defaultManager] ubiquityIdentityToken] == nil) {
    // iCloud is unavailable. You'll have to store the saved game locally.
}
```

To put a file in iCloud, you do this:

```
NSString* fileName = @"MySaveGame.save"; // this can be anything

// Moving into iCloud should always be done in a background queue, because it
// can take a bit of time
```

```
NSOperationQueue* backgroundQueue = [[NSOperationQueue alloc] init];
[backgroundQueue addOperationWithBlock:^{
    NSURL* containerURL = [[NSFileManager defaultManager]
                           URLForUbiquityContainerIdentifier:nil];
    NSURL* iCloudURL = [containerURL URLByAppendingPathComponent:fileName];

    NSError* error = nil;
    [[NSFileManager defaultManager] setUbiquitous:YES itemAtURL:saveGameURL
     destinationURL:iCloudURL error:&error];

    if (error != nil) {
        NSLog(@"Problem putting the file in iCloud: %@", error);
    }
}];
```

To find files that are in iCloud, you use the NSMetadataQuery class. This returns information about files that have been stored in iCloud, either by the current device or by
another device the user owns. NSMetadataQuery works like a search—you tell it what
you're looking for, register to be notified when the search completes, and then tell it to
start looking:

```
NSMetadataQuery* _query; // Keep this around in an instance variable

_query = [[NSMetadataQuery alloc] init];

[_query setSearchScopes:[NSArray arrayWithObjects:NSMetadataQueryUbiquitous
                         DocumentsScope, nil]];

// Search for all files ending in .save
[_query setPredicate:[NSPredicate predicateWithFormat:@"%K LIKE '*.save'",
                      NSMetadataItemFSNameKey]];

// Register to be notified of when the search is complete
NSNotificationCenter* notificationCenter = [NSNotificationCenter defaultCenter];
[notificationCenter addObserver:self selector:@selector(searchComplete)
    name:NSMetadataQueryDidFinishGatheringNotification object:nil];
[notificationCenter addObserver:self selector:@selector(searchComplete)
    name:NSMetadataQueryDidUpdateNotification object:nil];

[_query startQuery];
```

You then implement a method that's run when the search is complete:

```
- (void) searchComplete {
    for (NSMetadataItem* item in _query.results) {
        // Find the URL for the item
        NSURL* url = [item valueForAttribute:NSMetadataItemURLKey];

        if ([item valueForAttribute:NSMetadata
                UbiquitousItemDownloadingStatusKey] == NSMetadataUbiquitousItem
                DownloadingStatusCurrent) {
            // This file is downloaded and is the most current version
```

```
        [self doSomethingWithURL:url];
    } else {
        // The file is either not downloaded at all, or is out of date
        // We need to download the file from iCloud; when it finishes
        // downloading, NSMetadataQuery will call this method again
        NSError* error = nil;
        [[NSFileManager defaultManager] startDownloading
            UbiquitousItemAtURL:url error:&error];
        if (error != nil) {
            NSLog(@"Problem starting download of %@: %@", url, error);
        }
    }
  }
}
```

 An NSMetadataQuery runs until it's stopped. If you make a change to a file that the query is watching, you'll receive a new notification. If you're done looking for files in iCloud, you can stop the query using the stopQuery method:

```
[_query stopQuery];
```

When a file is in iCloud and you make changes to it, iCloud will automatically upload the changed file, and other devices will receive the new copy. If the same file is changed at the same time by different devices, the file will be in conflict. You can detect this by checking the NSMetadataUbiquitousItemHasUnresolvedConflictsKey attribute on the results of your NSMetadataQuery; if this is set to YES, then there are conflicts.

There are several ways you can resolve a conflict; one way is to simply say, "The most recent version that was saved is the current one; ignore conflicts." To indicate this to the system, you do this:

```
// Run this code when an NSMetadataQuery indicates that a file is in conflict

NSURL* fileURL = ...; // the URL of the file that has conflicts to be resolved

for (NSFileVersion* conflictVersion in [NSFileVersion unresolvedConflict
                                VersionsOfItemAtURL:fileURL]) {
    conflictVersion.resolved = YES;
}

[NSFileVersion removeOtherVersionsOfItemAtURL:fileURL];
```

Discussion

iCloud is a technology from Apple that syncs documents and information across the various devices that a user owns. "Devices," in this case, means both iOS devices and Macs; when you create a document and put it in iCloud, the same file appears on all devices that you're signed in to. Additionally, the file is backed up by Apple on the Web.

To use iCloud, you need to have an active iOS Developer account, because all iCloud activity in an app is linked to the developer who created the app. You don't have to do anything special with your app besides have Xcode activate iCloud support for it—all of the setup is handled for you automatically.

It's worth keeping in mind that not all users will have access to iCloud. If they're not signed in to an Apple ID, or if they've deliberately turned off iCloud, your game still needs to work without it. This means saving your game files locally, and not putting them into iCloud.

Additionally, it's possible that the user might have signed out of iCloud, and a different user has signed in. You can check this by asking the `NSFileManager` for the `ubiquityIdentityToken`, which you can store; if it's different to the last time you checked, you should throw away any local copies of your saved games, and redownload the files from iCloud.

You should always try to perform iCloud work on a background queue. iCloud operations can frequently take several dozen milliseconds to complete, which can slow down your game if you run them on the main queue.

5.4. Using the iCloud Key/Value Store

Problem

You want to store small amounts of information in iCloud.

Solution

Use `NSUbiquitousKeyValueStore`, which is like an `NSMutableDictionary` whose contents are shared across all of the user's devices:

```
NSUbiquitousKeyValueStore* store = [NSUbiquitousKeyValueStore defaultStore];

// Get the most recent level
int mostRecentLevel = (int)[store longLongForKey:@"mostRecentLevel"];

// Save the level
[store setLongLong:13 forKey:@"mostRecentLevel"];

// Sign up to be notified of when the store changes
[[NSNotificationCenter defaultCenter] addObserver:self
    selector:@selector(storeUpdated:)
    name:NSUbiquitousKeyValueStoreDidChangeExternallyNotification object:store];

// Elsewhere:
- (void) storeUpdated:(NSNotification*)notification {
    NSArray* listOfChangedKeys = [notification.userInfo
        objectForKey:NSUbiquitousKeyValueStoreChangedKeysKey];
```

```
    for (NSString* changedKey in listOfChangedKeys) {
        NSLog(@"%@ changed to %@", changedKey, [store objectForKey:changedKey]);
    }
}
```

Discussion

Many games don't need to store very much information in order to let the players keep their state around. For example, if you're making a puzzle game, you might only need to store the number of the level that the players reached. In these cases, the `NSUbiquitous KeyValueStore` is exactly what you need. The ubiquitous key/value store stores small amounts of data—strings, numbers, and so on—and keeps them synchronized.

You'll need to activate iCloud support in your app for `NSUbiquitous KeyValueStore` to work.

Unlike when you're working with files, conflict resolution in the ubiquitous key/value store is handled automatically for you by iCloud: the most recent value that was set wins. This can sometimes lead to problems. For example, consider the following user experience:

1. You have a puzzle game, and the highest level that's been unlocked is stored in the key/value store.
2. You play up to level 6 on your iPhone, and iCloud syncs the key/value store.
3. Later, you play the game on your iPad, but it's offline. You get up to level 2 on your iPad. Later, your iPad is connected to the Internet, and iCloud syncs this latest value. Because it's the latest value to be set, it overwrites the "older" value of 2.
4. You then play the game on your iPhone, and are very surprised to see that your progress has been "lost." You delete the app and leave a 1-star review on the App Store. The app developer goes bankrupt and dies alone in a gutter.

To solve this problem, you should keep data in the local user defaults, and update it only after comparing it to the ubiquitous store. When the store changes, compare it against the local user defaults; if the ubiquitous store's value is lower, copy the value from the local store into the ubiquitous store, overwriting it. If it's higher, copy the value from the ubiquitous store into the local store. Whenever you want to read the information, always consult the local store.

You're limited to 1 MB of data in the ubiquitous key/value store on a per-application basis. If you try to put more data than this into the key/value store, the value will be set to nil.

5.5. Loading Structured Information

Problem

You want to store and load structured information (e.g., NSArray and NSDictionary objects), in a way that produces files that are easy to read and write.

Solution

Use the NSJSONSerialization class to read and write JSON files.

To create and write out a file:

```
NSDictionary* informationToSave = @{
    @"playerName": @"Grabthar",
    @"weaponType": @"Hammer",
    @"hitPoints": 1000,
    @"currentQuests": @[@"save the universe", @"get home"]
};

NSURL* locationToSaveTo = ... // where to save the information

NSError* error = nil;
NSData* dataToSave = [NSJSONSerialization dataWithJSONObject:informationToSave
                      options:0 error:&error];

if (error != nil) {
    NSLog(@"Error converting data to JSON: %@", error);
}

[dataToSave writeToURL:locationToSaveTo atomically:YES];
```

The file created by the preceding code looks like this:

```
{
    "playerName": "Grabthar",
    "weaponType": "Hammer",
    "hitPoints": 1000,
    "currentQuests": [
        "save the galaxy",
        "get home"
    ]
}
```

You can load this file back in and convert it back to its original type, as well:

```
NSURL* locationToLoadFrom = ... // where to load the information from

NSError* error = nil;
NSData* loadedData = [NSData dataWithContentsOfURL:locationToLoadFrom
                            error:&error];

if (loadedData == nil) {
    NSLog(@"Error loading data: %@", error);
}

NSDictionary* loadedDictionary = [NSJSONSerialization
    JSONObjectWithData:loadedData options:0 error:&error];

if (loadedDictionary == nil) {
    NSLog(@"Error processing data: %@", error);
}

// ALWAYS ensure that the data that you've received is the type you expect:
if ([loadedData isKindOfClass:[NSDictionary class]] == NO) {
    NSLog(@"Error: loaded data is not what I expected!");
}
```

Discussion

JSON, which is short for JavaScript Object Notation, is a simple, easy-to-read format for storing structured information like dictionaries and arrays. NSJSONSerialization is designed to provide an easy way to convert objects into JSON data and back again.

Note that JSON can only store specific kinds of data. Specifically, you can only store the following types:

- Strings
- Numbers
- Boolean values (i.e., true and false)
- Arrays
- Dictionaries (JSON calls these "objects")

This means that NSJSONSerialization can only be given NSStrings, NSNumbers, NSArrays, and NSDictionary objects to process. If you don't do this, then the class won't produce JSON.

You can check to see if the object you're about to give to NSJSONSerialization is able to be converted to JSON by using the isValidJSONObject method:

```
NSDictionary* myDictionary = @{@"canIDoThis": @(YES)};

BOOL canBeConverted = [NSJSONSerialization isValidJSONObject:myDictionary];
```

```
// canBeConverted = YES
```

5.6. Deciding When to Use Files or a Database

Problem

You want to decide whether to store information as individual files, or as a database.

Solution

Use individual files when:

- You know that you'll need the entire contents of the file all at the same time.
- The file is small.
- The file is easy to read and process, and won't take lots of CPU resources to get information out of.

Use a database when:

- The file is large, and you don't need to load everything in at once.
- You only need a little bit of information from the file.
- You need to very quickly load specific parts of the file.
- You want to make changes to the file while continuing to read it.

Discussion

Games tend to load files for two different reasons:

- The file contains information that needs to be kept entirely in memory, because all of it is needed at once (e.g., textures, level layouts, and some sounds).
- The file contains a lot of information, but only parts of it need to be read at once (e.g., monster information, player info, dialogue).

Databases are much faster and more efficient at getting small amounts of information from a larger file, but the downside is *lots* of increased code complexity.

5.7. Using SQLite for Storage

Problem

You want to use SQLite, a fast database system, for storing and loading information.

Solution

To work with SQLite, you first create a `sqlite3` object. This represents your database, and you do all of your work using it.

You open a database using the `sqlite3_open` function:

```
const char* filename = ... // a C string containing a path to where you want
                           // the file to be

sqlite3* database = nil;
sqlite3_open(filename, &database);
```

When you're done with the database, you close it with the `sqlite3_close` function:

```
sqlite3_close(database);
```

You interact with SQLite by creating SQL statements, using the `sqlite3_prepare_v2` function. You then execute the statements by using the `sqlite3_step` function.

Data in SQLite databases is stored in *tables*. To create a table, you use the "CREATE TABLE" statement (note that this line has been broken here to fit within the page margins; you must enter it on a single line or a compiler error will be raised):

```
sqlite3_stmt* statement = nil;
const char* query = "CREATE TABLE IF NOT EXISTS monsters (id INTEGER
    PRIMARY KEY, type TEXT, hitpoints INTEGER);"
sqlite3_prepare_v2(database, query, strlen(query), &statement, NULL);

if (sqlite3_step(statement) != SQLITE_DONE) {
    // There was a problem
}

sqlite3_finalize(statement);
```

You can insert information into the table using the "INSERT INTO" statement:

```
sqlite3_stmt* statement = nil;

const char* typeName = "goblin";
int hitpoints = 45;

const char* query = "INSERT INTO monsters (type, hitpoints) VALUES (?, ?)";

sqlite3_prepare_v2(database, query, strlen(query), &statement, NULL);
sqlite3_bind_text(statement, 1, typeName, strlen(typeName), SQLITE_TRANSIENT);
```

```
sqlite3_bind_int(statement, 2, hitpoints);

if (sqlite3_step(statement) != SQLITE_DONE) {
    // There was a problem
}

sqlite3_finalize(statement);
```

To get information from the database, you use the "SELECT" statement:

```
sqlite3_stmt statement = nil;
const char* typeName = "monster";

// Create the query
const char* query = "SELECT (type, hitpoints) FROM monsters WHERE type=?";
sqlite3_prepare_v2(database, query, strlen(query), &statement, NULL);

// Bind the monster type name we're searching for to the query
sqlite3_bind_text(statement, 1, typeName, strlen(typeName), SQLITE_TRANSIENT);

// For each row in the database, get the data
while (sqlite3_step(statement) == SQLITE_ROW) {
    // Get the hitPoints, which is column 2 in the query we submitted
    int hitPoints = sqlite3_column_int(statement, 2);

    // Do something with hitPoints
}

sqlite3_finalize(statement);
```

When you create these kinds of statements, you first create the statement, and then you *bind* values to it.

Never create statements like this (note that the second statement should appear all on one line, without wrapping):

```
NSString* typeName = @"monster";
NSString* query = [NSString stringWithFormat:@"SELECT (type, hitpoints)
                   FROM monsters WHERE type=\"%@\"", typeName];
```

You should always bind values to your statements, using the `sqlite3_bind_` family of functions. These ensure that the types remain the same, and that the resulting SQL statement is valid. It leads to cleaner code, and prevents the security risk posed by SQL injection.

Discussion

SQLite is a public-domain library for working with databases. In SQLite, the databases are stored as local files—unlike in database systems like PostgreSQL or MySQL where you connect to a server, in SQLite all of your work is done on a file that's kept on the local filesystem. This means that SQLite is very well suited for "private" use, where a single application uses the database.

Because SQLite databases are files, you can put them anywhere, including iCloud. Apple also provides special support for databases in iCloud, through Core Data, but that's *much* more complicated, and we don't have room to give it justice in this book.

5.8. Managing a Collection of Assets

Problem

Your game has a large number of big files, and you want to manage them in folders.

Solution

First, put all of your assets—your textures, sounds, data files, and so on—in a folder, which is inside the folder where you're keeping your source code. Call this folder *Assets*.

Drag the folder into the Project Navigator. Turn off "Copy items into destination group's folder," and set the Folders option to "Create folder references for any added folders."

Create a new class, called `AssetManager`. Put the following code in *AssetManager.h*:

```
#import <Foundation/Foundation.h>

typedef void (^LoadingBlock)(NSData* loadedData);
typedef void (^LoadingCompleteBlock)(void);

@interface AssetManager : NSObject

@property (strong) NSURL* baseURL;

+ (AssetManager*) sharedManager;

- (NSURL*) urlForAsset:(NSString*) assetName;
- (void) loadAsset:(NSString* )assetName withCompletion:(LoadingBlock)
    completionBlock;
- (void) waitForResourcesToLoad:(LoadingCompleteBlock)completionBlock;

@end
```

And in *AssetManager.m* add the following:

```
#import "AssetManager.h"

static AssetManager* sharedAssetManager = nil;

@implementation AssetManager {
    dispatch_queue_t _loadingQueue;
}
```

```objc
+ (AssetManager *)sharedManager {
    // If the shared instance hasn't yet been created, create it now
    if (sharedAssetManager == nil) {
        sharedAssetManager = [[AssetManager alloc] init];
    }

    return sharedAssetManager;
}

- (id)init
{
    self = [super init];
    if (self) {
        // Find assets inside the "Assets" folder, which is copied in
        self.baseURL = [[[NSBundle mainBundle] resourceURL]
                        URLByAppendingPathComponent:@"Assets" isDirectory:YES];

        // Create the loading queue
        _loadingQueue = dispatch_queue_create("com.YourGame.LoadingQueue",
                        DISPATCH_QUEUE_SERIAL);

    }
    return self;
}

- (NSURL *)urlForAsset:(NSString *)assetName {
    // Determine where to find the asset
    return [self.baseURL URLByAppendingPathComponent:assetName];
}

- (void)loadAsset:(NSString *)assetName withCompletion:(LoadingBlock)
    completionBlock {
        // Load the asset in the background; when it's done, give the loaded
        // data to the completionBlock
        NSURL* urlToLoad = [self urlForAsset:assetName];

        dispatch_queue_t mainQueue = dispatch_get_main_queue();

        dispatch_async(_loadingQueue, ^{
            NSData* loadedData = [NSData dataWithContentsOfURL:urlToLoad];

            dispatch_sync(mainQueue, ^{
                completionBlock(loadedData);
            });
        });
}

- (void)waitForResourcesToLoad:(LoadingCompleteBlock)completionBlock {
    // Run the block on the main queue, after all of the load requests that
    // have been queued up are complete
    dispatch_queue_t mainQueue = dispatch_get_main_queue();
```

```
        dispatch_async(_loadingQueue, ^{
            dispatch_sync(mainQueue, completionBlock);
        });
    }
```

To use this code:

```
// In this example, there's a large file called "Spaceship.png" in the
// "Images" folder, which is in the Assets folder:

[[AssetManager sharedManager] loadAsset:@"Images/Spaceship.png"
    withCompletion:^(NSData* loadedData) {
        // Do something with the loaded data
}];

[[AssetManager sharedManager] waitForResourcesToLoad:^{
    // This will be called after the image and any other resources have
    // been loaded
}];

// In the meantime, continue running the game while we wait for the image
// to load
```

Discussion

In Xcode, a *folder reference* is a special kind of group whose contents are automatically updated when the files on disk change. Folder references are great for when you have a moderately complex folder structure that you'd like to preserve in your game.

 If you change the contents of the folder, it will automatically update in Xcode, but those changes won't necessarily copy over when you build your game. To fix this, do a Clean action after changing your resources (choose Clean from the Product menu, or press Command-Shift-K).

Large files can take a long time to load, and you don't want the player to be looking at a frozen screen while resources are loaded from disk. To address this, you can use a class that handles the work of loading resources in the background. The AssetManager class in this solution handles the work for you, by creating a new dispatch queue and doing the resource loading using the new queue.

If you want to load multiple resources and then run some code, you can use the wait ForResourcesToLoad: method, which runs a block of code *after* the images have finished loading in the background.

5.9. Storing Information in NSUserDefaults

Problem

You want to store small amounts of information, like the most recently visited level in your game.

Solution

The NSUserDefaults class is a very useful tool that lets you store small pieces of data—strings, dates, numbers, and so on—in the *user defaults* database. The user defaults database is where each app keeps its preferences and settings.

There's only a single NSUserDefaults object that you work with, which you access using the standardUserDefaults method:

```
NSUserDefaults* defaults = [NSUserDefaults standardUserDefaults];
```

Once you have this object, you can treat it like an NSMutableDictionary object:

```
// Store a string into the defaults
[defaults setObject:@"A string" forKey:@"mySetting"];

// Get this string back out
NSString* string = [defaults stringForKey:@"mySetting"];
```

You can store the following kinds of objects in the NSUserDefaults system:

- NSData
- NSNumber
- NSString
- NSDate
- NSArray, as long as it only contains objects in this list
- NSDictionary, as long as it only contains objects in this list

Discussion

When you store information into NSUserDefaults, it isn't stored to disk right away—instead, it's saved periodically, and at certain important moments (like when the user taps the home button). This means that if your application crashes before the information is saved, whatever you stored will be lost.

You can force the NSUserDefaults system to save to disk any changes you've made to NSUserDefaults by using the synchronize method:

```
[defaults synchronize];
```

Doing this will ensure that all data you've stored to that point has been saved. For performance reasons, you shouldn't call `synchronize` too often—it's really fast, but don't call it every frame.

Information you store in `NSUserDefaults` is backed up, either to iTunes or to iCloud, depending on the user's settings. You don't need to do anything to make this happen—this will just work.

Sometimes, it's useful for `NSUserDefaults` to provide you with a default value—that is, a value that you should use if the user hasn't already provided one of his own.

For example, let's say your game starts on level 1, and you store the level that your player has reached as `currentLevel` in `NSUserDefaults`. When your game starts up, you ask `NSUserDefaults` for the current level, and set up the game from there:

```
NSInteger levelNumber = [defaults integerForKey:@"currentLevel"];
```

However, what should happen the first time the player starts the game? If no value is provided for the `currentLevel` setting, the first time this code is called, you'll get a value of 0—which is incorrect, because your game starts at 1.

To address this problem, you can register default values. This involves giving the `NSUserDefaults` class a dictionary of keys and values that it should use if no other value has been provided:

```
[defaults registerDefaults:@{@"currentLevel": @1}];

NSInteger levelNumber = [defaults integerForKey:@"currentLevel"];
// levelNumber will be either 1, or whatever was last stored in NSUserDefaults.
```

 It's very, very easy for users to modify the information you've stored in `NSUserDefaults`. Third-party tools can be used to directly access and modify the information stored in the defaults database, making it very easy for people to cheat.

If you're making a multiplayer game, for example, and you store the strength of the character's weapon in user defaults, it's possible for players to modify the database and make their players have an unbeatable weapon.

That's not to say that you shouldn't use `NSUserDefaults`, but you need to be aware of the possibility of cheating.

5.10. Implementing the Best Data Storage Strategy

Problem

You want to make sure your game stores data sensibly, and doesn't annoy your users.

Solution

The solution here is simple: don't drop data. If your game can save its state, then it should be saving its state. You can't expect the user to manually save in an iOS game, and you should always persist data at every available opportunity.

Discussion

Nothing is more annoying than losing your progress in a game because a phone call came in. Don't risk annoying your users: persist the state of the game regularly!

5.11. In-Game Currency

Problem

You want to keep track of an in-game resource, like money, which the player can earn and spend.

Solution

The requirements for this kind of thing vary from game to game. However, having an in-game currency is a common element in lots of games, so here's an example of how you might handle it.

In this example, let's say you have two different currencies: *gems* and *gold*. Gems are permanent, and the player keeps them from game to game. Gold is temporary, and goes away at the end of a game.

To add support for these kinds of currencies, create a class that manages their storage:

```
@interface CurrencyManager

@property (nonatomic, assign) NSInteger gems;
@property (nonatomic, assign) NSInteger gold;

- (void) endGame;

@end

@implementation CurrencyManager
```

```
@dynamic gems;

- (void) setGems:(NSInteger)gems {
    // Set the updated count of gems in the user defaults system
    [[NSUserDefaults standardUserDefaults] setInteger:gems forKey:@"gems"];
}

- (void) gems {
    // Ask the user defaults system for the current number of gems
    return [[NSUserDefaults standardUserDefaults] integerForKey:@"gems"];
}

- (void) endGame {
    // Game ended; get rid of all of the gold (but don't do anything to gems)
    self.gold = 0;
}

@end
```

Discussion

In this solution, the `gems` property stores its information using the `NSUserDefaults` system, rather than simply leaving it in memory (as is done with the `gold` property).

When you create a property, Objective-C creates an instance variable in which the information is stored. However, if you mark a property as `@dynamic`, the instance variable won't be created, and the setter and getter methods for the property need to handle the data storage themselves.

In this solution, the information is stored in `NSUserDefaults`. From the perspective of other objects, the property works like everything else:

```
CurrencyManager* currencyManager = ...

currencyManager.gems = 50;
currencyManager.gold = 100;
```

When data is stored in user defaults, it persists between application launches. This means that your gems will stick around when the application exits—something that players will appreciate. Note that data stored in the user defaults system can be modified by the user, which means cheating is not impossible.

CHAPTER 6

2D Graphics and Sprite Kit

Just about every game out there incorporates 2D graphics on some level. Even the most sophisticated 3D games use 2D elements, such as in the menu or in the in-game interface.

Creating a game that limits itself to 2D graphics is also a good way to keep your game simple. 2D is simpler than 3D, and you'll end up with an easier-to-manage game, in terms of both gameplay and graphics. Puzzle games, for example, are a category of game that typically use 2D graphics rather than more complex 3D graphics.

2D is simpler for a number of reasons: you don't need to worry about how objects are going to look from multiple angles, you don't need to worry as much about lighting, and it's often simpler to create a great-looking scene with 2D images than it is to create a 3D version of the same scene.

iOS comes with a system for creating 2D graphics, called *Sprite Kit*. Sprite Kit takes care of low-level graphics tasks like creating OpenGL contexts and managing textures, allowing you to focus on game-related tasks like showing your game's sprites on the screen.

 Sprite Kit was introduced in iOS 7, and is available on both iOS and OS X Mavericks. The API for Sprite Kit is the same on both platforms, which makes porting your game from one platform to the other easier.

In this chapter, you'll learn how to work with Sprite Kit to display your game's graphics.

6.1. Getting Familiar with 2D Math

When you're working with 2D graphics, it's important to know at least a little bit of 2D math.

Coordinate System

In 2D graphics, you deal with a space that has two dimensions: x and y. The x-axis is the horizontal axis and goes from left to right, whereas the y-axis is the vertical axis and runs from top to bottom. We call this kind of space a *coordinate system*. The central point of the coordinate system used in graphics is called the *origin*.

To describe a specific location in a coordinate space, you just need to provide two numbers: how far away from the origin the location is on the horizontal axis (also known as the *x coordinate*), and how far away it is on the vertical axis (also known as the *y coordinate*). These coordinates are usually written in parentheses, like this: (*x* coordinate, *y* coordinate)

The coordinates for a location 5 units to the right of the origin and 2 units above it would be written as (5,2). The location of the origin itself is written as (0,0)—that is, zero units away from the origin on both the x- and y- axes.

 Coordinate spaces in 3D work in the exact same way as in 2D, with one difference: there's one more axis, called the *z-axis*. In this coordinate system, coordinates have one more number, as in (0,0,0).

Vectors

In the simplest terms, a vector is a value that contains two or more values. In games, vectors are most useful for describing two things: positions (i.e., coordinates) and velocities.

An empty two-dimensional vector—that is, one with just zeros—is written like this: [0, 0].

When you're working in iOS, you can use the CGPoint structure as a 2D vector, as illustrated in Figure 6-1:

```
CGPoint myPosition;
myPosition.x = 2;
myPosition.y = 2;
```

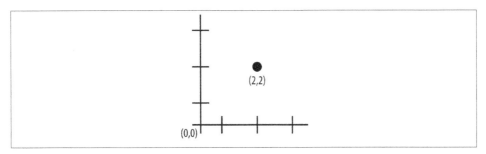

Figure 6-1. A vector used to define the position (2,2)

You can also use vectors to store *velocities*. A velocity represents how far a location changes over time; for example, if an object is moving 2 units right and 3 units down every second, you could write its velocity as [2, 3]. Then, every second, you would add the object's velocity to its current position.

While you can store velocities in CGPoint structures, it's slightly more convenient to store them in CGVector structures (see Figure 6-2). These are 100% identical to CGPoints, but the fields of the structure are named differently: x is named dx, and y is named dy. The d prefix stands for "delta," which means "amount of change of." So, "dx" means "delta x"—that is, "amount of change of x":

```
CGVector myVector;
myVector.dx = 2;
myVector.dy = 3;
```

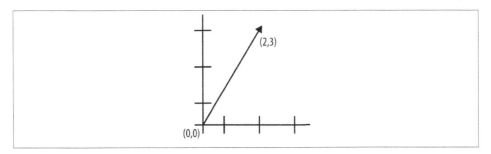

Figure 6-2. A vector used to define the direction (2,3)

Vector lengths

Let's say you've got a velocity vector [2, 3]. In a given second, how far will an object move?

The first thing you might think of is to add the two values together, giving a value of 5. However, this isn't correct, because the object is traveling in a straight line, not traveling a certain distance, turning, and traveling the rest of the distance.

To get the *length* of a vector (also sometimes referred to as the *magnitude*), you square each component of the vector, add them all up, and take the square root of the result:

```
CGVector myVector = CGVectorMake(4, 6);
float length = sqrt(myVector.dx * myVector.dx + myVector.dy * myVector.dy);
// float =~ 7.21
```

Moving vectors

When you want to move a point by a given velocity, you need to add the two vectors together.

To add two vectors together (also known as *translating* a vector), you just add the respective components of each vector—that is, you sum the x coordinates, then the y coordinates (Figure 6-3):

```
CGVector vector1 = CGVectorMake(1,2);
CGVector vector2 = CGVectorMake(1,1);

CGVector vector3;
vector3.dx = vector1.dx + vector2.dx;
vector3.dx = vector1.dy + vector2.dy;

// vector3 = (2, 3);
```

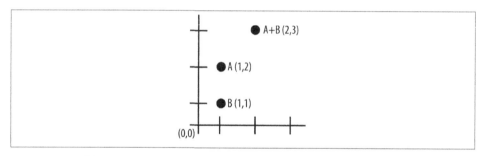

Figure 6-3. Adding vectors

The same thing applies to subtracting vectors: you just subtract the components, instead of adding them.

Rotating vectors

To rotate a vector, you first need to know the angle that you want to rotate it by.

In graphics, angles are usually given in *radians*. There are 2π radians in a full circle (and, therefore, π radians in half a circle, and $\pi/2$ radians in a quarter circle).

To convert from radians to degrees, multiply by 180 and divide by π:

```
float radians = 3.14159;
float degrees = radians * 180 / M_PI;
// degrees = 180
```

To convert from degrees to radians, divide by 180 and multiply by π:

```
float degrees = 45;
float radians = degrees * M_PI / 180;
// radians = ~0.785
```

When you have your angle in radians, you can rotate a vector like this:

```
CGFloat angle = M_PI / 4.0; // equals 45 degrees

CGPoint point = CGPointMake(4, 4);
CGPoint rotatedPoint;
rotatedPoint.x = point.x * cos(angle) - point.y * sin(angle);
rotatedPoint.y = point.y * cos(angle) + point.x * sin(angle);

// rotatedPoint = (0, 6.283)
```

Doing this will rotate the vector counterclockwise around the origin. If you want to rotate around another point, first subtract that point from your vector, perform your rotation, and then add the first point back.

Scaling vectors

Scaling a vector is easy—you just multiply each component of the vector by a value:

```
CGPoint myPosition = CGVectorMake(2, 7);

myPosition.dx *= 4;
myPosition.dy *= 4;
```

Dot product

The *dot product* is a useful way to find out how much two vectors differ in the direction that they point in.

For example, let's say you've got two vectors, [2, 2] and [2, 1], and you want to find out how much of an angle there is between them (Figure 6-4).

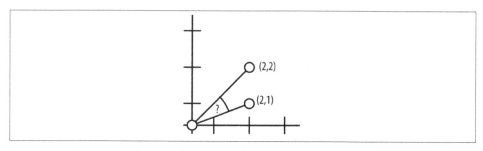

Figure 6-4. The dot product can be used to determine the angle between two vectors

You can figure this out by taking the dot product. The dot product can be calculated like this:

```
CGPoint v1 = CGPointMake(2,2);
CGPoint v2 = CGPointMake(2,1);

float dotProduct = (v1.x * v2.x + v1.y * v2.y);
```

An interesting property of the dot product is that the dot product of any two vectors is the same as the result of multiplying their lengths together along with the cosine of the angle between them:

```
A · B = |A| × |B| × cosα
```

This means that you can get the cosine of the angle by rearranging the equation as follows:

```
A · B ÷ (|A| × |B|) = cosα
```

Which means you can get the angle itself by taking the arc cosine, like this:

```
acos(A · B ÷ (|A| × |B|)) = α
```

The GLKit framework, discussed in Chapter 8, includes functions for working out the dot product of vectors without you having to write out all the math yourself:

```
GLKVector2 a = GLKVector2Make(1,2);
GLKVector2 b = GLKVector2Make(3,2);

float dotProduct = GLKVector2DotProduct(a, b);
```

6.2. Creating a Sprite Kit View

Problem

You want to display a Sprite Kit view, which you can use for showing 2D graphics.

Solution

To use any element of Sprite Kit, you need to add *SpriteKit.framework* to your project:

1. Select your project at the top of the Project Navigator, at the left of the Xcode window.

2. Go to the General tab, and scroll down until you see "Linked Frameworks and Libraries."

3. Click the + button, and type "SpriteKit" in the search box that appears (Figure 6-5).

4. Double-click on "SpriteKit.framework" to add the framework to your project.

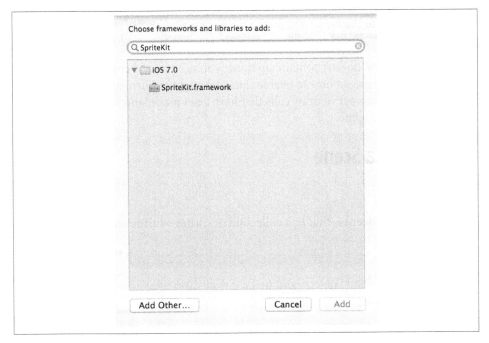

Figure 6-5. Adding Sprite Kit to the project

Once the framework has been added, go to your storyboard and select the view controller in which you want to show Sprite Kit content. Select the main view inside the view controller, and change its class to SKView.

Next, go to your view controller's implementation, and add the following code to the viewDidLoad method:

```
SKView* spriteView = (SKView*)self.view;
spriteView.showsDrawCount = YES;
```

```
spriteView.showsFPS = YES;
spriteView.showsNodeCount = YES;
```

Finally, run the application. You'll see a mostly empty screen; however, down in the lower-right corner of the screen, you'll see additional information about how well your game is performing.

Discussion

An `SKView` is the area in which Sprite Kit content is drawn. All of your 2D graphics drawing happens inside this area.

An `SKView` is a subclass of `UIView`, which means you can work with it in the interface builder. Given that you'll most likely want to use the entire screen for your sprites, it makes sense to make the view used by the view controller an `SKView` (rather than, for example, adding an `SKView` as a subview of the view controller's main view.)

By default, an `SKView` doesn't contain anything; you need to add content to it yourself. In this recipe, we've shown how to enable some debugging information: the frames per second (FPS), the number of draw calls that have been made, and the total number of nodes (items) in the scene.

6.3. Creating a Scene

Problem

You want to show a scene—that is, a collection of sprites—inside an `SKView`.

Solution

Create a new Objective-C object, and make it a subclass of `SKScene`. In this example, we'll call it `TestScene`.

Add a new property to `TestScene`:

```
@property BOOL contentCreated;
```

Add the following code to *TestScene.m*:

```
- (void)didMoveToView:(SKView *)view
{
    if (self.contentCreated == NO)
    {
        [self createSceneContents];
        self.contentCreated = YES;
    }
}
```

```
- (void)createSceneContents
{
    self.backgroundColor = [SKColor blackColor];
    self.scaleMode = SKSceneScaleModeAspectFit;

}
```

Import *TestScene.h* in your view controller's *.m* file.

Finally, add the following code to your view controller's viewWillAppear method:

```
- (void)viewWillAppear:(BOOL)animated {
    TestScene* hello = [[TestScene alloc] initWithSize:CGSizeMake(768, 1024)];
    SKView* spriteView = (SKView*)self.view;

    [spriteView presentScene:hello];
}
```

Discussion

When an SKScene is added to an SKView, it receives the didMoveToView: message. This is your scene's opportunity to prepare whatever content it wants to display.

However, it's important to keep in mind that an SKScene might be presented multiple times over its lifetime. For that reason, you should use a variable to keep track of whether the content of the scene has already been created:

```
- (void)didMoveToView:(SKView *)view
{
    if (self.contentCreated == NO)
    {
        [self createSceneContents];
        self.contentCreated = YES;
    }
}
```

In the createSceneContents method, the actual content that appears in the scene is prepared. In this example, the scene is empty, but shows a black background.

The black color is represented by an SKColor.

```
    self.backgroundColor = [SKColor blackColor];
```

SKColor isn't actually a class, but rather a macro that maps to the NSColor class on OS X, and to the UIColor class on iOS. This means that it's a little easier to port code from iOS to OS X.

Additionally, the scene's scaleMode is set. The scene's scaleMode property determines how the SKView scales the scene—because your scene might appear in different sizes (e.g., on iPhone screens versus iPad screens), it's important to know how the scene should be sized to fit into the SKView.

Several options exist for this:

SKSceneScaleModeFill
> The scene will be scaled to fill the SKView.

SKSceneScaleModeAspectFill
> The scene will be scaled to fill the SKView, preserving the aspect ratio of the scene. Some areas of the scene might be clipped off in order to achieve this.

SKSceneScaleModeAspectFit
> The scene will be scaled to fit inside the SKView. You might see some letterboxing (i.e., some blank areas at the top and bottom or sides).

SKSceneScaleModeResizeFill
> The scene will be resized—*not* scaled—in order to fill the SKView.

Once a scene has been prepared, it needs to be *presented* in order to appear in an SKView. This is quite straightforward—all you need to do is call presentScene:, and pass in an SKScene:

```
TestScene* hello = [[TestScene alloc] initWithSize:CGSizeMake(768, 1024)];
SKView* spriteView = (SKView*)self.view;

[spriteView presentScene:hello];
```

When you call presentScene:, the currently presented scene in the SKView is replaced with whatever you provided. Note that you have to cast self.view to an SKView before you can call presentScene:.

6.4. Adding a Sprite

Problem

You want to display a sprite in a Sprite Kit scene.

Solution

To show a sprite to the player, you create an SKSpriteNode, configure its size and position, and then add it to your SKScene object:

```
SKScene* scene = ... // an SKScene

SKSpriteNode* sprite = [[SKSpriteNode alloc] initWithColor:[SKColor grayColor]
                        size:CGSizeMake(32, 32)];

sprite.position = CGPointMake(100, 100);

[scene addChild:sprite];
```

Discussion

SKSpriteNode is a *node*: an object that can be put inside a scene. There are several different kinds of nodes, all of which are subclasses of the SKNode class.

SKSpriteNode is a type of node that can display either a colored rectangle, or an image. In this recipe, we're focusing on just colored rectangles; to show an image, see Recipe 6.10.

To create a colored rectangle sprite, you just need to provide the color you'd like to use, as well as the size of the rectangle:

```
SKSpriteNode* sprite = [[SKSpriteNode alloc] initWithColor:[SKColor grayColor]
                            size:CGSizeMake(32, 32)];
```

The position of the sprite is controlled by the sprite's position property, which is a CGPoint. The position that you provide determines the location of the sprite's *anchor point*, which is the center point of the sprite:

```
sprite.position = CGPointMake(100, 100);
```

Sprites aren't visible unless they're inside an SKScene, which means you need to call the addChild: method on the SKScene you want your sprite to appear in:

```
[scene addChild:sprite];
```

The position of a sprite—in fact, of any node—is determined relative to the position of the anchor point of the sprite's *parent*. This means that you can add sprites as children of *other sprites*. If you do this, the child sprites will move with their parents.

6.5. Adding a Text Sprite

Problem

You want to display some text in a Sprite Kit scene.

Solution

Create an SKLabelNode, and add it to your scene:

```
SKScene* scene = ... // an SKScene

SKLabelNode* helloWorldNode = [SKLabelNode labelNodeWithFontNamed:@"Zapfino"];

helloWorldNode.text = @"Hello, world!";
helloWorldNode.fontSize = 42;
helloWorldNode.position = CGPointMake(CGRectGetMidX(scene.frame),
                                      CGRectGetMidY(scene.frame));

helloWorldNode.name = @"helloNode";
```

```
[scene addChild:scene];
```

Discussion

An SKLabelNode is a node that displays text. Just like with other kinds of nodes, you add it to a scene to make it visible to the player (see Recipe 6.4.)

To create an SKLabelNode, all you need to provide is the font that the label should use:

```
SKLabelNode* helloWorldNode = [SKLabelNode labelNodeWithFontNamed:@"Zapfino"];
```

The specific font name that you provide to the labelNodeWithFontNamed: method needs to be one of the fonts that's included in iOS, or a custom font included with your application. To learn what fonts are available for use in your game, see Recipe 6.6; to learn how you can include a custom font in your app, see Recipe 6.7.

Once you've got an SKLabelNode to use, you just need to provide it with the text that it needs to display, as well as the font size that it should use:

```
helloWorldNode.text = @"Hello, world!";
helloWorldNode.fontSize = 42;
```

By default, the text is aligned so that it's centered horizontally on the x coordinate of the node's position, and the baseline (i.e., the bottom part of letters that don't have a descender—letter like e, a, and b) of the text is set to the y coordinate. However, you can change this: all you need to do is change the verticalAlignmentMode or horizontalAlignmentMode properties.

The verticalAlignmentMode property can be set to one of the following values:

SKLabelVerticalAlignmentModeBaseline
> The baseline of the text is placed at the origin of the node (this is the default).

SKLabelVerticalAlignmentModeCenter
> The center of the text is placed at the origin.

SKLabelVerticalAlignmentModeTop
> The top of the text is placed at the origin.

SKLabelVerticalAlignmentModeBottom
> The bottom of the text is placed at the origin.

Additionally, the horizontalAlignmentMode property can be set to one of the following values:

SKLabelHorizontalAlignmentModeCenter
> The text is center-aligned (this is the default).

```
SKLabelHorizontalAlignmentModeLeft
```
The text is left-aligned.

```
SKLabelHorizontalAlignmentModeRight
```
The text is right-aligned.

6.6. Determining Available Fonts

Problem

You want to know which fonts are available for your game to use.

Solution

The following code logs the name of every font available for use in your game to the
debugging console:

```
for (NSString* fontFamilyName in [UIFont familyNames]) {
    for (NSString* fontName in [UIFont fontNamesForFamilyName:fontFamilyName]) {
        NSLog(@"Available font: %@", fontName);
    }
}
```

Discusion

The UIFont class, which represents fonts on iOS, allows you to list all of the available
font families available to your code, using the familyNames method. This method returns an NSArray of NSString objects, each of which is the name of a font family.

However, a font family name isn't the same thing as the name of a usable font. For
example, the font Helvetica is actually a *collection* of different fonts: it includes Helvetica
Bold, Helvetica Light, Helvetica Light Oblique, and so on.

Therefore, to get a font name that you can use with an SKLabel (or, indeed, any other
part of iOS that deals in font names), you pass a font family name to the fontNamesFor
FamilyName method in UIFont. This returns *another* NSArray of NSString objects, each
of which is the name of a font you can use.

Alternatively, you can visit iOS Fonts (*http://iosfonts.com/*), which is a third-party site
that lists all of the available fonts and includes additional information about which fonts
are available on different versions of iOS.

6.7. Including Custom Fonts

Problem

You want to include a custom font in your game, so that you can show text using fancy letters.

Solution

First, you'll need a font file, in either TrueType or OpenType format—that is, a *.ttf* or *.otf* file.

Add the file to your project. Next, go to your project's Info tab, and add a new entry to the Custom Target Properties, called "Fonts provided by application." This is an array; for each of the fonts you want to add, add a new entry in this array.

For example, if you've added a font file called *MyFont.ttf*, add *MyFont.ttf* to the "Fonts provided by application" list.

Discussion

Any fonts you include in your application are available through `UIFont` (see Recipe 6.6); you don't have to do anything special to get access to them.

If you don't have a font, Dafont (*http://www.dafont.com*) is an excellent place to find free fonts—just be sure that any fonts you get are allowed to be used for commercial purposes.

6.8. Transitioning Between Scenes

Problem

You want to move from one scene to another.

Solution

Use the `presentScene:` method on an `SKView` to change which scene is being shown:

```
SKView* spriteView = ... // an SKView

SKScene* newScene = ... // the new SKScene you want to present

[spriteView presentScene:newScene];
```

Using `presentScene:` immediately switches over to the new scene. If you want to use a transition, you create an `SKTransition`, and then call `presentScene:transition::`

```
SKTransition* crossFade = [SKTransition crossFadeWithDuration:1.0];

[spriteView presentScene:newScene transition:crossFade];
```

Discussion

When an `SKScene` is presented, the scene that's about to be removed from the screen is sent the `willMoveFromView:` message. This gives the scene a chance to tidy up, or to remove any sprites that might take up a lot of memory. The `SKScene` that's about to be shown in the `SKView` is sent the `didMoveToView:` message, which is its chance to prepare the scene's content.

If you call `presentScene:`, the new scene will immediately appear. However, it's often good to use an animation to transition from one scene to another, such as a fade or push animation.

To do this, you use the `SKTransition` class, and provide that to the `SKView` through the `presentScene:transition:` method.

You create an `SKTransition` through one of the factory methods, and provide any additional information that that type of transition needs. All transitions need to know how long the transition should run for, and a few transitions need additional information, such as a direction. For example, you create a cross-fade transition like this:

```
SKTransition* crossFade = [SKTransition crossFadeWithDuration:1.0];
```

There are a variety of transitions available for you to use, each with a corresponding method for creating it. Try them out! Options include:

Cross-fade (`crossFadeWithDuration:`)
: The current scene fades out while the new scene fades in.

Doors close horizontal (`doorsCloseHorizontalWithDuration:`)
: The new scene comes in as a pair of horizontal closing "doors."

Doors close vertical (`doorsCloseVerticalWithDuration:`)
: The new scene comes in as a pair of vertical closing "doors."

Doors open horizontal (`doorsOpenHorizontalWithDuration:`)
: The current scene splits apart, and moves off as a pair of horizontally opening "doors."

Doors open vertical (`doorsOpenVerticalWithDuration:`)
: The current scene splits apart, and moves off as a pair of vertically opening "doors."

Doorway (`doorwayWithDuration:`)
: The current scene splits apart, revealing the new scene in the background; the new scene approaches the camera, and eventually fills the scene by the time the transition is complete.

Fade with color (`fadeWithColor:duration:`*)*
> The current scene fades out, revealing the color you specify; the new scene then fades in on top of this color.

Fade (`fadeWithDuration:`*)*
> The current scene fades to black, and then the new scene fades in.

Flip horizontal (`flipHorizontalWithDuration:`*)*
> The current scene flips horizontally, revealing the new scene on the reverse side.

Flip vertical (`flipVerticalWithDuration:`*)*
> The current scene flips vertically, revealing the new scene on the reverse side.

Move in (`moveInWithDirection:duration:`*)*
> The new scene comes in from off-screen, and moves in on top of the current scene.

Push in (`pushWithDirection:duration:`*)*
> The new scene comes in from off-screen, pushing the current scene off the screen.

Reveal (`revealWithDirection:duration:`*)*
> The current scene moves off-screen, revealing the new scene underneath it.

`CIFilter` *transition (*`transitionWithCIFilter:duration:`*)*
> You can use a `CIFilter` object to create a custom transition.

6.9. Moving Sprites and Labels Around

Problem

You want your sprites and labels to move around your scene.

Solution

You can use `SKAction` objects to make any node in the scene perform an *action*. An action is something that changes the position, color, transparency, or size of any node in your scene.

The following code makes a node move up and to the right while fading away, then runs some code, and finally removes the node from the scene:

```
SKNode* node = ... // an SKNode - this can be a sprite, label, or anything

// Move 100 pixels up and 100 pixels to the right over 1 second
SKAction* moveUp = [SKAction moveByX:100 y:100 duration:1.0];

// Fade out over 0.5 seconds
SKAction* fadeOut = [SKAction fadeOutWithDuration:0.5];
```

```
// Run a block of code
SKAction* runBlock = [SKAction runBlock:^{
    NSLog(@"Hello!");
}];

// Remove the node
SKAction* remove = [SKAction removeFromParent];

// Run the movement and fading blocks at the same time
SKAction* moveAndFade = [SKAction group:@[moveUp, fadeOut]];

// Move and fade, then run the block, then remove the node
SKAction* sequence = [SKAction sequence:@[moveAndFade, runBlock, remove]];

// Run these sequences on the node
[node runAction:sequence];
```

Discussion

An SKAction is an object that represents an action that a node can perform. There are heaps of different kinds of actions available for you to use—too many for us to list here, so for full information, check out Apple's documentation for SKAction (*https://develop er.apple.com/library/ios/documentation/SpriteKit/Reference/SKAction_Ref/Reference/ Reference.html*).

Generally, an action is something that changes some property of the node that it applies to. For example, the moveByX:y:duration: action in the preceding example changes the position of the node by making it move by a certain distance along the x- and y-axes. Some actions don't actually change the node, though; for example, you can create an action that simply waits for an amount of time, or one that runs some code.

To run an action, you first create an SKAction with one of the factory methods. Then, you call runAction: on the SKNode that you'd like to have perform that action.

You can add an action to multiple nodes—if you want several nodes to all do the same thing, just create the SKAction once and then call runAction: on each of the SKNodes that you want to perform the action.

Most actions are things that take place over a period of time: for example, moving, rotating, fading, changing color, and so on. Some actions take place immediately, however, such as running code or removing a node from the scene.

An action can work on its own, or you can combine multiple actions with *sequences* and *groups*. A sequence is an SKAction that runs *other* actions, one after the other. The first action is run, and once it's complete the next is run, and so on until the end; at this point, the sequence action is considered done. To create a sequence, use the se quence: method, which takes an NSArray of SKAction objects:

```
SKAction* sequence = [SKAction sequence:@[action1, action2, action3]];
```

A group, by contrast, runs a collection of actions simultaneously. A group action is considered complete when the longest-running of the actions it's been given has completed. Creating groups looks very similar to creating sequences. To create a group, you pass an NSArray of SKAction objects to the group: method:

```
SKAction* group = [SKAction group:@[action1, action2, action3]];
```

You can combine groups and sequences. For example, you can make two sequences run at the same time by combining them into a group:

```
SKAction* sequence1 = [SKAction sequence:@[action1, action2]];
SKAction* sequence2 = [SKAction sequence:@[action1, action2]];

SKAction* group = [SKAction group:@[sequence1, sequence2]];
```

You can also create sequences that contain groups; if, for example, you have a sequence with two groups in it, the second group will not run until all actions in the first group have finished.

Some actions are able to be reversed. By sending the reversedAction message to these actions, you get back an SKAction that performs the opposite action to the original. Not all actions can be reversed; for details on which can and can't, check the documentation for SKAction.

As we've already mentioned, you start actions by calling runAction: on an SKNode. You can also make Sprite Kit run a block when the action that you've submitted finishes running, using the runAction:completion: block:

```
SKAction* action = ... // an SKAction of any kind
SKNode* node = ... // an SKNode

[node runAction:action completion:^{
    NSLog(@"Action's done!");
}];
```

You can add multiple actions to a node, which will all run at the same time. If you do this, it's often useful to be able to keep track of the actions you add to a node. You can do this with the runAction:withKey: method, which lets you associate actions you run on an SKNode with a name:

```
[node runAction:action withKey:@"My Action"];
```

If you add two actions with the same name, the old action is removed before the new one is added.

Once you've added an action with a name, you can use the actionForKey: method to get the action back:

```
SKAction* action = [node actionForKey:@"My Action"];
```

You can also remove actions by name, using the removeActionForKey: method:

```
[node removeActionForKey:@"My Action"]
```

Finally, you can remove *all* actions from a node in one line of code using the removeAl
lActions method:

```
[node removeAllActions];
```

 When you remove an action, the action stops whatever it was doing. However, any changes that the action had *already* made to the
node remain.

For example, if you've added an action that moves the sprite, and you
remove it before the action finishes running, the sprite will be left
part-way between its origin point and the destination.

6.10. Adding a Texture Sprite

Problem

You want to create a sprite that uses an image.

Solution

First, add the image that you want to use to your project (see Recipe 2.5).

Next, create an SKSpriteNode with the initWithImageNamed: method:

```
SKScene* scene = ... // an SKScene

SKSpriteNode* imageSprite = [[SKSpriteNode alloc]
                              initWithImageNamed:@"ImageName"];

[scene addChild:]
```

Discussion

When you create a sprite with initWithImageNamed:, the size of the sprite is based on
the size of the image.

Once you've created the sprite, it works just like any other node: you can position it,
add it to the scene, run actions on it, and so on.

6.11. Creating Texture Atlases

Problem

You want to use texture atlases, which save memory and make rendering more efficient.

Solution

Create a folder named *Textures.atlas* and put all of the textures that you want to group in it.

Then, add this folder to your project by dragging the folder into the Project Navigator.

Finally, go to the Build Settings by clicking on the project at the top of the Project Navigator, and search for "SpriteKit." Set Enable Texture Atlas Generation to Yes.

Discussion

A *texture atlas* is a texture composed of other, smaller textures. Using a texture atlas means that instead of several smaller textures, you use one larger texture. This atlas uses slightly less memory than if you were to use lots of individual textures, and more importantly is more efficient for rendering. When a sprite needs to be drawn, a subregion of the texture atlas is used for drawing.

If your game involves lots of sprites that each use different images, the Sprite Kit renderer needs to switch images every time it starts drawing a different sprite. Switching images has a small performance cost, which adds up if you're doing it multiple times. However, if multiple sprites share the same texture, Sprite Kit doesn't have to switch images, making rendering faster.

When you put images in a folder whose name ends with *.atlas*, and turn on Texture Atlas Generation, Xcode will automatically create a texture atlas for you based on whatever images are in that folder. You images will be automatically trimmed for transparency, reducing the number of wasted pixels, and images are packed together as efficiently as possible.

When you're using texture atlases, your Sprite Kit code remains the same. The following code works regardless of whether you're using atlases or not:

```
SKSpriteNode* imageSprite = [[SKSpriteNode alloc]
                        initWithImageNamed:@"ImageName"];
```

6.12. Using Shape Nodes

Problem

You want to use shape nodes to draw vector shapes.

Solution

Use an SKShapeNode to draw shapes:

```
SKScene* scene = ... // an SKScene
```

```objc
UIBezierPath* path = [UIBezierPath bezierPathWithRoundedRect:CGRectMake(-100,
                        -100, 200, 200) cornerRadius:20 ];

SKShapeNode* shape = [[SKShapeNode alloc] init];
shape.path = [path CGPath];
shape.strokeColor = [SKColor greenColor];
shape.fillColor = [SKColor redColor];

shape.glowWidth = 4;

shape.position = CGPointMake(CGRectGetMidX(scene.frame),
                        CGRectGetMidY(scene.frame));

[scene addChild:shape];
```

Discussion

SKSceneNode draws *paths*, which are objects that represent shapes. A path can be a rectangle, a circle, or any shape you can possibly think of. For more information on working with paths, see Recipe 6.15.

The coordinates of the path that you provide are positioned relative to your node's anchor point. For example, a shape that has a line that starts at (−10,−10) and moves to (10,10) starts above and to the left of the node's position, and ends below and to the right of the position.

You can use the fillColor and strokeColor properties to change the colors used to draw the shape. Use SKColor to define the colors you want to use. The *fill color* is the color used to fill the contents of the shape, and the *stroke color* is the color used to draw the line around the outside of the shape. By default, the fill color is clear (i.e., no color, just empty space), while the stroke color is white.

Finally, you can specify how thick the line is. By default, the thickness is 1 point; Apple notes that specifying a line thickness of more than 2 pt may lead to rendering problems. In these cases, you're better off using an SKSpriteNode. In addition, you can make the stroke line glow by setting the glowWidth property to a value higher than 0.

6.13. Using Blending Modes

Problem

You want to use different blending modes to create visual effects.

Solution

Use the blendMode property to control how nodes are blended with the rest of the scene:

```
SKNode* node = ... // any SKNode
node.blendMode = SKBlendModeAdd;
```

Discussion

When a node is drawn into the scene, the way that the final scene looks depends on the node's *blend mode*. When a node is blended into the scene, the Sprite Kit renderer looks at the color of each pixel of the node, and the color underneath each pixel, and determines what the resulting color should be.

By default, all SKNodes use the same blending mode: SKBlendModeAlpha, which uses the alpha channel of the image multiplied by the sprite's alpha property to determine how much the node's color should contribute to the scene. This is generally the blending mode you want to use most of the time.

However, it isn't the *only* blending mode that you can use. Other options exist:

SKBlendModeAdd
> The colors of the node are added to the scene. This leads to a brightening, semi-transparent effect. (Good for lights, fires, laser beams, and explosions!)

SKBlendModeSubtract
> The colors of the node are subtracted from the scene. This creates a rather weird-looking darkening effect. (Not very realistic, but it can lead to some interesting effects.)

SKBlendModeMultiply
> The colors of the node are multiplied with the scene. This darkens the colors. (Very good for shadows, and for tinting parts of the scene.)

SKBlendModeMultiplyX2
> The same as SKBlendModeMultiply, but the colors of the sprite are doubled after the first multiplication. This creates a brighter effect than plain multiply.

SKBlendModeScreen
> The colors of the node are added to the scene, multiplied by the inverse of the scene's color. This creates a more subtle brightening effect than SKBlendModeAdd. (Good for glosses and shiny areas.)

SKBlendModeReplace
> The colors of the node replace the scene and are not blended with any existing colors. This means that any alpha information is completely ignored. This mode is also the fastest possible drawing mode, since no blending calculations need to take place.

6.14. Using Image Effects to Change the Way that Sprites Are Drawn

Problem

You want to use image effects on your sprites, to create different effects.

Solution

Use an SKEffectNode with a CIFilter to apply visual effects to nodes:

```
SKScene* scene = ... // an SKScene

SKEffectNode* effect = [[SKEffectNode alloc] init];
effect.position = CGPointMake(550, 300);

CIFilter* filter = [CIFilter filterWithName:@"CIGaussianBlur"];
[filter setValue:@(20.0) forKey:@"inputRadius"];

effect.filter = filter;

SKSpriteNode* sprite = [[SKSpriteNode alloc] initWithImageNamed:@"MySprite"];

[effect addChild:sprite];
[scene addChild:effect];
```

Discussion

A CIFilter is an object that applies an effect to images. CIFilters are incredibly powerful, and are used all over iOS and OS X. One of the most popular examples of where they're used is in the Photo Booth app, where they power the visual effects that you can apply to photos.

To use a CIFilter with Sprite Kit, you create an SKEffectNode and add any nodes that you want to have the effect apply to as children of that node. (Don't forget to add the SKEffectNode to your scene.)

Once you've done that, you get a CIFilter, configure it how you like, and provide it to the SKEffectNode. You get a CIFilter using the filterWithName: method of the CIFilter class, which takes an NSString: the name of the filter you'd like to use.

Different filters have different properties, which you can configure using the CIFilter's setValue:forKey: method.

There are dozens of CIFilters that you can use—lots more than we could sensibly list here. Here are a couple of especially cool ones:

CIGaussianBlur

Applies a Gaussian blur. The default blur radius is 10.0; change it by setting
inputRadius to something different.

CIPixellate

Makes the image all blocky and pixelated. The default pixel size is 8.0; change it by
setting inputScale to something different.

CIPhotoEffectNoir

Makes the image black and white, with an exaggerated contrast. This filter has no
parameters you can change.

6.15. Using Bézier Paths

Problem

You want to draw shapes using Bézier paths (custom shapes and lines).

Solution

Use the UIBezierPath class to represent shapes:

```
UIBezierPath* path = [UIBezierPath bezierPathWithRoundedRect:CGRectMake(-100,
                     -100, 200, 200) cornerRadius:20 ];

UIBezierPath* rectangle = [UIBezierPath bezierPathWithRect:CGRectMake(0, 0,
                          100, 200)];
UIBezierPath* roundedRectagle = [UIBezierPath bezierPathWithRoundedRect:
                                 CGRectMake(0, 0, 100, 200) cornerRadius:20];
UIBezierPath* oval = [UIBezierPath bezierPathWithOvalInRect:CGRectMake(0, 0,
                     100, 200)];

UIBezierPath* customShape = [UIBezierPath bezierPath];
[customShape moveToPoint:CGPointMake(0, 0)];
[customShape addLineToPoint:CGPointMake(0, 100)];
[customShape addCurveToPoint:CGPointMake(0, 0) controlPoint1:CGPointMake(100,
                             100) controlPoint2:CGPointMake(100, 0)];
[customShape closePath];
```

Discussion

UIBezierPath objects represent shapes, which you can display on the screen with an
SKShapeNode.

Creating a rectangle, rounded rectangle, or oval is pretty easy—there are built-in factory
methods for these. There's no built-in method for creating circles, but it's easy to make

one—just create an oval inside a square rectangle (i.e., a rectangle with an equal width and height).

In addition to these basic shapes, you can also create your own custom shapes. You do this by using the `moveToPoint:`, `addLineToPoint:`, and `addCurveToPoint:control Point1:controlPoint2:` methods.

When you're drawing a custom shape, it helps to imagine a virtual pen poised over a sheet of paper. When you call `moveToPoint:`, you're positioning your hand over a specific point. When you call `addLineToPoint:`, you place the pen down on the paper and draw a straight line from the pen's current location to the destination. You can call `moveToPoint:` again to lift the virtual pen from the paper and reposition your hand somewhere else.

The `addCurveToPoint:controlPoint1:controlPoint2:` method lets you draw a cubic Bézier curve. A Bézier curve is a curved line that starts at the pen's current location and moves toward the destination point you provide, bending toward the two control points. A Bézier curve is often useful for drawing smoothly curving things in games, such as roads.

When you're done creating a shape, you call `closePath`. Doing this draws a straight line from the pen's current position to the starting position.

To use a `UIBezierPath` with an `SKShapeNode`, you ask the `UIBezierPath` for its `CGPath` property, and give that to the `SKShapeNode`. For more information on how `SKShape Node` works, see Recipe 6.12.

6.16. Creating Smoke, Fire, and Other Particle Effects

Problem

You want to create fire, smoke, snow, or other visual effects.

Solution

You can use particle effects to simulate these kinds of effects. To create a particle effect, follow these steps:

1. From the File menu, choose New→File. Select Resource, and then select SpriteKit Particle File.

2. You'll be asked to pick a template to start from. Pick whichever you like—Jon happens to like the Fire template.

3. Open the newly created file, and you'll enter the Emitter editor. This component of Xcode allows you to play with the various properties that define how the particle

system looks, including how many particles are emitted, how they change over time, and how they're colored. Additionally, you can click and drag to see how the particle system looks when it's moving.

Once you're done configuring the particle system, you can add the effect to your scene with the following code (adjust the filenames to suit your needs.):

```
NSString *firePath = [[NSBundle mainBundle] pathForResource:@"Fire"
                            ofType:@"sks"];
SKEmitterNode *fire = [NSKeyedUnarchiver unarchiveObjectWithFile:firePath];

[self addChild:fire];
```

Discussion

Particle effects can be used for a variety of natural-looking effects that would be difficult to create with individual sprites. Individual particles in a particle system have much less overhead than creating the sprites yourself, so you can create rather complex-looking effects without dramatically affecting performance.

Because there are so many different parameters available to customize, creating a particle system that suits your needs is very much more an art than a science. Be prepared to spend some time playing with the available settings, and try the different built-in presets to get an idea of what's possible.

6.17. Shaking the Screen

Problem

You want the screen to shake—for example, an explosion has happened, and you want to emphasize the effect by rattling the player's view of the scene around.

Solution

Create an empty node, and call it cameraNode. Add it to the screen. Put all of the nodes that you'd normally put into the scene into this new node.

Add the following method to your scene's code:

```
- (void) shakeNode:(SKNode*)node {
    // Reset the camera's position
    node.position = CGPointZero;

    // Cancel any existing shake actions
    [node removeActionForKey:@"shake"];

    // The number of individual movements that the shake will be made up of
    int shakeSteps = 15;
```

```objc
// How "big" the shake is
float shakeDistance = 20;

// How long the shake should go on for
float shakeDuration = 0.25;

// An array to store the individual movements in
NSMutableArray* shakeActions = [NSMutableArray array];

// Start at shakeSteps, and step down to 0
for (int i = shakeSteps; i > 0; i--) {

    // How long this specific shake movement will take
    float shakeMovementDuration = shakeDuration / shakeSteps;

    // This will be 1.0 at the start and gradually move down to 0.0
    float shakeAmount= i / (float)shakeSteps;

    // Take the current position - we'll then add an offset from that
    CGPoint shakePosition = node.position;

    // Pick a random amount from -shakeDistance to shakeDistance
    shakePosition.x += (arc4random_uniform(shakeDistance*2) - shakeDistance)
                        * shakeAmount;
    shakePosition.y += (arc4random_uniform(shakeDistance*2) - shakeDistance)
                        * shakeAmount;

    // Create the action that moves the node to the new location, and
    // add it to the list
    SKAction* shakeMovementAction = [SKAction moveTo:shakePosition
                                         duration:shakeMovementDuration];
    [shakeActions addObject:shakeMovementAction];

}

// Run the shake!
SKAction* shakeSequence = [SKAction sequence:shakeActions];
[node runAction:shakeSequence withKey:@"shake"];
}
```

When you want to shake the screen, just call `shakeNode:` and pass in `cameraNode`:

```objc
[self shakeNode:cameraNode];
```

Discussion

Shaking the screen is a really effective way to emphasize to the player that something big and impressive is happening. If something forceful enough to shake the *world* around you is going on, then you know it means business!

So, what does a shake actually mean in terms of constructing an animation? Well, a shake is when you start at a neutral, resting point and begin moving large distances back and forth over that neutral point. An important element in realistic-looking shakes is that the shake gradually settles down, with the movements becoming less and less drastic as the shaking comes to an end.

To implement a shake, therefore, you need to construct several small movements. These can be implemented using SKActions: each step in the shake is an SKAction that moves the node from its current location to another location.

To attenuate the shake—that is, to make the movements smaller and smaller—the for loop that creates individual movements actually counts *down* to zero, and the number of steps remaining is divided by the total number of steps. This gives us a number from 0 to 1, by which the movement is multiplied. Eventually, the amount of movement is multiplied by 0—in other words, the movement settles back down to the neutral position.

6.18. Animating a Sprite

Problem

You want to make a SpriteKit animation using a collection of images. For example, you've got a "running" animation, and you want your sprite to play that animation.

Solution

In this solution, we're going to assume that you've already got all of your individual frames, and you've put them into a folder named **Animation.atlas**, which has been added to your project.

Use SKAction's animateWithTextures:timePerFrame: method to animate a collection of sprites:

```
// Load the texture atlas
SKTextureAtlas* atlas = [SKTextureAtlas atlasNamed:@"Animation"];

// Get the list of texture names, and sort them
NSArray* textureNames = [[atlas textureNames]
sortedArrayUsingSelector:@selector(compare:)];

// Load all textures
NSMutableArray* allTextures = [NSMutableArray array];

for (NSString* textureName in textureNames) {
    [allTextures addObject:[atlas textureNamed:textureName]];
}
```

```
// Create the sprite, and give it the initial frame; position it
// in the middle of the screen
SKSpriteNode* animatedSprite = [SKSpriteNode
                                spriteNodeWithTexture:allTextures[0]];
animatedSprite.position = CGPointMake(CGRectGetMidX(self.frame),
                                      CGRectGetMidY(self.frame));
[self addChild:animatedSprite];

// Make the sprite animate using the loaded textures, at a rate of
// 30 frames per second
SKAction* animationAction = [SKAction animateWithTextures:allTextures
                             timePerFrame:(1.0/30.0)];
[animatedSprite runAction:[SKAction repeatActionForever:animationAction]];
```

Discussion

The SKAction class is capable of changing the texture of a sprite over time. If you have a sequence of images that you want to use as an animation, all you need is an NSArray containing each of the textures you want, with each one stored as an SKTexture.

When you create the animation action using animateWithTextures:timePerFrame:, you provide the NSArray and the amount of time that each texture should be displayed. If you want to run your animation at 30 FPS, then each frame should be shown for 1/30th of a second (0.033 seconds per frame).

To get the SKTextures for display, you either need to load them using SKTexture's textureWithImageNamed: method, or else get them from a texture atlas that contains them. Texture atlases were discussed in Recipe 6.11, and are an excellent way to group the frames for your animation together. They're also better for memory, and ensure that all necessary frames are present for your animation—the game won't pause halfway through your animation to load more frames.

6.19. Parallax Scrolling

Problem

Using SpriteKit, you want to show a two-dimensional scene that appears to have depth, by making more *distant* objects move slower than *closer* objects when the *camera* moves.

Solution

The specific approach for implementing parallax scrolling will depend on the details of your game. In this solution, we're creating a scene where there are four components, listed in order of proximity:

- A dirt path

- Some nearby hills
- Some further distant hills
- The sky

You can see the final scene in Figure 6-6. (Unless you have magic paper, or possibly some kind of hyper-advanced *computer reader* technology yet to be invented, the image will not be scrolling.)

Figure 6-6. The final parallax scrolling scene.

In this scene, we've drawn the art so that each of these components is a separate image. Additionally, each of these images can tile horizontally without visible edges. The art has been put in a texture atlas (see Recipe 6.11 to learn how to use these). The names of the textures for each of the components are *Sky.png*, *DistantHills.png*, *Hills.png*, and *Path.png* (shown in Figure 6-7).

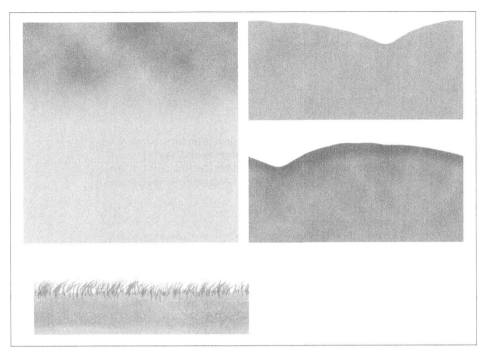

Figure 6-7. The components of the parallax scene. Note that all four components can tile horizontally.

With that out of the way, here's the source code for the SKScene that shows these four components scrolling horizontally at different speeds:

```
@implementation MyScene {

    // Sky
    SKSpriteNode* skyNode;
    SKSpriteNode* skyNodeNext;

    // Foreground hills
    SKSpriteNode* hillsNode;
    SKSpriteNode* hillsNodeNext;

    // Background hills
    SKSpriteNode* distantHillsNode;
    SKSpriteNode* distantHillsNodeNext;

    // Path
    SKSpriteNode* pathNode;
    SKSpriteNode* pathNodeNext;

    // Time of last frame
    CFTimeInterval lastFrameTime;
```

```
        // Time since last frame
        CFTimeInterval deltaTime;
}

-(id)initWithSize:(CGSize)size {
    if (self = [super initWithSize:size]) {

        // Prepare the sky sprites
        skyNode = [SKSpriteNode spriteNodeWithTexture:
                [SKTexture textureWithImageNamed:@"Sky"]];
        skyNode.position = CGPointMake(CGRectGetMidX(self.frame),
                                    CGRectGetMidY(self.frame));

        skyNodeNext = [skyNode copy];
        skyNodeNext.position =
            CGPointMake(skyNode.position.x + skyNode.size.width,
                    skyNode.position.y);

        // Prepare the background hill sprites
        distantHillsNode = [SKSpriteNode spriteNodeWithTexture:
            [SKTexture textureWithImageNamed:@"DistantHills"]];
        distantHillsNode.position =
            CGPointMake(CGRectGetMidX(self.frame),
                    CGRectGetMaxY(self.frame) - 284);

        distantHillsNodeNext = [distantHillsNode copy];
        distantHillsNodeNext.position =
            CGPointMake(distantHillsNode.position.x +
                    distantHillsNode.size.width,
                    distantHillsNode.position.y);

        // Prepare the foreground hill sprites
        hillsNode = [SKSpriteNode spriteNodeWithTexture:
            [SKTexture textureWithImageNamed:@"Hills"]];
        hillsNode.position =
            CGPointMake(CGRectGetMidX(self.frame),
                    CGRectGetMaxY(self.frame) - 384);

        hillsNodeNext = [hillsNode copy];
        hillsNodeNext.position =
            CGPointMake(hillsNode.position.x + hillsNode.size.width,
                    hillsNode.position.y);

        // Prepare the path sprites
        pathNode = [SKSpriteNode spriteNodeWithTexture:
            [SKTexture textureWithImageNamed:@"Path"]];
        pathNode.position =
            CGPointMake(CGRectGetMidX(self.frame),
                    CGRectGetMaxY(self.frame) - 424);

        pathNodeNext = [pathNode copy];
```

```
        pathNodeNext.position =
            CGPointMake(pathNode.position.x +
                        pathNode.size.width,
                        pathNode.position.y);

        // Add the sprites to the scene
        [self addChild:skyNode];
        [self addChild:skyNodeNext];

        [self addChild:distantHillsNode];
        [self addChild:distantHillsNodeNext];

        [self addChild:hillsNode];
        [self addChild:hillsNodeNext];

        [self addChild:pathNode];
        [self addChild:pathNodeNext];

    }
    return self;
}

// Move a pair of sprites leftward based on a speed value;
// when either of the sprites goes off-screen, move it to the
// right so that it appears to be seamless movement
- (void) moveSprite:(SKSpriteNode*)sprite
        nextSprite:(SKSpriteNode*)nextSprite
            speed:(float)speed {

    CGPoint newPosition;

    // For both the sprite and its duplicate:
    for (SKSpriteNode* spriteToMove in @[sprite, nextSprite]) {

        // Shift the sprite leftward based on the speed
        newPosition = spriteToMove.position;
        newPosition.x -= speed * deltaTime;
        spriteToMove.position = newPosition;

        // If this sprite is now offscreen (i.e., its rightmost edge is
        // farther left than the scene's leftmost edge):
        if (CGRectGetMaxX(spriteToMove.frame) < CGRectGetMinX(self.frame)) {

            // Shift it over so that it's now to the immediate right
            // of the other sprite.
            // This means that the two sprites are effectively
            // leap-frogging each other as they both move.
            spriteToMove.position =
                CGPointMake(spriteToMove.position.x +
                            spriteToMove.size.width * 2,
                            spriteToMove.position.y);
        }
```

```
            }
        }

        - (void)update:(CFTimeInterval)currentTime {

            // First, update the delta time values:

            // If we don't have a last frame time value, this is the first frame,
            // so delta time will be zero.
            if (lastFrameTime <= 0)
                lastFrameTime = currentTime;

            // Update delta time
            deltaTime = currentTime - lastFrameTime;

            // Set last frame time to current time
            lastFrameTime = currentTime;

            // Next, move each of the four pairs of sprites.
            // Objects that should appear move slower than foreground objects.
            [self moveSprite:skyNode nextSprite:skyNodeNext speed:25.0];
            [self moveSprite:distantHillsNode
             nextSprite:distantHillsNodeNext speed:50.0];
            [self moveSprite:hillsNode nextSprite:hillsNodeNext speed:100.0];
            [self moveSprite:pathNode nextSprite:pathNodeNext speed:150.0];
        }
```

Discussion

Parallax scrolling is no more complicated than moving some things quickly and other things slowly. In SpriteKit, the real trick is getting a sprite to appear to be continuously scrolling, showing no gaps.

In this solution, each of the four components in the scene—the sky, hills, distant hills, and path—are drawn with two sprites each: one shown onscreen, and one to its immediate right. For each pair of sprites, they both slide to the left until one of them has moved completely off the screen. At that point, it's repositioned so it's placed to the right of the other sprite.

In this manner, the two sprites are leap-frogging each other as they move. You can see the process illustrated in Figure 6-8.

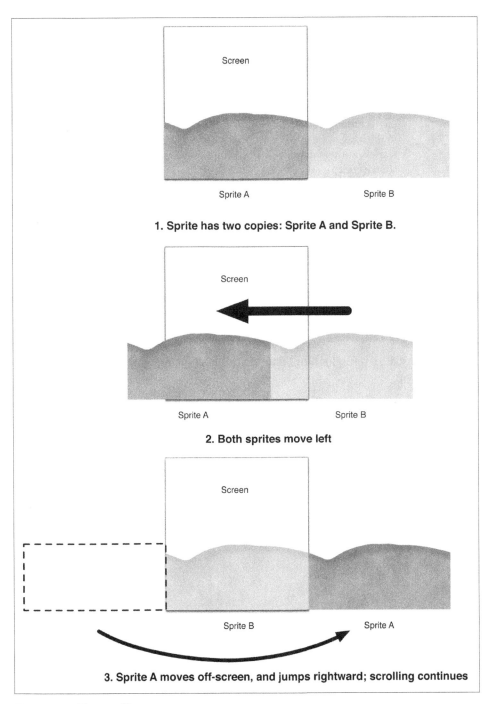

Figure 6-8. The scrolling process

Getting the speed values right for your scene is a matter of personal taste. However, the important thing is to make sure that the relationships between the speeds of the different layers makes sense: if you have an object that's in the foreground and is moving much, much faster than a relatively close background, it won't look right.

 Simulating perspective using parallax scrolling is a great and simple technique, but be careful with it. This recipe was written while in the back of a car that was driving down a winding road, and your fearless authors developed a little motion sickness while testing the source code.

Motion sickness in games, sometimes known as "simulation sickness," is a real thing that affects many game players around the world. If you're making a game that simulates perspective—either in a 3D game or a 2D game where you're faking perspective—make sure you test with as many people as you can find.

6.20. Creating Images Using Perlin Noise

Problem

You want to create organic-looking textures and effects using the Perlin noise algorithm.

Solution

The Perlin noise algorithm is a really useful method for creating natural-looking patterns. It's based on the idea of repeatedly adding successively more detailed layers of noise, and can be used for anything that needs to be random, but also look organic and natural. You can see an example of Perlin noise in Figure 6-9.

Figure 6-9. Perlin noise

The algorithm was invented by Ken Perlin in 1985, and was based on earlier work done for the Disney film *Tron* (1982). Perlin himself later won an Academy Award for Technical Achievement in 1997 for his work on Perlin noise.

The algorithm itself can be implemented in any language; the following is an example of an implementation you can use in Objective-C. This implementation is done inside a class, PerlinNoise, which provides a method that generates a UIImage on a background thread based on parameters that you provide.

To implement this class, create a new NSObject subclass called PerlinNoise by navigating to File→New→File…

Implement *PerlinNoise.h* as follows:

```
@interface PerlinNoise : NSObject

// The shared noise object.
+ (PerlinNoise*) noise;

// Begins generating a UIImage filled with perlin noise,
// given a size, a persistence value, the number of
// octaves, the random seed to use, and a block to call
```

```
// when the image is done.
- (void) imageWithSize:(CGSize)size persistence:(float)persistence
octaves:(int)octaves seed:(int) seed completion:(void (^)(UIImage* image))
completionBlock;

// Calculates Perlin noise at a position.
- (float) perlinNoiseAtPosition:(CGPoint)position persistence:(float)persistence
octaves:(int)octaves seed:(int)seed;

@end
```

Then, implement *PerlinNoise.m* as follows:

```
#import "PerlinNoise.h"

static PerlinNoise* _sharedNoise = nil;

@implementation PerlinNoise

// Returns the shared 'noise' object.
+ (PerlinNoise*) noise {
    static dispatch_once_t onceToken;
    dispatch_once(&onceToken, ^{
        _sharedNoise = [[PerlinNoise alloc] init];
    });

    return _sharedNoise;
}

// Interpolates from one value to the next, using the cosine
// function to smooth the values.
- (float) interpolateCosineWithStart:(float)start
                                 end:(float)end
                              amount:(float)amount {

    // Perform cosine interpolation, which creates a smooth transition
    // from one value to the next

    float ft = amount * M_PI;

    float f = (1 - cosf(ft)) * 0.5f;

    return start * (1 - f) + end * f;
}

// Returns a random number generated by combining the components of
// the position and the random seed.
// This random number generator is guaranteed to provide the same
// results for the same inputs.
- (float) noiseAtPosition:(CGPoint)position seed:(int)seed {


    int n = (int)position.x + (int)position.y * 57 * (seed * 131);
```

```
    n = (n<<13) ^ n;
    return ( 1.0 - ( (n * (n * n * 15731 + 789221) + 1376312589) & 0x7fffffff)
        / 1073741824.0);

}

// Given a position, return the noise value at that position based on the noise
// values of its neighbours.
- (float) smoothNoiseAtPosition:(CGPoint)position seed:(int)seed {

    // Get the noise values for points at the corners...
    float topLeftCorner     = [self noiseAtPosition:(CGPoint){position.x-1,
                                                        position.y - 1}
                                            seed:seed];
    float topRightCorner    = [self noiseAtPosition:(CGPoint){position.x+1,
                                                        position.y - 1}
                                            seed:seed];
    float bottomLeftCorner  = [self noiseAtPosition:(CGPoint){position.x-1,
                                                        position.y + 1}
                                            seed:seed];
    float bottomRightCorner = [self noiseAtPosition:(CGPoint){position.x+1,
                                                        position.y + 1}
                                            seed:seed];

    // ... the sides...
    float leftSide   = [self noiseAtPosition:(CGPoint){position.x - 1,
                                                        position.y}
                                            seed:seed];
    float rightSide  = [self noiseAtPosition:(CGPoint){position.x + 1,
                                                        position.y}
                                            seed:seed];
    float topSide    = [self noiseAtPosition:(CGPoint){position.x,
                                                        position.y - 1}
                                            seed:seed];
    float bottomSide = [self noiseAtPosition:(CGPoint){position.x,
                                                        position.y + 1}
                                            seed:seed];

    // ... and the center.
    float center = [self noiseAtPosition:(CGPoint){position.x, position.y}
                    seed:seed];

    // Merge them all together. The corners affect the result the least,
    // the center the most, and the sides halfway between.
    float corners = (topLeftCorner + topRightCorner +
                    bottomLeftCorner + bottomRightCorner) / 16.0f;
    float sides = (leftSide + rightSide + topSide + bottomSide) / 8.0f;
    center = center / 4.0f;

    // Return the result.
    return corners + sides + center;
```

```
        }

        // Given a position in the image, work out how the noise values blend
        // together in the image
        - (float) interpolatedNoiseAtPosition:(CGPoint)position seed:(int)seed {
            int integralX = (int)position.x;
            int integralY = (int)position.y;

            float fractionalX = position.x - integralX;
            float fractionalY = position.y - integralY;

            float v1 = [self smoothNoiseAtPosition:(CGPoint){integralX, integralY}
                                        seed:seed];
            float v2 = [self smoothNoiseAtPosition:(CGPoint){integralX+1, integralY}
                                        seed:seed];
            float v3 = [self smoothNoiseAtPosition:(CGPoint){integralX, integralY+1}
                                        seed:seed];
            float v4 = [self smoothNoiseAtPosition:(CGPoint){integralX+1, integralY+1}
                                        seed:seed];

            float i1 = [self interpolateCosineWithStart:v1 end:v2 amount:fractionalX];
            float i2 = [self interpolateCosineWithStart:v3 end:v4 amount:fractionalX];

            return [self interpolateCosineWithStart:i1 end:i2 amount:fractionalY];

        }


        // Calculate the value of the image at a given position by applying
        // Perlin noise.
        - (float) perlinNoiseAtPosition:(CGPoint)position
                    persistence:(float)persistence
                    octaves:(int)octaves seed:(int)seed {

            float total = 0.0;

            for (int i = 0; i <= octaves - 1; i++) {

                int frequency = pow(2, i);
                float amplitude = pow(persistence, i);

                total += [self interpolatedNoiseAtPosition:(CGPoint)
                            {(position.x * frequency),
                            (position.y * frequency)}
                            seed:seed * (i+1)] * amplitude;

            }

            return total;

        }

        // Generate an image filled with Perlin noise.
```

```objc
- (void) imageWithSize:(CGSize)size persistence:(float)persistence
        octaves:(int)octaves seed:(int) seed
        completion:(void (^)(UIImage* image))completionBlock {

    // If we don't have a completion block, immediately return
    // after logging an error.
    if (completionBlock == NULL) {
        NSLog(@"Error: %@ was called with no completion block, so there's no way
        to return the image. Provide a completion block.",
        NSStringFromSelector(_cmd));
        return;
    }

    // Create a background queue to run the operation on
    NSOperationQueue* backgroundQueue = [[NSOperationQueue alloc] init];

    // Run the work in the background
    [backgroundQueue addOperationWithBlock:^{

        // Begin a new graphics context
        UIGraphicsBeginImageContextWithOptions(size, YES,
                                               [UIScreen mainScreen].scale);

        // Get the graphics context as a CGContextRef
        // so that we can use CoreGraphics calls later
        CGContextRef context =  UIGraphicsGetCurrentContext();

        // For each pixel in the image, work out the value using the
        // Perlin noise algorithm.
        for (int x = 0; x <= size.width; x+= 1) {

            for (int y = 0; y <= size.height; y += 1) {

                // Work out the Perlin noise value
                // for this pixel.
                float value = [self perlinNoiseAtPosition:(CGPoint)
                              {x / size.width, y / size.height}
                              persistence:persistence octaves:octaves
                              seed:seed];

                // Example of banding the output (uncomment to apply)
                /*
                if (value > 0.5)
                    value = 0.9;
                else if (value > 0.3)
                    value = 0.5;
                else if (value > 0.2)
                    value = 0.3;
                else
                    value = 0.2;
                 */
```

```
            // Once we have the value, we turn that into a grayscale color...
            CGContextSetGrayFillColor(context, value, 1.0);

            // ...and fill the appropriate pixel.
            CGRect rect = CGRectMake(x, y, x+1, y+1);
            CGContextFillRect(context, rect);

        }

    }

    // Once the rendering is done, grab the image from the context
    UIImage* image = UIGraphicsGetImageFromCurrentImageContext();

    // And then call the completion block, making sure
    // to do it on the main queue
    [[NSOperationQueue mainQueue] addOperationWithBlock:^{
        completionBlock(image);
    }];

    // Finally, tidy up by removing the image context
    // we created.
    UIGraphicsEndImageContext();

    }];

    // We don't return anything in this method because the image
    // is returned to the caller via the completion block.
}

@end
```

Discussion

At its core, the Perlin noise algorithm is very simple: for each octave, a slightly more detailed amount of noise is overlaid on top.

The three key parameters that you feed into the algorithm are as follows:

Random seed

> Used to determine the specific pattern that the algorithm generates. You'll note that the built-in random number generator function, random(), isn't used. This is because we don't actually want properly random numbers, in which it (hopefully) isn't possible to determine what the next random number is going to be.

> Instead, we want *random-like* numbers, which change based on the input and nothing else. This allows the Perlin noise algorithm to be able to calculate noise values relative to neighboring pixels because the values for neighboring pixels aren't going to change between different calculations.

octaves

The number of octaves controls how many times the algorithm is run. Each time it's run, an additional level of detail is added to the result, which means that more octaves means higher levels of detail in the final result, and fewer octaves means less-detailed, blurrier noise.

persistence value

Controls how much of an effect higher octaves have on the final result. High persistence values mean a greater contrast between the dark and light areas of the noise image.

 You can tweak and tune the number of octaves and the persistence value to get the kind of noise you want. The sample code provided with this book contains an app that lets you play around with these values.

Perlin noise is an incredibly effective method for creating natural, organic looking textures. You can use it for a number of things, including fire, fog, smoke, lightning; additionally, its uses aren't limited to and terrain generation—all you need to do is change how you're using the results that the Perlin noise algorithm gives you. Perlin noise works best when blended with other images.

For example, instead of using Perlin noise only for images, consider a case where you use it to work out how a bumblebee randomly moves about as it hovers. To do that, all you need to do is to generate two Perlin noise values, each with their own random seed:

```
- (void) updateBumblebeePositionAtTime:(float)time {

    CGPoint inputPosition = CGPointMake(time,0);

    float movementX = [[PerlinNoise noise] perlinNoiseAtPosition:inputPosition
                                                     persistence:0.75
                                                         octaves:10
                                                            seed:18273];

    float movementY = [[PerlinNoise noise] perlinNoiseAtPosition:inputPosition
                                                     persistence:0.75
                                                         octaves:10
                                                            seed:21516];

    CGPoint bumblebeeMovement = CGPointMake(movementX, movementY);

    // The perlin method returns values from 0 to 1, so multiply by 2
    // and subtract 1  to get values from -1 to 1
    bumblebeeMovement.x *= 2;
    bumblebeeMovement.y *= 2;
```

```
        bumblebeeMovement.x -= 1;
        bumblebeeMovement.y -= 1;

        // The bumblebeeMovement variable now contains a position somewhere
        // from (-1, -1) to (1, 1). Additionally, as time increases, this position
        // will smoothly and randomly change.

        // The bumblebeeMovement position can now be used to change the position
        // of the bee, e.g.:
        [self moveBumblebeeByPosition:bumblebeeMovement];

    }
```

CHAPTER 7

Physics

If, like us, you've existed on a planet that has gravity, you'll be familiar with the fact that objects react to forces and collide with other objects. When you pick up an object and let go, it falls down until it hits something. When it hits something, it bounces (or shatters, depending on what you dropped). In games, we can make objects have this kind of behavior through *physics simulation*.

Physics simulation lets you do things like:

- Make objects have gravity and fall to the ground
- Give objects properties like weight, density, friction, and bounciness
- Apply forces to objects, and make them move around realistically
- Attach objects together in a variety of configurations

In short, adding physics simulation to your game often gives you a lot of realism for free.

Sprite Kit has built-in support for simulating physics in two dimensions, and we'll mostly be talking about physics in Sprite Kit in this chapter. (If you're not familiar with Sprite Kit yet, go check out Chapter 6.) Before we get to the recipes, though, let's go over some terminology.

7.1. Reviewing Physics Terms and Definitions

Physics simulation has its basis in math, and math people tend to like giving everything its own name. These terms are used by the physics simulation system built in to iOS, and it's important to know what's being referred to when you encounter, say, a *polygon collision body*.

In this section, before we get stuck into the recipes themselves, we're going to present a list of definitions that you're very likely to run into when working with physics. Some of these are terms that you've probably heard in other contexts, and others are fairly specific to physics:

World

A physics world is the "universe" in which all of your objects exist. If an object isn't in the world, it isn't being physically simulated, and nothing will interact with it. A physics world contains settings that apply to all objects in the world, such as the direction and strength of gravity.

Mass

Mass is a measure of how much stuff is inside an object. The more mass there is, the heavier it is.

Velocity

Velocity is a measure of how quickly an object is moving, and in which direction. In 2D physics, velocity has two components: horizontal velocity, or "x-velocity," and vertical velocity, or "y-velocity."

Body

A body is an object in the physics simulation. Bodies react to forces, and can collide with other bodies. Bodies have mass and velocity. You can optionally make a body be *static*, which means that it never reacts to forces and never moves.

Force

A force is something that causes a body to move. For example, when you throw a ball, your arm is imposing a force on the ball; when your hand releases the ball, the ball's got a large amount of built-up velocity, and it flies out of your hand. Gravity is another force, and it applies to all objects in your physics world. The amount of force needed to make an object move depends on how much mass is in that object. If you apply the exact same force to a heavy object and to a light object, the light object will move further.

Friction

When an object rubs against something else, it slows down. This is because of friction. In the real world, friction converts kinetic energy (i.e., movement) into heat, but in Sprite Kit, the energy is just lost. You can configure how much friction an object has. For example, if you make an object have very low friction, it will be slippery.

Collider

A collider defines the shape of an object. Common shapes include squares, rectangles, circles, and polygons. In Sprite Kit, all bodies have a collider, which you define when you create the body. (In some other physics engines, bodies and colliders are separate entities.)

Edge collider

An edge collider is a collider that is composed of one or more infinitely thin lines. Edge colliders are useful for creating walls and obstacles, because they're simple to create and very efficient to simulate. A body with an edge collider never moves; they're always static.

Collision

A collision is when two objects come into contact. Note that a *collision* is different from a *collider*: A collision is an event that happens, while a collider is a shape. When a collision happens, you can get information about it, such as which objects collided, where they collided, and so on.

Joint

A joint is a relationship between two objects. Several different kinds of joints exist; some common ones include "pin" joints, in which one object is allowed to rotate freely but isn't allowed to move away from a certain point relative to another body, and "spring" joints, in which one object is allowed to move away from another but, if it moves beyond a threshold, begins to be pushed back toward the first object.

7.2. Adding Physics to Sprites

Problem

You want to make sprites be affected by gravity and other physical forces.

Solution

To make an SKSpriteNode be physically simulated, create an SKPhysicsBody and then set the sprite's physicsBody property to it:

```
SKScene* scene = ... // an SKScene

SKSpriteNode* sprite = [SKSpriteNode spriteNodeWithColor:[SKColor whiteColor]
                        size:CGSizeMake(100, 50)];
sprite.position = CGPointMake(CGRectGetMidX(scene.frame),
                  CGRectGetMidY(scene.frame));

sprite.physicsBody = [SKPhysicsBody bodyWithRectangleOfSize:sprite.size];

[scene addChild:sprite];
```

Discussion

When you add an SKPhysicsBody to an SKSpriteNode, Sprite Kit physically simulates the sprite's movement in the scene.

This has the following effects:

- The physics engine will start keeping track of physical forces that apply to the body, such as gravity.
- The position and rotation of the body will be updated every frame, based on these forces.
- The body will collide with other SKPhysicsBody objects.

When you run the sample code, you'll notice that the sprite falls off the bottom of the screen. This is because there's nothing for the sprite to land on—the physics body that you added to the sprite is the only physically simulated body in the entire scene. To learn how to create objects for your sprite's body to land on, see Recipe 7.3.

7.3. Creating Static and Dynamic Objects

Problem

You want to create an immobile object—one that never moves, but that other objects can collide with.

Solution

Set the dynamic property of your SKPhysicsBody to NO:

```
SKScene* scene = ... // an SKScene

SKSpriteNode* staticSprite = [SKSpriteNode spriteNodeWithColor:
                              [SKColor yellowColor]
                              size:CGSizeMake(200, 25)];

staticSprite.position = CGPointMake(CGRectGetMidX(scene.frame),
                        CGRectGetMidY(scene.frame));

staticSprite.physicsBody = [SKPhysicsBody bodyWithRectangleOfSize:
                            staticSprite.size];

staticSprite.physicsBody.dynamic = NO;

[scene addChild:staticSprite];
```

Discussion

There are two kinds of physics bodies used in Sprite Kit:

- *Dynamic bodies* respond to physical forces, and move around the scene.

- *Static bodies* don't respond to physical forces—they're fixed in place, and dynamic bodies can collide with them.

When you set the `dynamic` property of an `SKPhysicsBody` to `NO`, the body immediately stops responding to forces and stops moving and rotating. However, you can still reposition it by setting the sprite's `position` and `rotation`, or by using actions (see Recipe 6.9 to learn how to do this).

7.4. Defining Collider Shapes

Problem

You want to specify a custom shape for physics bodies.

Solution

To make your physics bodies use a shape other than a rectangle, you create them by using a different method, such as `bodyWithCircleOfRadius:` or `bodyWithPolygonFromPath:`, as shown here:

```
SKScene* scene = ... // an SKScene

SKShapeNode* circleSprite = [[SKShapeNode alloc] init];
circleSprite.path = [UIBezierPath bezierPathWithOvalInRect:CGRectMake(-50, -50,
                  100, 100)].CGPath;
circleSprite.lineWidth = 1;
circleSprite.physicsBody = [SKPhysicsBody bodyWithCircleOfRadius:50];
circleSprite.position = CGPointMake(CGRectGetMidX(scene.frame)+40,
                  CGRectGetMidY(scene.frame) + 100);

[scene addChild:circleSprite];
```

Discussion

There are a number of different ways that you can create an `SKPhysicsBody`. When you create one, you specify what sort of *collider* the body is using—that is, the actual shape of the body (a circle, a rectangle, or some other shape).

The easiest way to create a body is with the `bodyWithRectangleOfSize:` method, which lets you (as you might expect, given the name), create a rectangle given a size (you don't set the position of the body—that's determined by the position of the node that the body's attached to):

```
// A box, 100x100
CGSize size = CGSizeMake(100,100);
sprite.physicsBody = [SKPhysicsBody bodyWithRectangleOfSize:size];
```

You can also create a body with a circular collider like so:

```
sprite.physicsBody = [SKPhysicsBody bodyWithCircleOfRadius:50];
```

> A circular collider is the simplest possible collider, and requires the least amount of computation to simulate. If you need to create a large number of colliders, consider making them circular where possible.

In addition to creating rectangular or circular colliders, you can define your own custom shapes by defining a path and creating an SKPhysicsBody with it:

```
UIBezierPath* path = [[UIBezierPath alloc] init];
[path moveToPoint:CGPointMake(-25, -25)];
[path addLineToPoint:CGPointMake(25, 0)];
[path addLineToPoint:CGPointMake(-25, 25)];
[path closePath];

sprite.physicsBody = [SKPhysicsBody bodyWithPolygonFromPath:path.CGPath];
```

You can learn more about creating paths using UIBezierPath in Recipe 6.15.

When you create a path for use as a polygon body, the points in the path need to be defined in clockwise order. For example, the following code will *not* work:

```
UIBezierPath* path = [[UIBezierPath alloc] init];
[path moveToPoint:CGPointMake(-25, -25)];
[path addLineToPoint:CGPointMake(-25, 25)];
[path addLineToPoint:CGPointMake(25, 0)];
[path closePath];

sprite.physicsBody = [SKPhysicsBody bodyWithPolygonFromPath:path.CGPath];
```

Additionally, the path you provide isn't allowed to contain any curves—it can only contain straight lines. (You won't get any crashes if you use curves, but the resulting shape will behave strangely.)

If you want to more easily visualize the custom shapes you're creating for use with physics bodies, you can attach the same path that you've created to an SKShapeNode, as illustrated in Figure 7-1. See Recipe 6.12 for more information about this.

> You can't change the shape of a body's collider after it's been created. If you want a sprite to have a different shape, you need to replace the sprite's SKPhysicsBody.

Figure 7-1. SKShapeNodes being used to visually represent custom collider shapes

7.5. Setting Velocities

Problem

You want to make an object start moving at a specific speed and in a specific direction.

Solution

To change the velocity of an object, you modify the velocity property:

```
SKSpriteNode* sprite = ... // an SKSpriteNode

sprite.physicsBody = [SKPhysicsBody bodyWithRectangleOfSize:sprite.size];

// Start moving upward at 100 pixels per second
sprite.velocity = CGVectorMake(0, -100);
```

Discussion

The simplest way to change the velocity of a physics body is to directly set the `veloci` `ty` property. This is a `CGVector` that represents the velocity, in pixels per second, at which the body is moving.

Note that directly setting the velocity tends to have the best-looking results when you use the technique to set the initial velocity of an object. For example, if you want to create rockets that come out of a rocket launcher, those rockets should start out moving quickly. In this case, you'd create the rocket sprite, and then immediately set the velocity of its physics body to make it start moving.

If you want things to *change* their movement in a realistic way, consider using forces on your bodies (see Recipe 7.14). Alternatively, if you want precise frame-by-frame control over how your objects move, make the physics bodies static (see Recipe 7.3), and manually set the position of the objects or use actions (see Recipe 6.9.)

7.6. Working with Mass, Size, and Density

Problem

You want to control how heavy your objects are.

Solution

Set the `density` or `mass` properties of your physics bodies to control how heavy they are:

```
SKSpriteNode* sprite = ... // an SKSpriteNode

sprite.physicsBody = [SKPhysicsBody bodyWithRectangleOfSize:sprite.size];

// Make this object be twice as massy
sprite.physicsBody.density = 2.0;

// Alternatively, make the object be a fixed mass regardless of its size
sprite.physicsBody.mass = 4.0;
```

Discussion

An object's *mass* is how much matter the object is composed of. Note that this is different from how much the object *weighs*, which is the amount of force applied to an object by gravity, dependent on the object's mass and how strong gravity is.

Objects with more mass require more force to move around. If you apply the same force to an object with low mass and one with high mass, the object with lower mass will move further.

The mass of an object is calculated based on the volume of the object (i.e., its size) and the object's *density*. The mass of an object is automatically calculated when you create the body, based on the size of the body and a default density of 1; however, you can change an object's mass and density at any time you like.

The initial mass of an object is calculated like this:

```
Mass = Area x Density
```

The default density of an object is 1.0. The area depends on the shape of the body:

- The area of a rectangle is width × height.
- The area of a circle is $\pi \times r^2$ (where r is the radius).
- The area of a polygon depends on its shape; search the Web for "irregular polygon area" for different kinds of formulae. A common strategy is to break the polygon into triangles, calculate the area for each one, and then add them together.

The actual units you use for density and mass don't matter—you can use pounds, kilograms, or grapnars (if you are from Venus). However, the values you choose should be consistent across the objects in your scene. For example, if you create two crates, both of the same size, and you set the mass of the first to 2 (kilograms) and the second to 4 (pounds), it won't be apparent to the user why one appears lighter than the other.

Because mass and density are linked, if you change an object's density, the mass will change (and vice versa).

7.7. Creating Walls in Your Scene

Problem

You want to create walls for your collision scene.

Solution

The most efficient way to create walls is to use edge colliders:

```
SKScene* scene = ... // an SKScene

SKNode* wallsNode = [SKNode node];
wallsNode.position = CGPointMake(CGRectGetMidX(scene.frame),
```

```
                    CGRectGetMidY(scene.frame));

    // Reposition the rectangle so that it's centered on (0,0)
    CGRect rect = CGRectOffset(self.frame, -scene.frame.size.width / 2.0,
                            -scene.frame.size.height / 2.0);
    wallsNode.physicsBody = [SKPhysicsBody bodyWithEdgeLoopFromRect:rect];

    [scene addChild:wallsNode];
```

Discussion

An *edge collider* is a collider that's just a single line, or a collection of connected lines. Edge colliders are different from other kinds of colliders in that they have no volume, no mass, and are always treated as static colliders.

There are two different types of edge colliders: *edge loops* and *edge chains*. An edge chain is a linked collection of lines; an edge loop always links from the end point to the start point.

Edge colliders can have almost any shape you want. The easiest ways to create them are either to create a single line from one point to another:

```
    CGPoint point1 = CGPointMake(-50, 0);
    CGPoint point2 = CGPointMake(50, 0);
    SKPhysicsBody* line = [SKPhysicsBody bodyWithEdgeFromPoint:point1
                            toPoint:point2];
```

or with a rectangle:

```
    CGRect rect = CGPointMake(0, 0, 50, 50);
    SKPhysicsBody* box = [SKPhysicsBody bodyWithEdgeLoopFromRect:rect]
```

In addition to lines and rectangles, you can create arbitrary shapes. These can be either edge chains or edge loops.

You create these shapes using a path, much like when you make polygon bodies (see Recipe 7.4). In this case, though, there's a difference: you don't have to close your paths, since edge chains don't have to form a closed polygon:

```
    UIBezierPath* path = [UIBezierPath bezierPath];
    [path moveToPoint:CGPointMake(-50, -10)];
    [path addLineToPoint:CGPointMake(-25, 10)];
    [path addLineToPoint:CGPointMake(0, -10)];
    [path addLineToPoint:CGPointMake(25, 10)];
    [path addLineToPoint:CGPointMake(50, -10)];

    SKPhysicsBody* body = [SKPhysicsBody bodyWithEdgeChainFromPath:path.CGPath];
```

7.8. Controlling Gravity

Problem

You want to customize the gravity in your scene.

Solution

To change the gravity in your scene, you must first get access to your scene's `physics World`. Once you have that, you can change the physics world's `gravity` property:

```
SKScene* scene = ... // an SKScene

SKPhysicsWorld* world = scene.physicsWorld;
world.gravity = CGPointMake(0, -0.45); // half normal gravity
```

Discussion

For the purposes of a physics simulation, *gravity* is a constant force that's applied to all bodies. (Gravity in the real universe is quite a bit more complex than that, but this simplification is more than adequate for most games.)

 A game that deals with gravity in a much more realistic way than "gravity equals down" is Kerbal Space Program (*http://www.kerbal spaceprogram.com*), in which players launch rockets and use orbital mechanics to travel to other planets. In this kind of game, the force of gravity depends on how close you are to various planets, each of which has a different mass.

By default, the gravity in a scene is set to (0, –9.81). That is to say, all bodies have a constant force that's pushing them down (i.e., toward the bottom of the screen), at a rate of 9.81 pixels per second per second. By changing this property, you can make gravity nonexistent:

```
world.gravity = CGPointMake(0, 0);
```

Or, you can reverse gravity:

```
world.gravity = CGPointMake(0, 9.81); // note the lack of a minus sign
```

You can also make an individual physics body be unaffected by gravity by changing the body's `affectedByGravity` property:

```
SKPhysicsBody* body = ... // an SKPhysicsBody

body.affectedByGravity = NO;
```

Note that a body that isn't affected by gravity still has mass, and still responds to other forces. A really heavy object that's floating in the air will still require quite a bit of force to move.

7.9. Keeping Objects from Falling Over

Problem

You want to prevent certain objects, such as the player, from rotating.

Solution

Change the `allowsRotation` property of your body:

```
SKPhysicsBody* body = ... // an SKPhysicsBody

body.allowsRotation = NO;
```

Discussion

In many games with 2D physics, it's useful to have some objects that move around, but never rotate. For example, if you're making a platform game, you almost never want the player to actually rotate.

Locking the rotation of a body means that it won't ever rotate, no matter how many forces are applied to it. However, you can change the angle of the body by manually setting the `zRotation` of the node, or by using an action (see Recipe 6.9.)

7.10. Controlling Time in Your Physics Simulation

Problem

You want to pause or speed up the physics simulation.

Solution

Change the `speed` property of your scene's `SKPhysicsWorld` to control how quickly time passes in your scene's physics simulation:

```
SKScene* scene = ... // an SKScene

SKPhysicsWorld* world = scene.physicsWorld;

world.speed = 2.0; // double the simulation speed

world.speed = 0.0; // pause all physics simulation
```

Discussion

The `speed` property of your scene's `SKPhysicsWorld` controls the rate at which time passes in your physics simulation. For example, setting the speed to 2.0 makes things move twice as fast (note, however, that increasing the speed of the simulation can lead to some instability in your simulation).

You can also use this to create slow-motion effects: if you set the `speed` property to a value between 0 and 1, time will be slowed down, which you can use to highlight totally sweet stunts or explosions.

7.11. Detecting Collisions

Problem

You want to detect when objects collide.

Solution

First, make your `SKScene` subclass conform to the `SKPhysicsContactDelegate` protocol.

Next, implement the `didBeginContact:` and `didEndContact:` methods in your `SKScene`:

```
- (void)didBeginContact:(SKPhysicsContact *)contact {
    NSLog(@"Contact started between %@ and %@", contact.bodyA, contact.bodyB);
}

- (void)didEndContact:(SKPhysicsContact *)contact {
    NSLog(@"Contact ended between %@ and %@", contact.bodyA, contact.bodyB);
}
```

When you're setting up your scene's contents, set the `contactDelegate` property of your scene's `physicsWorld` to the scene:

```
self.physicsWorld.contactDelegate = self;
```

Next, make every physics body for which you want to get notifications about collisions set its `contactTestBitMask` to `0x01`:

```
SKNode* node = ... // an SKNode

node.physicsBody = [SKPhysicsBody bodyWithRectangleOfSize:node.size];

node.physicsBody.contactTestBitMask = 0x01;
```

Now, every object collision that occurs will make your `didBeginContact:` and `didEnd Contact:` methods get called.

Discussion

If you want an object to be notified about objects coming into contact with each other, you make that object conform to the SKPhysicsContactDelegate protocol, and then set the scene's physicsWorld to use the object as its contactDelegate.

The contact delegate methods, didBeginContact: and didEndContact:, will only be called when two objects that have an intersecting contactTestBitMask come into contact with each other.

The contact test bitmask lets you define categories of objects. By default, it's set to zero, which means that objects aren't in any collision category.

The contact delegate methods receive an SKPhysicsContact object as their parameter, which contains information about which bodies collided, at which point they collided, and with how much force.

7.12. Finding Objects

Problem

You want to find physics objects in the scene.

Solution

Use the enumerateBodiesInRect:usingBlock:, enumerateBodiesAtPoint:using Block:, and enumerateBodiesAlongRayStart:end:usingBlock: methods to find SKPhysicsBody objects in your world:

```
SKScene* scene = ... // an SKScene

CGRect searchRect = CGRectMake(10, 10, 200, 200);

[scene.physicsWorld enumerateBodiesInRect:searchRect usingBlock:^(SKPhysicsBody
    *body, BOOL *stop) {
        NSLog(@"Found a body: %@", body);
}];

CGPoint searchPoint = CGPointMake(40, 100);

[scene.physicsWorld enumerateBodiesAtPoint:searchPoint usingBlock:^(
    SKPhysicsBody *body, BOOL *stop) {
        NSLog(@"Found a body: %@", body);
}];

CGPoint searchRayStart = CGPointMake(0, 0);
CGPoint searchRayEnd = CGPointMake(320, 480);
```

```
[scene.physicsWorld enumerateBodiesAlongRayStart:searchRayStart end:searchRayEnd
    usingBlock:^(SKPhysicsBody *body, CGPoint point, CGVector normal, BOOL *stop)
        { NSLog(@"Found a body: %@ (normal: %.1f, %.1f)", body, normal.dx,
        normal.dy);
}];
```

Discussion

You can use these methods to find SKPhysicsBody objects in a rectangle, at a certain point, or along a line. When you call them, you pass in the location you want to search, as well as a block; this block is called for each body that is found.

All of the results blocks used by these methods receive as parameters the body that was found and stop, which is a pointer to a BOOL variable. If you set this variable to YES, the search will stop. This means that if you're looking for a specific body, you can stop the search when you find it, which saves time:

```
[scene.physicsWorld enumerateBodiesAtPoint:searchPoint usingBlock:^(
    SKPhysicsBody *body, BOOL *stop) {
        if (body == theBodyWeWant) {
            *stop = YES; // note the asterisk!
        }
}];
```

Note that when you call enumerateBodiesAlongRayStart:end:usingBlock:, the results block takes *three* parameters: the block, a *normal*, and the stop variable. The normal is a vector that indicates the direction at which the line bounces off the body it hit. (This is useful for determining, for example, the directions that sparks should fly in when something hits a surface.)

If you're looking for a single body and don't care which one, you can use the bodyAt Point:, bodyInRect:, and bodyAlongRayStart:end: methods, which just return the first body they find:

```
SKPhysicsBody* body = [self.physicsWorld bodyAtPoint:searchPoint];
```

or

```
SKPhysicsBody* body = [self.physicsWorld bodyInRect:searchRect];
```

or

```
SKPhysicsBody* body = [self.physicsWorld bodyAlongRayStart:searchRayStart
                        end:searchRayEnd];
```

These methods won't find nodes that don't have an SKPhysicsBody attached to them—they only check the physics simulation. If you're looking for nodes that have no physics body, use the nodeAtPoint:, nodesAtPoint:, childNodeWithName:, or enumerate ChildNodesWithName:usingBlock: methods on your SKScene.

7.13. Working with Joints

Problem

You want to connect physics objects together.

Solution

Use one of the several SKPhysicsJoint classes available:

```
SKScene* scene = ... // an SKScene

// Create a static body and add it
SKSpriteNode* anchor = [SKSpriteNode spriteNodeWithColor:[SKColor whiteColor]
                        size:CGSizeMake(100, 100)];
anchor.position = CGPointMake(CGRectGetMidX(scene.frame),
                    CGRectGetMidY(scene.frame));
anchor.physicsBody = [SKPhysicsBody bodyWithRectangleOfSize:anchor.size];
anchor.physicsBody.dynamic = NO;

[self addChild:anchor];

SKSpriteNode* attachment = [SKSpriteNode spriteNodeWithColor:[SKColor
                            yellowColor] size:CGSizeMake(100, 100)];
attachment.position = CGPointMake(CGRectGetMidX(self.frame) + 100,
                    CGRectGetMidY(self.frame) - 100);
attachment.physicsBody = [SKPhysicsBody bodyWithRectangleOfSize:attachment.size];

[self addChild:attachment];

SKPhysicsJointPin* pinJoint = [SKPhysicsJointPin jointWithBodyA:
    anchor.physicsBody bodyB:attachment.physicsBody anchor:anchor.position];

[self.physicsWorld addJoint:pinJoint];
```

Discussion

A *joint* is an object that constrains the movement of one or more objects. Joints are pretty straightforward to work with: you create your joint object, configure it, and then give it to your scene's SKPhysicsWorld.

In this example, we're using a pin joint, which pins two bodies together at a point, and lets them rotate around that point. There are several different types of joints available:

- *Pin joints*, as we've just mentioned, let you pin two objects together. The objects can rotate around that pin point.

- *Fixed joints* fuse two objects together. Once they're joined, they're not allowed to move relative to each other, and they're not allowed to rotate relative to each other. This is very useful for creating larger objects that you want to break apart later.
- *Slider joints* let you create objects that can move away from or closer to each other, but only along a certain line.
- *Limit joints* make it so that the two objects can move freely relative to each other, but aren't allowed to move past a certain radius. This makes them act as if they're tethered with a rope.

Once you've created your joint, you add it to the physics simulation by using the add Joint: method:

```
[self.physicsWorld addJoint:myJoint];
```

You can remove a joint from an SKPhysicsWorld by using the removeJoint: method. Once you remove a joint, the bodies that it affected are able to move freely once again:

```
[self.physicsWorld removeJoint:myJoint];
```

A body can have multiple joints acting on it at once. Try connecting several bodies together with joints, and see what you come up with!

7.14. Working with Forces

Problem

You want to apply a force to an object.

Solution

Use the applyForce: or applyTorque: methods:

```
SKNode* node = ... // An SKNode

// Move it up
[node.physicsBody applyForce:CGVectorMake(0, 100)];

// Rotate counter-clockwise
[node.physicsBody applyTorque:0.5];
```

Discussion

When you apply a force, you change the movement of a body. When you're using the Sprite Kit physics engine, there's a constant gravitational force being applied to all bodies in the scene, which makes them move downward.

You can apply your own forces to bodies using the `applyForce:` method, which takes a `CGVector` that describes the amount of force you'd like to apply. Forces get applied immediately.

When you call `applyForce:`, the force is evenly applied across the entire body. If you need to apply the force to a specific point on the body, you can use `applyForce:atPoint::`

```
// Apply a force just to the right of the center of the body
CGPoint position = CGPointMake(10, 0);
[node.physicsBody applyForce:CGVectorMake(0, 100) atPoint:position];
```

The point that you provide to `applyForce:atPoint:` is defined in scene coordinates.

In addition to force, which changes the position of a body, you can also apply *torque*, which is a change to the angular movement (i.e., the spin) of a body.

The units that you use with `applyForce:` and `applyTorque:` don't really matter as long as they're consistent. Technically, they're measured in newtons and newton-meters, respectively.

7.15. Adding Thrusters to Objects

Problem

You want to make an object move continuously in a certain direction.

Solution

First, add this property to your `SKScene` subclass:

```
@property (assign) float lastTime;
```

Then, in your scene's `update:` method, apply whatever forces and torque you need:

```
- (void)update:(NSTimeInterval)currentTime {
    if (self.lastTime == 0)
        self.lastTime = currentTime;

    float deltaTime = currentTime - self.lastTime;

    SKNode* node = [self childNodeWithName:@"Box"];

    [node.physicsBody applyForce:CGVectorMake(0 * deltaTime, 10 * deltaTime)];
    [node.physicsBody applyTorque:0.5 * deltaTime];
}
```

Discussion

The `update:` method is called on your `SKScene` subclass every frame, immediately before physics simulation and rendering. This is your opportunity to apply any continuous forces to your objects.

The `update:` method receives one parameter: a float named `currentTime`. This variable contains the current system time, measured in seconds. To apply an even amount of force per second, you need to know how long each frame takes to render. You can calculate this by subtracting the system time at the last frame from the system time at the current frame (you can learn more about this in Recipe 1.4):

```
deltaTime = time at start of current frame - time at start of last frame
```

Once you have that, you can multiply forces by that number.

7.16. Creating Explosions

Problem

You want to apply an explosion force to some objects.

Solution

Add this method to your `SKScene`:

```
- (void) applyExplosionAtPoint:(CGPoint)point radius:(float)radius power:
(float)power{

    // Determine which bodies are in range of the explosion by creating a
    // rectangle
    CGRect explosionRect = CGRectMake(point.x - radius, point.y - radius,
                                      radius*2, radius*2);

    // For each body, apply an explosion force
    [self.physicsWorld enumerateBodiesInRect:explosionRect usingBlock:^(
        SKPhysicsBody *body, BOOL *stop) {

        // Determine the direction we should apply the force in for this body
        CGVector explosionOffset = CGVectorMake(body.node.position.x -
            point.x, body.node.position.y - point.y);

        // Calculate the distance from the explosion point
        CGFloat explosionDistance = sqrtf(explosionOffset.dx *
            explosionOffset.dx + explosionOffset.dy * explosionOffset.dy);

        // Normalize the explosion force
        CGVector explosionForce = explosionOffset;
        explosionForce.dx /= explosionDistance;
        explosionForce.dy /= explosionDistance;
```

```
        // Multiply by power
        explosionForce.dx *= power;
        explosionForce.dy *= power;

        // Finally, apply the force
        [body applyForce:explosionForce];

    }];
}
```

When you want an explosion to happen, call this method like so:

```
CGPoint explosionPoint = CGPointMake(100,100);
[self applyExplosionAtPoint:explosionPoint radius:100 power:150];
```

Discussion

An explosion is simply a force that's applied to a group of nearby bodies, which pushes those bodies away from a point.

So, to make an explosion, you need to do the following:

1. Determine which bodies are affected by the explosion.

2. Decide which direction each body should be sent in.

3. Calculate how much force should be applied.

4. Apply that force to each body!

Simple, right?

You can determine which bodies are affected by the explosion by using the `enumerate` `BodiesInRect:usingBlock:` method on your scene's SKPhysicsWorld. This calls a block for each body that it finds, which gives you your opportunity to calculate the forces for each body.

To calculate the amount of force you need to apply to each body, you do the following:

1. Subtract the body's position from the explosion's position. This is the *explosion offset*, calculated as follows:

```
CGVector explosionOffset = CGVectorMake(body.node.position.x - point.x,
                                        body.node.position.y - point.y);
```

2. Determine the distance from the body's position by *normalizing* the explosion offset. This means calculating the length (or *magnitude*) of the vector, and then dividing the vector by that magnitude.

   To calculate the magnitude of the vector, you take the square root of the sums of the squares of the components of the offset vector:

```
CGFloat explosionDistance = sqrtf(explosionOffset.dx * explosionOffset.dx
    + explosionOffset.dy * explosionOffset.dy);
```

Once you have that, you divide the offset by this length, and then multiply it by the power. This ensures that all affected objects get the same total amount of power, regardless of their position:

```
CGVector explosionForce = explosionOffset;
explosionForce.dx /= explosionDistance;
explosionForce.dy /= explosionDistance;

explosionForce.dx *= power;
explosionForce.dy *= power;
```

3. Finally, you apply this calculated force vector to the body:

```
[body applyForce:explosionForce];
```

7.17. Using Device Orientation to Control Gravity

Problem

You want the direction of gravity to change when the player rotates her device.

Solution

First, make your application only use the portrait orientation by selecting the project at the top of the Project Navigator, selecting the General tab, scrolling down to "Device Orientation," and turning off everything except Portrait.

Next, add the Core Motion framework to your project. Scroll down to "Linked Frameworks and Libraries," click the + button, and type "CoreMotion"; then double-click "CoreMotion.framework."

Next, open your SKScene subclass. Import the Core Motion header file:

```
#import <CoreMotion/CoreMotion.h>
```

and add a new instance variable to your class:

```
@implementation PhysicsScene {
    CMMotionManager* motionManager;
}
```

Finally, when your scene is being set up, add the following code:

```
motionManager = [[CMMotionManager alloc] init];

[motionManager startDeviceMotionUpdatesToQueue:[NSOperationQueue mainQueue]
    withHandler:^(CMDeviceMotion *motion, NSError *error) {
```

```
    CGVector gravityVector = CGVectorMake(motion.gravity.x, motion.gravity.y);

    gravityVector.dx *= 9.81;
    gravityVector.dy *= 9.81;

    self.physicsWorld.gravity = gravityVector;

}];
```

Discussion

When you create a CMMotionManager and call startDeviceMotionUpdatesTo
Queue:withHandler:, the motion system will call a block that you provide and give it
information on how the player's device is moving.

To get the direction of gravity, you ask the motion object that gets passed in as a parameter for its gravity property. Gravity has three components: x, y, and z. These
correspond to how much gravity is pulling on the sides of the device, the top and bottom
edges of the device, and the front and back of the device.

In a 2D game, there are only two dimensions you care about: x and y. Therefore, we can
just discard the z component of gravity.

However, the values contained in the gravity property are measured in *gravities*—that
is, if you lay your phone perfectly flat with the back of the phone pointed down, there
will be precisely one gravity of force on the z-axis. In Sprite Kit, however, gravity is
measured in meters per second (by default). So, you need to convert between the two
units.

The conversion is very easy: one gravity is equal to 9.81 meters per second. So, all that
needs to happen is to multiply both the x and y components of the gravity vector by
9.81.

Finally, this updated gravity vector is given to the scene's physicsWorld, which in turn
affects the physics objects in the scene.

7.18. Dragging Objects Around

Problem

You want the player of your game to be able to drag physics objects on the screen.

Solution

First, create two new instance variables: an SKNode object called dragNode, and an
SKPhsyicsJointPin called dragJoint.

In the code for your SKScene, add the following methods:

```
-(void)touchesBegan:(NSSet *)touches withEvent:(UIEvent *)event {
    // Called when a touch begins

    // We only care about one touch at a time
    UITouch* touch = [touches anyObject];

    // Determine which node got touched
    CGPoint touchPosition = [touch locationInNode:self];
    SKNode* touchedNode = [self nodeAtPoint:touchPosition];

    // Make sure that the user is touching something that can be dragged
    if (touchedNode == nil || touchedNode == dragNode)
        return;

    // Make sure that the object we touched has a physics body
    if (touchedNode.physicsBody == nil)
        return;

    // Create the invisible drag node, with a small static body
    dragNode = [SKNode node];
    dragNode.position = touchPosition;
    dragNode.physicsBody = [SKPhysicsBody bodyWithRectangleOfSize:
                            CGSizeMake(10, 10)];
    dragNode.physicsBody.dynamic = NO;

    [self addChild:dragNode];

    // Link this new node to the object that got touched
    dragJoint = [SKPhysicsJointPin jointWithBodyA:touchedNode.physicsBody
                                  bodyB:dragNode.physicsBody
                                  anchor:touchPosition];

    [self.physicsWorld addJoint:dragJoint];

}

- (void)touchesMoved:(NSSet *)touches withEvent:(UIEvent *)event {
    UITouch* touch = [touches anyObject];

    // When the touch moves, move the static drag node. The joint will drag
    // the connected object with it.
    CGPoint touchPosition = [touch locationInNode:self];

    dragNode.position = touchPosition;

}

- (void)touchesEnded:(NSSet *)touches withEvent:(UIEvent *)event {
    [self stopDragging];
}
```

```
- (void)touchesCancelled:(NSSet *)touches withEvent:(UIEvent *)event {
    [self stopDragging];
}

- (void) stopDragging {
    // Remove the joint and the drag node.
    [self.physicsWorld removeJoint:dragJoint];
    dragJoint = nil;

    [dragNode removeFromParent];
    dragNode = nil;
}
```

Discussion

The first thing that often comes into people's heads when they start thinking about how to do this is something like this: "When a touch begins, store a reference to the object that got touched. Then, when the touch moves, update the position property, and it'll move with it!"

This has a couple of problems, though. First, if you're only setting the position of the object that the user is dragging when the touch updates, gravity's going to be dragging the object down. This will have the effect of making the object's position flicker quite noticeably as it's moved around.

Second, if you're directly setting the position of an object, it becomes possible to make an object move through walls or through other objects, which may not be what you want.

A better solution, which is what we're doing in this recipe, is to create a static, invisible object, and connect it to the object that you want to actually let the user drag around. When the touch moves, you change the position of this static object, not the object you want dragged—as a result, the joint will move the object around. Because we're not overriding the physics system, the object being dragged around won't do impossible things like intersect with other objects.

You'll notice that in both the touchesEnded: and touchesCancelled: methods, a new method called stopDragging is called. It's important to call stopDragging in both the ended and cancelled phases of the touch—a touch can get cancelled while the user's dragging the object around (such as when a phone call comes in), in which case you'll need to act as if the finger has been deliberately lifted up.

7.19. Creating a Car

Problem

You want to create a vehicle with wheels.

Solution

A vehicle is composed of at least two main parts: the body of the vehicle, and one or more wheels. In the case of a car (at least, a two-dimensional car) we can model this with a box and two wheels—in other words, a rectangular SKSpriteNode and two SKShapeNodes that are set up to draw circles (see Figure 7-2).

Figure 7-2. The car object described in this recipe, composed of a rectangular main body, two circles for wheels, and two pin joints to connect the wheel to the main body

In addition to creating the nodes, the wheels need to be linked to the body with two SKPhysicsJointPin objects:

```
- (void) createCar {
```

```
// Create the car
SKSpriteNode* carNode = [SKSpriteNode spriteNodeWithColor:[SKColor
                            yellowColor] size:CGSizeMake(150, 50)];
carNode.position = CGPointMake(CGRectGetMidX(self.frame),
                    CGRectGetMidY(self.frame));
carNode.physicsBody = [SKPhysicsBody bodyWithRectangleOfSize:carNode.size];
[self addChild:carNode];

// Create the left wheel
SKNode* leftWheelNode = [self createWheelWithRadius:30];
leftWheelNode.position = CGPointMake(carNode.position.x-80,
                                carNode.position.y);
leftWheelNode.physicsBody = [SKPhysicsBody bodyWithCircleOfRadius:30];
[self addChild:leftWheelNode];

// Create the right wheel
SKNode* rightWheelNode = [self createWheelWithRadius:30];
rightWheelNode.position = CGPointMake(carNode.position.x+80,
                                carNode.position.y);
rightWheelNode.physicsBody = [SKPhysicsBody bodyWithCircleOfRadius:30];
[self addChild:rightWheelNode];

// Attach the wheels to the body
CGPoint leftWheelPosition = leftWheelNode.position;
CGPoint rightWheelPosition = rightWheelNode.position;

SKPhysicsJointPin* leftPinJoint = [SKPhysicsJointPin
    jointWithBodyA:carNode.physicsBody bodyB:leftWheelNode.physicsBody
    anchor:leftWheelPosition];
SKPhysicsJointPin* rightPinJoint = [SKPhysicsJointPin
    jointWithBodyA:carNode.physicsBody bodyB:rightWheelNode.physicsBody
    anchor:rightWheelPosition];

[self.physicsWorld addJoint:leftPinJoint];
[self.physicsWorld addJoint:rightPinJoint];
}

- (SKNode*) createWheelWithRadius:(float)wheelRadius {
    CGRect wheelRect = CGRectMake(-wheelRadius, -wheelRadius, wheelRadius*2,
                            wheelRadius*2);

    SKShapeNode* wheelNode = [[SKShapeNode alloc] init];
    wheelNode.path = [UIBezierPath bezierPathWithOvalInRect:wheelRect].CGPath;

    return wheelNode;
}
```

Discussion

When you create an SKPhysicsJointPin, the anchor point you define is defined in scene
coordinates, not relative to any other body. In this recipe, the pin anchors are set at the

---

center of each wheel, which makes them rotate around their axes; if you set the anchor to be somewhere else, you'll end up with bumpy wheels (which may actually be what you want!).

While writing this recipe, we noticed something that appears to be a bug in Sprite Kit, at least in iOS 7.0: if you set the position of your nodes *after* you give them physics bodies, your joints will not work correctly. That is, this code won't work correctly:

```
carNode.physicsBody = [SKPhysicsBody bodyWithRectangleOfSize:carNode.size];
carNode.position = CGPointMake(CGRectGetMidX(self.frame),
                    CGRectGetMidY(self.frame));
```

Instead, you need to set `position` *before* setting the physics body, like this:

```
carNode.position = CGPointMake(CGRectGetMidX(self.frame),
                    CGRectGetMidY(self.frame));
carNode.physicsBody = [SKPhysicsBody bodyWithRectangleOfSize:carNode.size];
```

This bug appears to be fixed in iOS 7.1, but keep an eye out.

CHAPTER 8

3D Graphics

Using 3D graphics is the most popular approach for games these days. However, 3D is *complicated*. It's so complicated, in fact, that we're going to dedicate three whole chapters to it. The first chapter (this one) covers introductory 3D—setup, basic drawing, and understanding how 3D works overall. The next two chapters cover more intermediate and advanced topics in 3D rendering on the iPhone and iPad.

When you work in 3D, you use a library called *OpenGL ES*. OpenGL ES is the "embedded" version of OpenGL, the industry-standard library for computer graphics. OpenGL is *everywhere*—you'll find it in desktop computers, in games consoles, in industrial hardware, and in mobile computers like iOS devices.

Because OpenGL is designed to be cross-platform, it doesn't have the same nice API as you might be used to from working with other tools on iOS. Apple's put quite a bit of effort into making things as easy as possible for developers, introducing a framework called *GLKit* that helps with the setup and integration of OpenGL in your game. However, you'll still need to get used to how OpenGL works.

Because it's not really possible to talk about 3D graphics features in isolation, this chapter is actually designed to be read in sequence. Whereas in other chapters you can basically jump straight to any recipe, we recommend that you start this one at the beginning and read through. As a precursor to the recipes, we'll begin with an introduction to 3D math.

8.1. Working with 3D Math

In addition to providing lots of useful support classes and functions for working with 3D graphics, GLKit also includes a number of types and functions that are helpful for working with 3D math.

The two most common kinds of mathematical constructs that you'll see when doing 3D math are *vectors* and *matrices*. We talked about two-dimensional vectors in "Vectors" on page 148; the 3D equivalent is a three-dimensional vector.

3D Vectors and GLKit

A 3D vector has three components. By convention, these are referred to as *x*, *y*, and *z*. In GLKit, a 2D vector is represented by the GLKVector2 structure, and 3D vectors are represented by GLKVector3 objects:

```
GLKVector2 myVector2D;
myVector2D.x = 1;
myVector2D.y = 2;

GLKVector3 myVector3D;
myVector2D.x = 1;
myVector2D.y = 2;
myVector2D.z = 4;
```

GLKit provides a number of useful functions for working with vectors:

GLKVector3Add *and* GLKVector2Add
   Add two vectors together.

GLKVector3Subtract *and* GLKVector2Subtract
   Subtract one vector from another.

GLKVector3Distance *and* GLKVector2Distance
   Get the distance from one vector to another.

GLKVector3Length *and* GLKVector2Length
   Get the length (or magnitude) of a vector.

GLKVector3Normalize *and* GLKVector2Normalize
   Get the normalized version of a vector (i.e., a vector with the same direction as the original but with a length of 1).

GLKVector3DotProduct *and* GLKVector2DotProduct
   Get the dot product between two vectors.

For more information on what these functions involve, see "Vectors" on page 148.

Matrices

A *matrix* is a grid of numbers (see Figure 8-1).

$$M = \begin{bmatrix} 1 & 2 & 3 \\ 4 & 5 & 7 \\ 0 & 1 & 2 \end{bmatrix}$$

Figure 8-1. A matrix

On their own, matrices are just a way to store numbers. However, matrices are especially useful when they're combined with vectors. This is because you can multiply a matrix with a vector, which results in a changed version of the original vector.

Additionally, if you multiply two matrices together, the result is a matrix that, if you multiply it with a vector, has the same result as if you had multiplied the vector with each matrix individually. This means that a single matrix can be used to represent a combination of operations.

Additionally, there's a single matrix that, if multiplied with a vector, returns a vector with no changes (i.e., it returns the original vector). This is referred to as the *identity matrix*, and it's a good starting point for building a matrix: you start with the identity matrix and then translate it, rotate it, and so on.

The three most useful things a matrix can do with a vector are:

Translation
    Moving the vector

Rotation
    Rotating the vector in 3D space

Scaling
    Increasing or decreasing the distance of the vector from the origin

Another common kind of matrix, called a *perspective projection transform matrix*, does the work of making objects get smaller as they move away from the origin point. You can multiply a vector with a perspective projection transform matrix, just like any other transform.

Conversely, if you use an *orthographic projection transform matrix*, objects remain the same size no matter how far away they get. In both of these cases, you define the height and width of the view area, and objects outside of the view area aren't visible.

In GLKit, the GLKMatrix4 structure represents a 4-by-4 matrix, which you use with vectors to apply transforms. GLKMatrix4Identity is the identity matrix.

You can create matrices that represent specific transformations by using the GLKMatrix4MakeTranslation, GLKMatrix4MakeRotation, and GLKMatrix4MakeScale functions:

```
// Make a matrix that represents a translation of 1 unit on the y-axis
GLKMatrix4 translationMatrix = GLKMatrix4MakeTranslation(0, 1, 0)
```

```
// Make a matrix that represents a rotation of π radians around the x-axis
GLKMatrix4 rotationMatrix = GLKMatrix4MakeRotation(M_PI, 1, 0, 0);

// Make a matrix that represents a scaling of 0.9 on the x-axis,
// 1.2 on the y-axis, and 1 on the z-axis
GLKMatrix4 scaleMatrix = GLKMatrix4MakeScale(0.9, 1.2, 1);
```

Once you have a matrix, you can create additional matrices, and combine them together using `GLKMatrixMultiply`:

```
GLKMatrix4 translationMatrix = GLKMatrix4MakeTranslation(0, 1, 0)
GLKMatrix4 rotationMatrix = GLKMatrix4MakeRotation(M_PI, M_PI_2, 0);

GLKMatrix4 translateAndRotateMatrix = GLKMatrix4Multiply(translationMatrix,
                                                         rotationMatrix);
```

Once you're done constructing your matrices, you give them to GLKit when it needs a *model view matrix*. Model view matrices are discussed in Recipe 8.5.

Finally, you can create projection matrices using the `GLKMatrix4MakePerspective` and `GLKMatrix4MakeOrtho` functions.

When you create a perspective projection, you need to provide four pieces of information:

Field of view
How "wide" the viewable region should be, measured in radians. The field of view is the angle from the leftmost viewable point to the rightmost viewable point.

Aspect ratio
The width of the viewable area, as a ratio to its height. For example, if you want the viewable region to be twice as wide as the height, the aspect ratio is 2; if you want the viewable region to be one-third the height, the aspect ratio is 0.333.

Near clipping plane
The minimum distance from the camera at which objects are allowed to be.

Far clipping plane
The maximum distance from the camera at which objects are allowed to be.

 Humans have a field of view of almost 180° (i.e., π radians), but using this setting can cause problems in a game because the screen takes up a much smaller section of the player's field of view. Play around with 90° to 70° (i.e., π/2, or 1.57 radians to 1.22 radians).

Creating an orthographic projection requires different information. You need to provide the following:

- The *left* coordinate of the viewable region, relative to the center (i.e., the coordinate (0,0) is the center of the viewable region; if you want objects 5 units to the left of the camera to be viewable, you set this to −5)

- The *right* coordinate of the viewable region

- The *bottom* coordinate

- The *top* coordinate

- The *near* coordinate (i.e., the minimum distance that objects can be from the camera)

- The *far* coordinate (the maximum distance that objects can be from the camera)

Here's how you create perspective and orthographic matrices:

```
// Make a perspective projection with a n/2 (i.e., 90°) field of view,
// a 1.5:1 aspect ratio (the viewable area is 1.5x as wide as it is high),
// a near clipping plane 0.1 units away, and a far clipping plane 200
// units away
GLKMatrix4 perspectiveMatrix = GLKMatrix4MakePerspective(M_PI_2, 1.5, 0.1, 1.0);

// Make an orthographic projection with left coordinate -5,
// right coordinate 5, bottom coordinate -5, top coordinate 5,
// near coordinate 0.1, and far coordinate 200

GLKMatrix4 orthographicMatrix = GLKMatrix4MakeOrtho(-5, 5, -5, 5, 0.1, 100);
```

With this math primer in mind, it's on to the recipes!

8.2. Creating a GLKit Context

Problem

You want to create an application that draws using OpenGL.

Solution

Note that while Xcode includes a template that sets up a lot of this for you, in this exercise we're going to go through each part of it step by step, so you can understand it better:

1. Create a new single-view application.

2. Import *GLKit.framework* and *OpenGLES.framework*.

3. Open *ViewController.xib*.

4. Select the view, open the Identity inspector, and set the view's class to GLKView.

5. Open *ViewController.h*, import *GLKit/GLKit.h*, and change ViewController's parent class from UIViewController to GLKViewController.

6. Add the following code to `viewDidLoad`:

```
GLKView* view = (GLKView*)self.view;
view.context = [[EAGLContext alloc] initWithAPI:kEAGLRenderingAPIOpenGLES2];
```

7. Then add the following method:

```
- (void)glkView:(GLKView *)view drawInRect:(CGRect)rect {
    glClearColor(0.0, 0.5, 0.0, 1.0);
    glClear(GL_COLOR_BUFFER_BIT);
}
```

Discussion

When you create a GLKit context, you're creating the space in which all of your 3D graphics will be drawn. GLKit contexts are contained inside `GLKView` objects, which are just `UIView` objects that know how to draw OpenGL content.

When the context gets created, you need to specify which version of the OpenGL ES API you want to use. There are three different versions that you can use:

- *OpenGL ES 1.0*, which supports very simple, fixed-function rendering
- *OpenGL ES 2.0*, which adds support for *pixel shaders* (small programs that let you customize a great deal of the rendering process)
- *OpenGL ES 3.0*, which adds a number of low-level features that improve rendering speed and flexibility

 The changes from OpenGL ES 1.0 to 2.0 were much more significant than the changes from 2.0 to 3.0. The new stuff in 3.0 isn't as relevant to people starting out using OpenGL ES, so what we're covering in this book is largely content that was added in 2.0.

OpenGL works by continuously redrawing the entire scene every time a frame needs to be shown. Every time this happens, your `GLKView` calls the `glkView:drawInRect:` method. In this example, the only thing that happens is that the content of the view is cleared:

```
glClearColor(0.0, 0.5, 0.0, 1.0);
glClear(GL_COLOR_BUFFER_BIT);
```

The first line of the code calls `glClearColor`, which effectively tells OpenGL that the clear color should be set to the RGBA value (0.0, 0.5, 0.0, 1.0)—that is, fully opaque, dark green.

The next line instructs OpenGL to actually clear the *color buffer*—that is, it fills the entire screen with the clear color that was set on the previous line (see Figure 8-2).

Figure 8-2. The final result of this recipe: a screen filled with solid color

8.3. Drawing a Square Using OpenGL

Problem

You want to draw a square on the screen using OpenGL.

Solution

Make *ViewController.m* contain this code:

```
#import "ViewController.h"

typedef struct {
    GLKVector3 position;
} Vertex;

const Vertex SquareVertices[] = {
```

```
        {-1, -1 , 0}, // bottom left
        {1, -1 , 0},  // bottom right
        {1, 1 , 0},   // top right
        {-1, 1 , 0},  // top left
};

const GLubyte SquareTriangles[] = {
        0, 1, 2, // BL->BR->TR
        2, 3, 0  // TR->TL->BL
};

@interface ViewController () {
    GLuint _vertexBuffer; // contains the collection of vertices used to
                          // describe the position of each corner
    GLuint _indexBuffer;  // indicates which vertices should be used in each
                          // triangle used to make up the square

    GLKBaseEffect* _squareEffect; // describes how the square is going to be
                                  // rendered
}

@end

@implementation ViewController

- (void)viewDidLoad
{
    [super viewDidLoad];
        // Do any additional setup after loading the view, typically from a nib

    GLKView* view = (GLKView*)self.view;
    view.context = [[EAGLContext alloc] initWithAPI:kEAGLRenderingAPIOpenGLES2];

    [EAGLContext setCurrentContext:view.context];

    // Create the vertex array buffer, in which OpenGL will store the vertices

    // Tell OpenGL to give us a buffer
    glGenBuffers(1, &_vertexBuffer);

    // Make this buffer be the active array buffer
    glBindBuffer(GL_ARRAY_BUFFER, _vertexBuffer);

    // Put this data into the active array buffer. It's as big as the
    // 'SquareVertices' array, so we can use the data from that array;
    // also, this data isn't going to change.
    glBufferData(GL_ARRAY_BUFFER, sizeof(SquareVertices), SquareVertices,
                GL_STATIC_DRAW);


    // Now do the same thing for the index buffer, which indicates which
    // vertices to use when drawing the triangles
```

```
    glGenBuffers(1, &_indexBuffer);
    glBindBuffer(GL_ELEMENT_ARRAY_BUFFER, _indexBuffer);
    glBufferData(GL_ELEMENT_ARRAY_BUFFER, sizeof(SquareTriangles),
                 SquareTriangles, GL_STATIC_DRAW);

    // Prepare the GL effect, which tells OpenGL how to draw our triangle
    _squareEffect = [[GLKBaseEffect alloc] init];

    // First, we set up the projection matrix
    float aspectRatio = self.view.bounds.size.width /
                        self.view.bounds.size.height;
    float fieldOfViewDegrees = 60.0;
    GLKMatrix4 projectionMatrix = GLKMatrix4MakePerspective(
                          GLKMathDegreesToRadians(fieldOfViewDegrees),
                          aspectRatio, 0.1, 10.0);

    _squareEffect.transform.projectionMatrix = projectionMatrix;

    // Next, we describe how the square should be positioned (6 units away
    // from the camera)
    GLKMatrix4 modelViewMatrix = GLKMatrix4MakeTranslation(0.0f, 0.0f, -6.0f);
    _squareEffect.transform.modelviewMatrix = modelViewMatrix;

    // Tell the effect that it should color everything with a single color
    // (in this case, red)
    _squareEffect.useConstantColor = YES;
    _squareEffect.constantColor = GLKVector4Make(1.0, 0.0, 0.0, 1.0);

}

- (void)glkView:(GLKView *)view drawInRect:(CGRect)rect {

    // Erase the view by filling it with black
    glClearColor(0.0, 0.0, 0.0, 1.0);
    glClear(GL_COLOR_BUFFER_BIT);

    // Tell the effect that it should prepare OpenGL to draw using the
    // settings we've configured it with
    [_squareEffect prepareToDraw];

    // OpenGL already knows that the vertex array (GL_ARRAY_BUFFER) contains
    // vertex data. We now tell it how to find useful info in that array.

    // Tell OpenGL how the data is laid out for the position of each
    // vertex in the vertex array
    glEnableVertexAttribArray(GLKVertexAttribPosition);
    glVertexAttribPointer(GLKVertexAttribPosition, 3, GL_FLOAT, GL_FALSE, 0, 0);

    // Now that OpenGL knows where to find vertex positions, it can draw them
    int numberOfVertices = sizeof(SquareTriangles)/sizeof(SquareTriangles[0]);
    glDrawElements(GL_TRIANGLES, numberOfVertices, GL_UNSIGNED_BYTE, 0);
```

```
    }

    - (void)didReceiveMemoryWarning
    {
        [super didReceiveMemoryWarning];
        // Dispose of any resources that can be re-created
    }

    @end
```

Discussion

Drawing triangles in OpenGL is easier than drawing squares or more complex polygons, because triangles are always coplanar—that is, all of the points in the shape are on the same plane.

So, to draw a square, what we do is draw two triangles that share an edge, as illustrated in Figure 8-3.

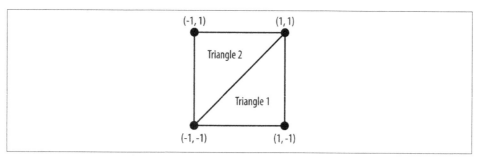

Figure 8-3. The vertices that define the triangles

This means that we need to tell OpenGL about two different things:

- Where each of these vertices are
- Which of these vertices are used in each triangle

To tell OpenGL about where the vertices are, we start by defining a structure for vertices and making an array. This will later be uploaded to OpenGL, so that it can be used:

```
typedef struct {
    GLKVector3 position;
} Vertex;

const Vertex SquareVertices[] = {
    {-1, -1 , 0}, // vertex 0: bottom left
    {1, -1 , 0}, // vertex 1: bottom right
    {1, 1 , 0},  // vertex 2: top right
```

```
    {-1, 1 , 0}, // vertex 3: top left
};
```

The positions used in each vertex are defined in arbitrary "units." These units can be anything you like: inches, centimeters, or whatever.

Once the vertices have been laid out, we need to define which triangles use which vertices. In OpenGL, we do this by numbering each vertex, and then describing triangles by giving OpenGL three numbers at a time:

```
const GLubyte SquareTriangles[] = {
    0, 1, 2, // BL->BR->TR
    2, 3, 0  // TR->TL->BL
};
```

In this case, the first triangle uses vertices 0, 1, and 2, and the second triangle uses vertices 2, 3, and 0. Note that both triangles use vertices 0 and 2. This means that they share an edge, which means that there won't be any gap between the two triangles.

This data needs to be passed to OpenGL before it can be used. Both the `SquareVerti ces` and `SquareTriangles` arrays need to be stored in a *buffer*, which is OpenGL's term for a chunk of information that it can use for rendering.

When you create a buffer, OpenGL gives you a number, which is the buffer's *name*. (A name is still a number, not text—it's just a weird OpenGL terminology thing.) When you want to work with a buffer, you use that buffer's name. In this code, we store the names as instance variables:

```
@interface ViewController () {
    GLuint _vertexBuffer; // contains the collection of vertices used to
                          // describe the position of each corner
    GLuint _indexBuffer;  // indicates which vertices should be used in each
                          // triangle used to make up the square

    GLKBaseEffect* _squareEffect; // describes how the square is going to be
                                  // rendered
}

@end
```

That last instance variable is a `GLKBaseEffect`, which is used to control the position of the square on the screen, as well as its color. We'll come back to this in a few moments.

The first part of the actual code that gets executed is in `viewDidLoad:`. First, we set up the `GLKView` with an OpenGL context. Because we're about to start issuing OpenGL commands, we also make that context the current context (if you don't do this, none of your OpenGL commands will do anything):

```
GLKView* view = (GLKView*)self.view;
view.context = [[EAGLContext alloc] initWithAPI:kEAGLRenderingAPIOpenGLES2];
```

```
[EAGLContext setCurrentContext:view.context];
```

Next, we create the buffers, starting with the vertex buffer. It's also bound to GL_AR RAY_BUFFER, which instructs OpenGL that whenever we're talking about "the GL_AR RAY_BUFFER," we mean _vertexBuffer. If you're making a game where you have more than one array buffer (which is common), you call glBindBuffer every time you want to start working with a different array buffer:

```
glGenBuffers(1, &_vertexBuffer);
glBindBuffer(GL_ARRAY_BUFFER, _vertexBuffer);
```

The vertex buffer is then filled with the vertex information:

```
glBufferData(GL_ARRAY_BUFFER, sizeof(SquareVertices),
        SquareVertices, GL_STATIC_DRAW);
```

The call to glBufferData basically says this: "Hey, OpenGL, I want you to put data into the currently bound GL_ARRAY_BUFFER. The size of the data is however big the Square Vertices array is, and the data should come from the SquareVertices array. Also, this data is unlikely to change, so you can optimize for that."

The same thing is then done for the index buffer, which you'll recall stores information on which vertices the two triangles will use:

```
glGenBuffers(1, &_indexBuffer);
glBindBuffer(GL_ELEMENT_ARRAY_BUFFER, _indexBuffer);
glBufferData(GL_ELEMENT_ARRAY_BUFFER, sizeof(SquareTriangles), SquareTriangles,
        GL_STATIC_DRAW);
```

Once this is done, all of the information has been passed to OpenGL. The next step is to configure how the object will be presented when OpenGL renders the scene.

GLKit provides *GLKit effects*, which are objects that contain information like color, lighting information, position, and orientation. This information can be configured ahead of time and is used at the moment of rendering. GLKit effects encapsulate a lot of the complexity that can go along with configuring how a rendered objects gets drawn.

In this simple example, we want the square to be red and to be positioned in the middle of the screen.

The first step is to create the effect object, and then provide it with a projection matrix. The projection matrix controls the overall sizes of things on the screen, and effectively acts as the lens in front of the camera. In this case, we create a projection matrix that uses the aspect ratio of the screen and uses a field of view of 60 degrees:

```
_squareEffect = [[GLKBaseEffect alloc] init];

float aspectRatio = self.view.bounds.size.width /
                    self.view.bounds.size.height;
float fieldOfViewDegrees = 60.0;
```

```
GLKMatrix4 projectionMatrix = GLKMatrix4MakePerspective(
                    GLKMathDegreesToRadians(fieldOfViewDegrees),
                    aspectRatio, 0.1, 10.0);

_squareEffect.transform.projectionMatrix = projectionMatrix;
```

Once we've set up the projection matrix, we provide a model view matrix. The model view matrix controls the position of the object, relative to the camera:

```
GLKMatrix4 modelViewMatrix = GLKMatrix4MakeTranslation(0.0f, 0.0f, -6.0f);
_squareEffect.transform.modelviewMatrix = modelViewMatrix;
```

Finally, we tell the effect that whenever it's used to render anything, everything should be rendered with a constant color of red:

```
_squareEffect.useConstantColor = YES;
_squareEffect.constantColor = GLKVector4Make(1.0, 0.0, 0.0, 1.0);
```

The actual work of rendering is done in the `glkView:drawInRect:` method. The first thing that happens in this is that the view is cleared, by filling the screen with black:

```
glClearColor(0.0, 0.0, 0.0, 1.0);
glClear(GL_COLOR_BUFFER_BIT);
```

The GLKit effect is then told to "prepare to draw." This means that it configures OpenGL in such a way that anything you draw will use that effect's settings. If you have multiple GLKit effects, you call `prepareToDraw` on each one before you start drawing:

```
[_squareEffect prepareToDraw];
```

At this point, OpenGL knows that the `GL_ARRAY_BUFFER` contains per-vertex data, and that the `GL_ELEMENT_ARRAY_BUFFER` contains information on what data in the array buffer should be used for each triangle. This is because both of these buffers were bound during the `viewDidLoad` method.

In the next step, we tell OpenGL how to use the data in the `GL_ARRAY_BUFFER`. There's only one piece of information relevant in this app: the *position* of each vertex. (In more complex apps, there's often much more information that each vertex needs, such as color information, normals, and texture coordinates. We're keeping it simple.)

To tell OpenGL where the position information is in the vertex array, we first tell OpenGL that we're going to be working with positions, and then tell OpenGL where to find the position information in the vertex data:

```
glEnableVertexAttribArray(GLKVertexAttribPosition);
glVertexAttribPointer(GLKVertexAttribPosition, 3, GL_FLOAT, GL_FALSE, 0, 0);
```

The call to `glVertexAttribPointer` is interpreted by OpenGL like this: "OK, OpenGL, here's where you'll find the position information I just mentioned. There are three numbers, and they're all floating point. They're not normalized. Once you've read the three numbers, don't skip any information, because the next position will be right after that. Also, the position information starts right at the start of the array."

Finally, the triangles can actually be drawn:

```
int numberOfTriangles = sizeof(SquareTriangles)/sizeof(SquareTriangles[0]);
glDrawElements(GL_TRIANGLES, numberOfTriangles, GL_UNSIGNED_BYTE, 0);
```

First, we need to know how many vertices we're asking OpenGL to draw. This can be figured out by taking the size of the entire index array, and dividing that by the size of one element in that array. In our case, the array is made up of unsigned bytes, and there are six bytes in the array, so we're going to be asking OpenGL to render six vertices.

This call translates to: "OK, OpenGL! I want you to draw triangles (i.e., three vertices at a time). The number of triangles is 2. Each entry in the triangle list is an unsigned byte. Don't skip over any items in the element array."

OpenGL will then draw the two triangles on the screen, as shown in Figure 8-4.

Figure 8-4. A square being drawn by OpenGL

8.4. Loading a Texture

Problem

You want to display a texture on an OpenGL surface.

Solution

In this solution, we'll be loading a texture and applying it to the square that was drawn in the previous recipe.

First, in your vertex structure, you need to include texture coordinate information:

```
typedef struct {
    GLKVector3 position; // the location of each vertex in space
    GLKVector2 textureCoordinates; // the texture coordinates for each vertex
} Vertex;

const Vertex SquareVertices[] = {
    {{-1, -1 , 0}, {0,0}}, // bottom left
    {{1, -1 , 0}, {1,0}}, // bottom right
    {{1, 1 , 0}, {1,1}},  // top right
    {{-1, 1 , 0}, {0,1}}, // top left
};
```

Next, when preparing for rendering in `viewDidLoad`:

```
NSString* imagePath = [[NSBundle mainBundle]
pathForResource:@"Texture" ofType:@"png"];
NSError* error = nil;

GLKTextureInfo* texture = [GLKTextureLoader
textureWithContentsOfFile:imagePath options:nil error:&error];

if (error != nil) {
    NSLog(@"Problem loading texture: %@", error);
}

_squareEffect.texture2d0.name = texture.name;
```

If you're modifying the previous recipe, remove these lines:

```
_squareEffect.useConstantColor = YES;
_squareEffect.constantColor = GLKVector4Make(1.0, 0.0, 0.0, 1.0);
```

Finally, when rendering in `glkView:drawInRect:`, you indicate to OpenGL where to find texture coordinates in the vertex information:

```
glEnableVertexAttribArray(GLKVertexAttribTexCoord0);
glVertexAttribPointer(GLKVertexAttribTexCoord0, 2, GL_FLOAT, GL_FALSE,
        sizeof(Vertex), (void*)offsetof(Vertex, textureCoordinates));
```

When the square is rendered, you'll see your image appear on it.

Discussion

GLKTextureLoader allows you to take an image and upload it to the graphics chip that's built into your device. To get an image, you use the pathForResource:ofType: method on NSBundle, which gives you the location of the image that you specify.

Once you've got that location, you pass it to GLKTextureLoader using the textureWith ContentsOfFile:options:error: method. This sends the image to the graphics chip, and returns a GLKTextureInfo object. This object contains information about the texture, including its name.

In OpenGL, a texture's name is a number used to identify that specific texture. To use a texture, you provide its name to the GLKEffect that you're using to render your geometry.

In addition to loading a texture, you need to indicate to OpenGL which parts of the texture are attached to the geometry you're drawing. This is done by defining *texture coordinates.*

Texture coordinates indicate points in the texture. As illustrated in Figure 8-5, the position (0,0) refers to the lower-left corner of the texture, while the position (1,1) refers to the upper-right corner.

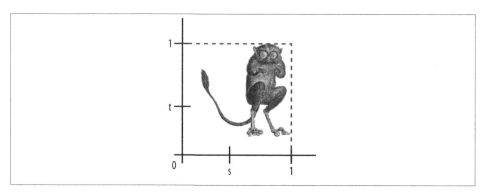

Figure 8-5. Texture coordinates

Texture coordinates are given to OpenGL by using the glEnableVertexAttribArray and glVertexAttribPointer functions. The first function tells OpenGL that you want to enable the use of texture coordinates, and the second tells OpenGL where in the vertex data the texture coordinates will be found (Figure 8-6).

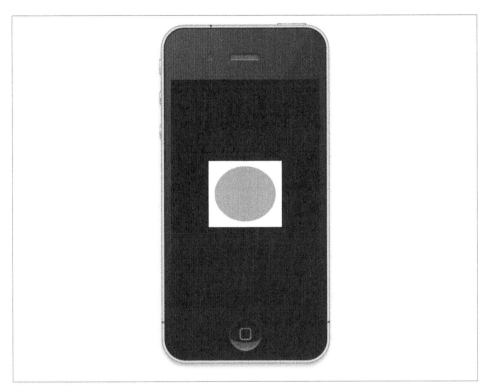

Figure 8-6. A textured square drawn by OpenGL

8.5. Drawing a Cube

Problem

You want to draw a three-dimensional cube, and draw a texture on its faces.

Solution

This solution builds from Recipe 8.4.

A cube is made up of eight vertices, one for each of its corners. To draw the cube, therefore, you need to provide information for each vertex, including its position and texture coordinates.

Additionally, you'll need to tell OpenGL how to build the triangles that make up each of the cube's six faces. (Recall from Recipe 8.3 that a square is drawn by drawing two triangles that share an edge.)

Note that in this example, we've renamed SquareVertices to CubeVertices and SquareTriangles to CubeTriangles:

```
const Vertex CubeVertices[] = {
    {{-1, -1, 1}, {0,0}}, // bottom left front
    {{1, -1, 1}, {1,0}},  // bottom right front
    {{1, 1, 1}, {1,1}},   // top right front
    {{-1, 1, 1}, {0,1}},  // top left front

    {{-1, -1, -1}, {1,0}}, // bottom left back
    {{1, -1, -1}, {0,0}},  // bottom right back
    {{1, 1, -1}, {0,1}},   // top right back
    {{-1, 1, -1}, {1,1}},  // top left back
};

const GLubyte CubeTriangles[] = {
    0, 1, 2, // front face 1
    2, 3, 0, // front face 2

    4, 5, 6, // back face 1
    6, 7, 4, // back face 2

    7, 4, 0, // left face 1
    0, 3, 7, // left face 2

    2, 1, 5,  // right face 1
    5, 6, 2,  // right face 2

    7, 3, 6, // top face 1
    6, 2, 3, // top face 2

    4, 0, 5, // bottom face 1
    5, 1, 0, // bottom face 2
};
```

The next step is a purely aesthetic one: the cube will be rotated, in order to illustrate that it is in fact a three-dimensional object.

Replace these lines:

```
GLKMatrix4 modelViewMatrix = GLKMatrix4MakeTranslation(0.0f, 0.0f, -6.0f);
_squareEffect.transform.modelviewMatrix = modelViewMatrix;
```

with the following:

```
GLKMatrix4 modelViewMatrix = GLKMatrix4MakeTranslation(0.0f, 0.0f, -6.0f);
modelViewMatrix = GLKMatrix4RotateX(modelViewMatrix,
                                    GLKMathDegreesToRadians(45));
modelViewMatrix = GLKMatrix4RotateY(modelViewMatrix,
                                    GLKMathDegreesToRadians(45));
_squareEffect.transform.modelviewMatrix = modelViewMatrix;
```

On its own, this is almost enough: as we saw in the previous recipe, the call to glDrawElements uses the size of the triangles array to determine how many triangles (and, consequently, how many vertices) it needs to use.

However, to draw our cube a depth buffer needs to be added and enabled.

Add this code immediately after the call to EAGLContext's setCurrentContext method:

```
view.drawableDepthFormat = GLKViewDrawableDepthFormat24;
glEnable(GL_DEPTH_TEST);
```

Finally, replace this line:

```
glClear(GL_COLOR_BUFFER_BIT);
```

with this:

```
glClear(GL_COLOR_BUFFER_BIT | GL_DEPTH_BUFFER_BIT);
```

The result is shown in Figure 8-7.

Figure 8-7. A cube rendered in OpenGL

Discussion

A *depth buffer* is a region of memory that keeps track of how far away each pixel is from the camera. This makes it possible to draw, for example, a close object before drawing one further away—without a depth buffer, you'd need to make sure that you drew your farthest objects before drawing closer ones, or you'd end up with distant objects overlapping closer ones. If you want to learn more about this, check out the Wikipedia article on the Painter's Algorithm (*http://en.wikipedia.org/wiki/Painter's_algorithm*).

Depth buffers work like this: every time a pixel is drawn onto the screen, OpenGL calculates how far away that pixel is from the camera. When the pixel is right up against the camera, a 0 is written into the depth buffer, and when the pixel is very, very far away from the camera, a 1 is written into the depth buffer. Pixels that fall somewhere between get written in as numbers in between (0.1, 0.12, and so on.)

When GL_DEPTH_TEST is turned on, OpenGL checks the depth buffer to see if the pixel it's about to draw is further away than the most recently drawn pixel. If the pixel is closer to the camera than the nearest existing pixel, that means that it's closer than the existing pixels, so it's drawn on the screen and the distance of the new pixel replaces the old one in the depth buffer. However, if it's further away than any existing pixel, it's behind the old ones, and consequently it's not drawn.

Just like with the color buffer, you have to clear the depth buffer every time you begin a new frame; if you don't, you'll end up with rendering glitches, because OpenGL will start comparing the depth values of pixels against an out-of-date depth buffer.

8.6. Rotating a Cube

Problem

You want to animate movement in a scene, such as rotation.

Solution

This solution builds upon the previous recipe.

Add the following instance variable to the ViewController class:

```
float rotation;
```

Next, add the following method to the class:

```
- (void) update {

    // Find out how much time has passed since the last update
    NSTimeInterval timeInterval = self.timeSinceLastUpdate;

    // We want to rotate at 15 degrees per second, so multiply
```

```
    // this amount times the time since the last update and
    // update the "rotation" variable.
    float rotationSpeed = 15 * timeInterval;
    rotation += rotationSpeed;

    // Now construct a model view matrix that places the object 6 units away
    // from the camera and rotates it appropriately
    GLKMatrix4 modelViewMatrix = GLKMatrix4MakeTranslation(0.0f, 0.0f, -6.0f);

    modelViewMatrix = GLKMatrix4RotateX(modelViewMatrix,
                                        GLKMathDegreesToRadians(45));
    modelViewMatrix = GLKMatrix4RotateY(modelViewMatrix,
                                        GLKMathDegreesToRadians(rotation));

    // Apply this to the effect so that the drawing will use this positioning
    _squareEffect.transform.modelviewMatrix = modelViewMatrix;
}
```

When you run the application, your cube will be rotating.

Discussion

The update method on a GLKViewController is called once per frame, and this is your game's opportunity to update in-game content.

In this solution, we're creating a GLKMatrix4, which defines the position and orientation of the object. You create it using the GLKMatrix4MakeTranslation function, and then rotate it around the x- and y-axes. Finally, the matrix is given to the object's GLKEffect, which sets the position and orientation.

8.7. Moving the Camera in 3D Space

Problem

You want to be able to move the camera based on user input.

Solution

First, we'll define how quickly the camera moves. Add the following line of code at the top of *ViewController.m*:

```
const float dragSpeed = 1.0f / 120.0f;
```

Next, add the following instance variable to ViewController:

```
GLKVector3 _cameraPosition;
```

Then add this code to the end of viewDidLoad:

```
UIPanGestureRecognizer* pan =
[[UIPanGestureRecognizer alloc] initWithTarget:self action:@selector(dragged:)];
[self.view addGestureRecognizer:pan];

_cameraPosition.z = -6;
```

Add this method to `ViewController`:

```
- (void) dragged:(UIPanGestureRecognizer*)pan {
    if (pan.state == UIGestureRecognizerStateBegan ||
        pan.state == UIGestureRecognizerStateChanged) {
        CGPoint translation = [pan translationInView:pan.view];
        _cameraPosition.x += translation.x * dragSpeed;
        _cameraPosition.y -= translation.y * dragSpeed;

        [pan setTranslation:CGPointZero inView:pan.view];
    }
}
```

And finally, update this line in the update method:

```
GLKMatrix4 modelViewMatrix = GLKMatrix4MakeTranslation(0, 0, -6);
```

with this code:

```
GLKMatrix4 modelViewMatrix =
GLKMatrix4MakeTranslation(_cameraPosition.x, _cameraPosition.y,
                          _cameraPosition.z);
```

Discussion

The term "camera" in OpenGL is actually kind of a misnomer. In OpenGL, you don't
create a camera object and move it around; instead, the camera is always positioned at
(0,0,0), and you position objects in front of it. In practical terms, this just means that
the matrices that define the position and orientation of your objects need to be *reversed*
—that is, when you want your object to be positioned 6 units in front of the camera,
you set the z-position of the object to be –6.

 In Recipe 9.5, you'll see how to create a movable camera in OpenGL.

CHAPTER 9

Intermediate 3D Graphics

Once you've got OpenGL drawing basic 3D content, you'll likely want to create more complicated scenes. In this chapter, you'll learn how to load meshes from files, how to compose complex objects by creating parent-child relationships between objects, how to position a camera in 3D space, and more.

This chapter builds on the basic 3D graphics concepts covered in Chapter 8, and makes use of the component-based layout shown in Recipe 1.3.

9.1. Loading a Mesh

Problem

You want to load meshes from files, so that you can store 3D objects in files.

Solution

First, create an empty text file called *MyMesh.json*. Put the following text in it:

```json
{
    "vertices":[
        {
                "x":-1, "y":-1, "z":1
                },
        {
                "x":1, "y":-1, "z":1
                },
        {
                "x":-1, "y":1, "z":1
                },
        {
            "x":1, "y":1, "z":1
                },
```

```
        {
                "x":-1, "y":-1, "z":-1
                },
        {
                "x":1, "y":-1, "z":-1
                },
        {
                "x":-1, "y":1, "z":-1
                },
                {
                        "x":1, "y":1, "z":-1
                }
        ],
        "triangles":[
                [0,1,2],
                [2,3,1],
                [4,5,6],
                [6,7,5]
        ]
}
```

 JSON is but one of many formats for storing 3D mesh data; many popular 3D modeling tools, such as the open source Blender (*http://www.blender.org/*), support it.

This mesh creates two parallel squares, as seen in Figure 9-1.

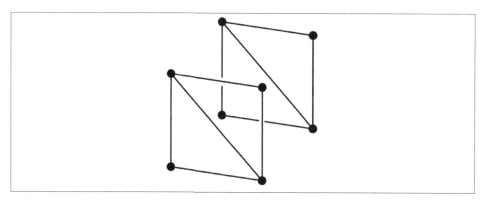

Figure 9-1. The mesh

Next, create a new subclass of NSObject, called Mesh. Put the following code in *Mesh.h*:

```
#import <GLKit/GLKit.h>
```

```
typedef struct {
    GLKVector3 position;
    GLKVector2 textureCoordinates;
    GLKVector3 normal;
} Vertex;

typedef struct {
    GLuint vertex1;
    GLuint vertex2;
    GLuint vertex3;
} Triangle;

@interface Mesh : NSObject

+ (Mesh*) meshWithContentsOfURL:(NSURL*)url error:(NSError**)error;

// The name of the OpenGL buffer containing vertex data
@property (readonly) GLuint vertexBuffer;

// The name of the OpenGL buffer containing the triangle list
@property (readonly) GLuint indexBuffer;

// A pointer to the loaded array of vector info
@property (readonly) Vertex* vertexData;

// The number of vertices
@property (readonly) NSUInteger vertexCount;

// A pointer to the triangle list data
@property (readonly) Triangle* triangleData;

// The number of triangles
@property (readonly) NSUInteger triangleCount;

@end
```

Next, put the following methods into *Mesh.m*. The first of these, meshWithContentsO fURL:error:, attempts to load an NSDictionary from disk, and then tries to create a new Mesh object with its contents:

```
+ (Mesh *)meshWithContentsOfURL:(NSURL *)url
error:(NSError *__autoreleasing *)error {

    // Load the JSON text into memory

    NSData* meshJSONData = [NSData dataWithContentsOfURL:url options:0
                            error:error];

    if (meshJSONData == nil)
        return nil;

    // Convert the text into an NSDictionary,
```

```
        // then check to see if it's actually a dictionary
        NSDictionary* meshInfo =
        [NSJSONSerialization JSONObjectWithData:meshJSONData options:0
         error:error];

        if ([meshInfo isKindOfClass:[NSDictionary class]] == NO)
            return nil;

        // Finally, attempt to create a mesh with this dictionary
        return [[Mesh alloc] initWithMeshDictionary:meshInfo];

    }
```

The next method, initWithMeshDictionary:, checks the contents of the provided
NSDictionary and loads the mesh information into memory. It then prepares OpenGL
buffers so that the mesh information can be rendered:

```
- (id)initWithMeshDictionary:(NSDictionary*)dictionary
{
    self = [super init];
    if (self) {

        // Get the arrays of vertices and triangles, and ensure they're arrays
        NSArray* loadedVertexDictionary = dictionary[@"vertices"];
        NSArray* loadedTriangleDictionary = dictionary[@"triangles"];

        if ([loadedVertexDictionary isKindOfClass:[NSArray class]] == NO) {
            NSLog(@"Expected 'vertices' to be an array");
            return nil;
        }

        if ([loadedTriangleDictionary isKindOfClass:[NSArray class]] == NO) {
            NSLog(@"Expected 'triangles' to be an array");
            return nil;
        }

        // Calculate how many vertices and triangles we have
        _vertexCount = loadedVertexDictionary.count;
        _triangleCount = loadedTriangleDictionary.count;

        // Allocate memory to store the vertices and triangles in
        _vertexData = calloc(sizeof(Vertex), _vertexCount);
        _triangleData = calloc(sizeof(Triangle), _triangleCount);

            if (_vertexData == NULL || _triangleData == NULL) {
            NSLog(@"Couldn't allocate memory!");
            return nil;
        }

        // For each vertex in the list, read information about it and store it
        for (int vertex = 0; vertex < _vertexCount; vertex++) {
```

```
NSDictionary* vertexInfo = loadedVertexDictionary[vertex];

if ([vertexInfo isKindOfClass:[NSDictionary class]] == NO) {
    NSLog(@"Vertex %i is not a dictionary", vertex);
    return nil;
}

// Store the vertex data in memory, at the correct position:

// Position:
_vertexData[vertex].position.x = [vertexInfo[@"x"] floatValue];
_vertexData[vertex].position.y = [vertexInfo[@"y"] floatValue];
_vertexData[vertex].position.z = [vertexInfo[@"z"] floatValue];

// Texture coordinates
_vertexData[vertex].textureCoordinates.s =
[vertexInfo[@"s"] floatValue];
_vertexData[vertex].textureCoordinates.t =
[vertexInfo[@"t"] floatValue];

// Normal
_vertexData[vertex].normal.x = [vertexInfo[@"nx"] floatValue];
_vertexData[vertex].normal.y = [vertexInfo[@"ny"] floatValue];
_vertexData[vertex].normal.z = [vertexInfo[@"nz"] floatValue];



}

// Next, for each triangle in the list, read information and store it
for (int triangle = 0; triangle < _triangleCount; triangle++) {
    NSArray* triangleInfo = loadedTriangleDictionary[triangle];

    if ([triangleInfo isKindOfClass:[NSArray class]] == NO) {
        NSLog(@"Triangle %i is not an array", triangle);
        return nil;
    }

    // Store the index of each referenced vertex
    _triangleData[triangle].vertex1 =
    [triangleInfo[0] unsignedIntegerValue];
    _triangleData[triangle].vertex2 =
    [triangleInfo[1] unsignedIntegerValue];
    _triangleData[triangle].vertex3 =
    [triangleInfo[2] unsignedIntegerValue];

    // Check to make sure that the vertices referred to exist

    if (_triangleData[triangle].vertex1 >= _vertexCount) {
        NSLog(@"Triangle %i refers to an unknown vertex %i", triangle,
                _triangleData[triangle].vertex1);
        return nil;
```

```
        }

        if (_triangleData[triangle].vertex2 >= _vertexCount) {
            NSLog(@"Triangle %i refers to an unknown vertex %i", triangle,
                _triangleData[triangle].vertex2);
            return nil;
        }

        if (_triangleData[triangle].vertex3 >= _vertexCount) {
            NSLog(@"Triangle %i refers to an unknown vertex %i", triangle,
                _triangleData[triangle].vertex3);
            return nil;
        }
    }

    // We've now loaded all of the data into memory. Time to create
    // buffers and give them to OpenGL!

    glGenBuffers(1, &_vertexBuffer);
    glGenBuffers(1, &_indexBuffer);

    glBindBuffer(GL_ARRAY_BUFFER, _vertexBuffer);
    glBufferData(GL_ARRAY_BUFFER, sizeof(Vertex) * _vertexCount, _vertexData,
            GL_STATIC_DRAW);

    glBindBuffer(GL_ELEMENT_ARRAY_BUFFER, _indexBuffer);
    glBufferData(GL_ELEMENT_ARRAY_BUFFER, sizeof(Triangle) * _triangleCount,
            _triangleData, GL_STATIC_DRAW);


    }
    return self;
}
```

The final method, `dealloc`, releases the resources that are created in the `init` method:

```
- (void)dealloc {
    // We're going away, so we need to tell OpenGL to get rid of the
    // data we uploaded
    glDeleteBuffers(1, &_vertexBuffer);
    glDeleteBuffers(1, &_indexBuffer);

    // Now free the memory that we allocated earlier
    free(_vertexData);
    free(_triangleData);
}
```

Discussion

In this solution, we're creating a `Mesh` object, which represents a loaded mesh. One of the advantages of this approach is that you can load a mesh once, and then reuse it multiple times.

At minimum, a mesh is a collection of vertices combined with information that links the vertices up into polygons. This means that when you load a mesh, you need to get the positions of every vertex, as well as information describing which vertices make up which polygons.

The specific format that you use to store your mesh on disk can be anything you like. In this solution, we went with JSON, since it's easy to read and write, and iOS has a built-in class designed for reading it. However, it's not the only format around, and not necessarily the best one for your uses. Other popular mesh formats include Wavefront OBJ, which is a text-based format, and Autodesk FBX, which is binary and supports a number of handy features like embedded animations and hierarchical meshes.

As we discussed in Recipe 8.3, to draw a mesh, you first need to load the information for its vertices and how the vertices are linked together into memory. The actual format for how this information is stored in memory is up to you, since you describe to OpenGL where to find the specific types of information that it needs.

When you load a mesh and give it to OpenGL to draw, you first allocate a chunk of memory, fill it with information, and then create an OpenGL buffer. You then tell OpenGL to fill the buffer with the information you've loaded. This happens twice: once for the vertices, and again for the list of indices that describe how the vertices are linked into triangles.

In this solution, the format for vertices is a structure that looks like this:

```
typedef struct {
    GLKVector3 position;
    GLKVector2 textureCoordinates;
} Vertex;
```

However, a mesh is almost always going to contain more than one vertex, and it isn't possible to know how many vertices you're going to be dealing with at compile time. To deal with this, the memory that contains the vertices needs to be *allocated*, using the calloc function. This function takes two parameters, the size of each of the pieces of memory you want to allocate and the number of pieces:

```
_vertexData = calloc(sizeof(Vertex), _vertexCount);
```

So, to create the memory space that contains the list of vertices, you need to know how big each vertex is, and how many vertices you need. To find out the size of any structure, you use the sizeof function, and to find out the number of vertices, you check the file that you're loading.

Once this memory has been allocated, you can work with it: for each vertex, you read information about it and fill in the data. The same process is done for the triangle list.

When you allocate memory using calloc (or any of its related methods, including malloc and realloc), you need to manually free it, using the free function. You do this in your `Mesh` object's `dealloc` method, which is called when the `Mesh` is in the process of being removed from memory.

 It's very important that any memory that you allocate using `calloc` or `malloc` gets freed with `free`. If you don't do this, you end up with a memory leak: memory that's been allocated but never freed and is never referred to again. Memory leaks waste memory, which is something you *really* don't want in the memory-constrained environment of iOS.

9.2. Parenting Objects

Problem

You want to attach objects to other objects, so that multiple animations can combine.

Solution

The code in this solution uses the component-based architecture discussed in Recipe 1.3, though the idea can also be applied to hierarchy-based architectures (see Recipe 1.2). In this solution, we'll be creating a `Transform` component.

Create a new class named `Transform`, and put the following contents in *Transform.h*:

```
@interface Transform : Component

@property (weak) Transform* parent;
@property (strong, readonly) NSSet* children;

- (void) addChild:(Transform*)child;
- (void) removeChild:(Transform*)child;

// Position relative to parent
@property (assign) GLKVector3 localPosition;

// Rotation angles relative to parent, in radians
@property (assign) GLKVector3 localRotation;

// Scale relative to parent
@property (assign) GLKVector3 localScale;

// The matrix that maps local coordinates to world coordinates
@property (readonly) GLKMatrix4 localToWorldMatrix;

// Vectors relative to us
@property (readonly) GLKVector3 up;
@property (readonly) GLKVector3 forward;
@property (readonly) GLKVector3 left;
```

```
// Position in world space
@property (readonly) GLKVector3 position;

// Rotation in world space
@property (readonly) GLKQuaternion rotation;

// Scale, taking into account parent object's scale
@property (readonly) GLKVector3 scale;

@end
```

And in *Transform.m*:

```
#import "Transform.h"

@interface Transform () {
    NSMutableSet* _children;
}

@end

@implementation Transform

@dynamic position;
@dynamic rotation;
@dynamic scale;

@dynamic up;
@dynamic left;
@dynamic forward;

- (id)init
{
    self = [super init];
    if (self) {
        // The list of children
        _children = [NSMutableSet set];

        // By default, we're scaled to 1 on all 3 axes
        _localScale = GLKVector3Make(1, 1, 1);
    }
    return self;
}

// Add a transform as a child of us
- (void)addChild:(Transform *)child {
    [_children addObject:child];
    child.parent = self;
}

// Remove a transform from the list of children
- (void)removeChild:(Transform *)child {
```

```
        [_children removeObject:child];
        child.parent = nil;
}

// Rotate a vector by our local axes
- (GLKVector3)rotateVector:(GLKVector3)vector {
    GLKMatrix4 matrix = GLKMatrix4Identity;
    matrix = GLKMatrix4RotateX(matrix, self.localRotation.x);
    matrix = GLKMatrix4RotateY(matrix, self.localRotation.y);
    matrix = GLKMatrix4RotateZ(matrix, self.localRotation.z);

    return GLKMatrix4MultiplyVector3(matrix, vector);
}

- (GLKVector3)up {
    return [self rotateVector:GLKVector3Make(0, 1, 0)];
}

- (GLKVector3)forward {
    return [self rotateVector:GLKVector3Make(0, 0, 1)];
}

- (GLKVector3)left {
    return [self rotateVector:GLKVector3Make(1, 0, 0)];
}

// Create a matrix that represents our position, rotation, and scale in
// world space
- (GLKMatrix4)localToWorldMatrix {

    // First, get the identity matrix
    GLKMatrix4 matrix = GLKMatrix4Identity;

    // Next, get the matrix of our parent
    if (self.parent)
        matrix = GLKMatrix4Multiply(matrix, self.parent.localToWorldMatrix);

    // Translate it
    matrix = GLKMatrix4TranslateWithVector3(matrix, self.localPosition);

    // Rotate it
    matrix = GLKMatrix4RotateX(matrix, self.localRotation.x);
    matrix = GLKMatrix4RotateY(matrix, self.localRotation.y);
    matrix = GLKMatrix4RotateZ(matrix, self.localRotation.z);

    // And scale it!
    matrix = GLKMatrix4ScaleWithVector3(matrix, self.localScale);

    return matrix;
}

// Get a quaternion that describes our orientation in world space
```

```
- (GLKQuaternion)rotation {

    // First, get the identity quaternion (i.e. no rotation)
    GLKQuaternion rotation = GLKQuaternionIdentity;

    // Now, multiply this rotation with its parent, if it has one
    if (self.parent)
        rotation = GLKQuaternionMultiply(rotation, self.parent.rotation);

    // Finally, rotate around our local axes
    GLKQuaternion xRotation = GLKQuaternionMakeWithAngleAndVector3Axis(
        self.localRotation.x, GLKVector3Make(1, 0, 0));
    GLKQuaternion yRotation = GLKQuaternionMakeWithAngleAndVector3Axis(
        self.localRotation.y, GLKVector3Make(0, 1, 0));
    GLKQuaternion zRotation = GLKQuaternionMakeWithAngleAndVector3Axis(
        self.localRotation.z, GLKVector3Make(0, 0, 1));

    rotation = GLKQuaternionMultiply(rotation, xRotation);
    rotation = GLKQuaternionMultiply(rotation, yRotation);
    rotation = GLKQuaternionMultiply(rotation, zRotation);

    return rotation;

}


// Get our position in world space
- (GLKVector3)position {
    GLKVector3 position = self.localPosition;

    if (self.parent)
        position = GLKVector3Add(position, self.parent.position);

    return position;
}

// Get our scale in world space
- (GLKVector3)scale {
    GLKVector3 scale = self.localScale;

    if (self.parent)
        scale = GLKVector3Multiply(scale, self.parent.scale);

    return scale;
}
```

To get the model-view matrix for an object at a given position, you just ask for its localToWorldMatrix, which you can then provide to a GLKBaseEffect's trans form.modelViewMatrix property.

Discussion

It's often the case that you'll have an object (called the "child" object) that needs to be attached to another object (called the "parent"), such that when the parent moves, the child moves with it. You can make this happen by allowing objects to keep a reference to their parent and use the position, orientation, and scale of the parent when calculating their own position, orientation, and scale:

```
my world position = parent's position + my local position
my world rotation = parent's rotation + my local rotation
my world scale = parent's scale + my local scale
```

When you do this, you can have a long chain of parents: one can be the parent of another, which can be the parent of yet another, and so on.

The easiest way to represent this is by making each object calculate a matrix, which is a single value that represents the *transform* of an object (i.e., the position, rotation, and scale of the object). Matrices are useful, both because a single matrix represents all three operations and because matrices can be combined. So, if you get the transform matrix of the parent and multiply that by your own transform matrix, you end up with a matrix that combines the two.

It just so happens that a transform matrix is exactly what's needed when you render a mesh: the model-view matrix, which converts the coordinates of vertices in a mesh to world space, *is* a transform matrix.

9.3. Animating a Mesh

Problem

You want to animate objects by moving them over time.

Solution

The code in this solution uses the component-based architecture discussed in Recipe 1.3, though the idea can also be applied to hierarchy-based architectures (see Recipe 1.2). In this solution, we'll be creating an Animation component.

Add a new class called Animation, and put the following contents in *Animation.h*:

```
#import "Component.h"
#import <GLKit/GLKit.h>

// Animates a property on "object"; t is between 0 and 1
typedef void (^AnimationBlock)(GameObject* object, float t);

@interface Animation : Component
```

```
@property (assign) float duration;

- (void) startAnimating;
- (void) stopAnimating;

- (id) initWithAnimationBlock:(AnimationBlock)animationBlock;

@end
```

And in *Animation.m*:

```
#import "Animation.h"

@implementation Animation {
    AnimationBlock _animationBlock;

    float _timeElapsed;

    BOOL _playing;

}

- (void)startAnimating {
    _timeElapsed = 0;
    _playing = YES;
}

- (void)stopAnimating {
    _playing = NO;
}

- (void) update:(float)deltaTime {

    // Don't do anything if we're not playing
    if (_playing == NO)
        return;

    // Don't do anything if the duration is zero or less
    if (self.duration <= 0)
        return;

    // Increase the amount of time that this animation's been running for
    _timeElapsed += deltaTime;

    // Go back to the start when time elapsed > duration
    if (_timeElapsed > self.duration)
        _timeElapsed = 0;

    // Dividing the time elapsed by the duration returns a value between 0 and 1
    float t = _timeElapsed / self.duration;

    // Finally, call the animation block
    if (_animationBlock) {
```

```
            _animationBlock(self.gameObject, t);
        }
    }

    - (id)initWithAnimationBlock:(AnimationBlock)animationBlock
    {

        self = [super init];
        if (self) {
            _animationBlock = animationBlock;
            _duration = 2.5;
        }
        return self;
    }

    @end
```

To use the animation component, you create one and provide a block that performs an animation:

```
GameObject* myObject = ... // a GameObject

// Create an animation that rotates around the y-axis
Animation* rotate =
[[Animation alloc] initWithAnimationBlock:^(GameObject *object, float t) {
    float angle = 2*M_PI*t;

    object.transform.localRotation = GLKVector3Make(0, angle, 0);
}];

// The animation takes 10 seconds to complete
rotate.duration = 10;

// Add the animation to the object
[myObject addComponent:rotate];

// Kick off the animation
[rotate startAnimating];
```

Discussion

An animation is a change in value over time. When you animate an object's position, you're changing the position from a starting point to the ending point.

An animation can take as long as you want to complete, but it's often very helpful to think of the animation's time scale as going from 0 (animation start) to 1 (animation end). This means that the animation's duration can be kept separate from the animation itself.

You can use this value as part of an *easing equation*, which smoothly animates a value over time.

If t is limited to the range of 0 to 1, you can write the equation for a linear progression from value v1 to value v2 like this:

```
result = v1 + (v2 - v1) * t;
```

Imagine that you want to animate the *x* coordinate of an object from 1 to 5. If you plot this position on a graph, where the y-axis is the position of the object and the x-axis is time going from 0 to 1, the coordinates looks like Table 9-1.

Table 9-1. Plot points to animate x

Position	t
1	0.00
2	0.25
3	0.50
4	0.75
5	1.00

This equation moves smoothly from the first value to the second, and maintains the same speed the entire way.

There are other equations that you can use:

```
// Ease-in - starts slow, reaches full speed by the end
result = v1 + (v2 - v1) * pow(t,2);

// Ease-out - starts at full speed, slows down toward the end
result = v1 + (v1 - v2) * t * (t-2)
```

You can also create more complex animations by combining multiple animations, using parenting (see Recipe 9.2).

9.4. Batching Draw Calls

Problem

You have a number of objects, all of which have the same texture, and you want to improve rendering performance.

Solution

This solution uses the Mesh class discussed in Recipe 9.1.

If you have a large number of objects that can be rendered with the same GLKEffect (but with varying positions and orientations), create a new vertex buffer and, for each copy of the object, copy each vertex into the buffer.

For each vertex you copy in, multiply the vertex by the object's transform matrix (see Recipe 9.2). Next, create an index buffer and copy each triangle from each object into it. (Because they're triangles, they don't get transformed.)

When you render the contents of these buffers, all copies of the object will be rendered at the same time.

Discussion

The glDrawElements function is the slowest function involved in OpenGL. When you call it, you kick off a large number of complicated graphics operations: data is fetched from the buffers, vertices are transformed, shaders are run, and pixels are written into the frame buffer. The more frequently you call glDrawElements, the more work needs to happen, and as discussed in Recipe 14.1, the more work you do, the lower your frame rate's going to be.

To reduce the number of calls to glDrawElements and improve performance, it's better to group objects together and render them at the same time. If you have a hundred crates, instead of drawing a crate 100 times, you draw 100 crates once.

There are a couple of limitations when you use this technique, though:

- All objects have to use the same texture and lights, because they're all being drawn at the same time.
- More space in memory gets taken up, because you have to store a duplicate set of vertices for each copy of the object.
- If any of the objects are moving around, you have to dynamically create a new buffer and fill it with vertex data every frame, instead of creating a buffer once and reusing it.

9.5. Creating a Movable Camera Object

Problem

You want your camera to be an object that can be moved around the scene like other objects.

Solution

This solution builds on the component-based architecure discussed in Recipe 1.3 and uses the Transform component from Recipe 9.2.

Create a new subclass of Component called Camera, and put the following contents in *Camera.h*:

```
#import "Component.h"
#import <GLKit/GLKit.h>

@interface Camera : Component

// Return a matrix that maps world space to view space
- (GLKMatrix4) viewMatrix;

// Return a matrix that maps view space to eye space
- (GLKMatrix4) projectionMatrix;

// Field of view, in radians
@property (assign) float fieldOfView;

// Near clipping plane, in units
@property (assign) float nearClippingPlane;

// Far clipping plane, in units
@property (assign) float farClippingPlane;

// Clear screen contents and get ready to draw
- (void) prepareToDraw;

// The color to erase the screen with
@property (assign) GLKVector4 clearColor;

@end
```

And in *Camera.m*:

```
#import "Camera.h"
#import "Transform.h"
#import "GameObject.h"

@implementation Camera

// By default, start with a clear color of black (RBGA 1,1,1,0)
- (id)init
{
    self = [super init];
    if (self) {
        self.clearColor = GLKVector4Make(0.0, 0.0, 0.0, 1.0);
    }
    return self;
}

- (void) prepareToDraw {
    // Clear the contents of the screen
    glClearColor(self.clearColor.r, self.clearColor.g, self.clearColor.b,
                 self.clearColor.a);
```

```
        glClear(GL_COLOR_BUFFER_BIT | GL_DEPTH_BUFFER_BIT);
    }

    // Return a matrix that maps world space to view space
    - (GLKMatrix4)viewMatrix {

        Transform* transform = self.gameObject.transform;

        // The camera's position is its transform's position in world space
        GLKVector3 position = transform.position;

        // The camera's target is right in front of it
        GLKVector3 target = GLKVector3Add(position, transform.forward);

        // The camera's up direction is the transform's up direction
        GLKVector3 up = transform.up;

        return GLKMatrix4MakeLookAt(position.x, position.y, position.z,
                                    target.x, target.y, target.z,
                                    up.x, up.y, up.z);

    }

    // Return a matrix that maps view space to eye space
    - (GLKMatrix4)projectionMatrix {

        // We'll assume that the camera is always rendering into the entire screen
        // (i.e., it's never rendering to just a subsection if it).
        // This means the aspect ratio of the camera is the screen's aspect ratio.

        float aspectRatio = [UIScreen mainScreen].bounds.size.width /
                            [UIScreen mainScreen].bounds.size.height;

        return GLKMatrix4MakePerspective(self.fieldOfView, aspectRatio,
                                         self.nearClippingPlane,
                                         self.farClippingPlane);
    }

    @end
```

Discussion

The idea of a "camera" in OpenGL is kind of the reverse of how people normally think of viewing a scene. While it's easy to think of a camera that moves around in space, looking at objects, what's really going on in OpenGL is that objects get rearranged to be in front of the viewer. That is, when the camera "moves forward," what's really happening is that objects are moving closer to the camera.

When objects in your 3D scene are rendered, they get transformed through a variety of *coordinate spaces*. The first space that vertices begin in is *model space*, where all vertices are defined relative to the point of the model. Because we don't want all the meshes to be drawn on top of one another, they need to be transformed into *world space*, in which all vertices are defined relative to the origin point of the world.

Once they're in world space, they need to be rearranged such that they're in front of the camera. This is done by calculating a view matrix, which you do by taking the position of the camera in world space, the position of a point it should be looking toward, and a vector defining which direction is "up" for the camera, and calling `GLKMatrix4Make LookAt`.

The view matrix rearranges vertices so that the camera's position is at the center of the coordinate space, and arranges things so that the camera's "up" and "forward" directions become coordinate space's y- and z-axes.

So, when you "position" a camera, what you're really doing is preparing a matrix that arranges your vertices in a way that puts the camera in the center, with everything else arranged around it.

CHAPTER 10

Advanced 3D Graphics

OpenGL provides a huge amount of flexibility in how objects get rendered, and you can do all kinds of interesting things with light and material. In this chapter, we're going to look at *shaders*, which are small programs that give you complete control over how OpenGL should draw your 3D scene. We'll look at lighting, texturing, bump-mapping, and non-photorealistic rendering.

This chapter builds on beginning and intermediate concepts covered in Chapters 8 and 9, respectively.

10.1. Understanding Shaders

Problem

You want to create shader programs, which control how objects are drawn onscreen, so that you can create different kinds of materials.

Solution

A shader is comprised of three elements: a *vertex shader*, a *fragment shader*, and a *shader program* that links the vertex and fragment shaders together. To make a shader, you first write the vertex and fragment shaders, then load them in to OpenGL, and then tell OpenGL when you want to use them.

First, create the vertex shader. Create a file called *SimpleVertexShader.vsh*, and add it to your project:

```
uniform mat4 modelViewMatrix;
uniform mat4 projectionMatrix;

attribute vec3 position;
```

```
void main()
{

    // "position" is in model space. We need to convert it to camera space by
    // multiplying it by the modelViewProjection matrix.
    gl_Position = (projectionMatrix* modelViewMatrix) * vec4(position,1.0);
}
```

 When you drag and drop the file into your project, Xcode won't add it to the list of files that get copied into the app's resources. Instead, it will add it to the list of files that should be compiled. You don't want this.

To fix it, open the project build phases by clicking on the project at the top of the Project Navigator and clicking Build Phases, and move the file from the Compile Sources to the Copy Bundle Resources list, by dragging and dropping it.

Next, create the fragment shader by creating a file called *SimpleFragmentShader.fsh*, and putting the following code in it:

```
void main()
{
    // All pixels in this object will be pure red
    gl_FragColor = vec4(1.0, 0.0, 0.0, 1.0);
}
```

Finally, provide your shader code to OpenGL. You do this by first creating two shaders, using the glCreateShader function. You then give each shader its source code using the glShaderSource function, and then compile the shader with the glCompileShad er function. This needs to be done twice, once for each of the two shaders. Note that you'll need to keep the GLuint variable around in your Objective-C code (not the shader code):

```
// Keep this variable around as an instance variable
GLuint _shaderProgram;

// Compile the vertex shader
NSString* vertexSource = ... // an NSString containing the source code of your
                             // vertex shader. Load this string from a file.
GLuint _vertexShader = glCreateShader(GL_VERTEX_SHADER);
const char* vertexShaderSourceString =
[vertexSource cStringUsingEncoding:NSUTF8StringEncoding];
glShaderSource(_vertexShader, 1, &vertexShaderSourceString, NULL);
glCompileShader(_vertexShader);

// Compile the fragment shader
NSString* fragmentSource = ... // contains the fragment shader's source code
GLuint _fragmentShader = glCreateShader(GL_FRAGMENT_SHADER);
const char* fragmentShaderSourceString =
```

```
[fragmentSource cStringUsingEncoding:NSUTF8StringEncoding];

glShaderSource(_fragmentShader, 1, &fragmentShaderSourceString, NULL);
glCompileShader(_fragmentShader);
```

After you give the shader source to OpenGL, you then need to check to see if there were any errors. You do this by creating a variable called success and giving its address to the glGetShaderiv function, asking it for the shader's compile status. After the function returns, success will contain a 1 if it succeeded, and a 0 if it didn't. If a shader didn't succeed, you can get information on what went wrong using the glGetShaderInfo Log function:

```
// Check to see if both shaders compiled
int success;

// Check the vertex shader
glGetShaderiv(_vertexShader, GL_COMPILE_STATUS, &success);
if (success == 0) {
    char errorLog[1024];
    glGetShaderInfoLog(_vertexShader, sizeof(errorLog), NULL, errorLog);}
    NSLog(@"Error: %s");
    return;
}

glGetShaderiv(_fragmentShader, GL_COMPILE_STATUS, &success);
if (success == 0) {
    char errorLog[1024];
    glGetShaderInfoLog(_fragmentShader, sizeof(errorLog), NULL, errorLog);}
    NSLog(@"Error: %s");
    return;
}
```

Once the shaders have been checked, you then create the shader program, which links the shaders together. You do this with the glCreateProgram function, and then attach the two shaders with the glAttachShader function:

```
_shaderProgram = glCreateProgram();
glAttachShader(_shaderProgram, _vertexShader);
glAttachShader(_shaderProgram, _fragmentShader);
```

Next, we need to tell OpenGL how we want to pass information to the shader. We do this by creating a variable and setting it to 1, and then instructing OpenGL that we want to refer to a specific shader variable by this number. When you have multiple variables in a shader that you want to work with this way, you create another variable and set it to 2, and so on:

```
const MaterialAttributePosition = 1;

// Tell OpenGL that we want to refer to the "position" variable by the number 1
glBindAttribLocation(_shaderProgram, MaterialAttributePosition, "position");
```

Once the program is appropriately configured, you tell OpenGL to link the program. Once it's linked, you can check to see if there were any problems, in much the same way as when you compiled the individual shaders:

```
glLinkProgram(_shaderProgram);

int success;
glGetProgramiv(program, GL_LINK_STATUS, &success);
if (success == 0) {
    char errorLog[1024];
    glGetProgramInfoLog(program, sizeof(errorLog), NULL, errorLog);
    NSLog(@"Error: %s", errorLog);
    return;
}
```

This completes the setup process for the shader program. When you want to render using the program, you first tell OpenGL you want to use the program by calling glUseProgram, and pass information to the shader using the glVertexAttribPointer function. When glDrawElements is called, the shader will be used to draw the objects:

```
glUseProgram(_shaderProgram);

glEnableVertexAttribArray(MaterialAttributePosition);
glVertexAttribPointer(MaterialAttributePosition, 3, GL_FLOAT, GL_FALSE,
                      sizeof(Vertex), (void*)offsetof(Vertex, position));

glDrawElements(GL_TRIANGLES, self.mesh.triangleCount * 3, GL_UNSIGNED_INT, 0);
```

Discussion

A shader program gives you a vast amount of control over how objects are rendered by OpenGL. Prior to OpenGL ES 2.0 (which became available in iOS 3 on the iPhone 3GS), the only way you could draw graphics was using the built-in functions available on the graphics chip. While these were useful, they didn't allow programmers to create their own custom rendering effects. Shaders let you do that.

Shaders are small programs that run on the graphics chip. Vertex shaders receive the vertex information provided by your code, and are responsible for transforming the vertices from object space into screen space.

Once each vertex has been transformed, the graphics chip determines which pixels on the screen need to have color drawn into them, which is a process called *rasterization*. Once rasterization is complete, the graphics chip then runs the shader program for each pixel to determine exactly what color needs to be shown.

Even though shaders appear to have very limited responsibilities, they have tremendous amounts of power. It's up to shaders to apply effects like lighting, cartoon effects, bump mapping, and more.

10.2. Working with Materials

Problem

You want to separate the appearance of an object from its geometry.

Solution

This solution makes use of the component architecture discussed in Recipe 1.3 and elaborated on in Chapter 9. In this solution, we're going to create a Material class, which loads shaders and keeps material information separate from mesh information.

Create a new class called Material, which is a subclass of GLKBaseEffect. Put the following code in *Material.h*:

```
enum MaterialAttributes {
    MaterialAttributePosition,
    MaterialAttributeNormal,
    MaterialAttributeColor,
    MaterialAttributeTextureCoordinates
};

@interface Material : GLKBaseEffect <GLKNamedEffect>

+ (Material*)effectWithVertexShaderNamed:(NSString*)vertexShaderName
fragmentShaderNamed:(NSString*)fragmentShaderName error:(NSError**)error;

- (void) prepareToDraw;

@end
```

Now, put the following code in *Material.m*. We're going to show one method at a time, because this file is kind of big. First, the instance variables. These store information about the shader, including where to find various variables. Not all of the variables will be used at the same time:

```
@interface Material () {
    // References to the shaders and the program
    GLuint _vertexShader;
    GLuint _fragmentShader;
    GLuint _shaderProgram;

    // Uniform locations:

    // Matrices, for converting points into different coordinate spaces
    GLuint _modelViewMatrixLocation;
    GLuint _projectionMatrixLocation;
    GLuint _normalMatrixLocation;

    // Textures, for getting texture info
```

```
    GLuint _texture0Location;
    GLuint _texture1Location;

    // Light information
    GLuint _lightPositionLocation;
    GLuint _lightColorLocation;
    GLuint _ambientLightColorLocation;
}

// Where to find the shader files
@property (strong) NSURL* vertexShaderURL;
@property (strong) NSURL* fragmentShaderURL;

@end
```

Next, add the methods that create the `Material` objects:

```
// Create a material by looking for a pair of named shaders
+ (Material*)effectWithVertexShaderNamed:(NSString*)vertexShaderName
fragmentShaderNamed:(NSString*)fragmentShaderName error:(NSError**)error {

    NSURL* fragmentShaderURL =
    [[NSBundle mainBundle] URLForResource:fragmentShaderName
                                          withExtension:@"fsh"];
    NSURL* vertexShaderURL =
    [[NSBundle mainBundle] URLForResource:vertexShaderName withExtension:@"vsh"];

    return [Material effectWithVertexShader:vertexShaderURL
    fragmentShader:fragmentShaderURL error:error];
}

// Create a material by loading shaders from the provided URLs.
// Return nil if the shaders can't be loaded.
+ (Material*)effectWithVertexShader:(NSURL *)vertexShaderURL
fragmentShader:(NSURL *)fragmentShaderURL error:(NSError**)error {

    Material* material = [[Material alloc] init];
    material.vertexShaderURL = vertexShaderURL;
    material.fragmentShaderURL = fragmentShaderURL;

    if ([material prepareShaderProgramWithError:error] == NO)
        return nil;

    return material;

}
```

Then, add the method that loads and prepares the shaders:

```
// Load and prepare the shaders. Returns YES if it succeeded, or NO otherwise.
- (BOOL)prepareShaderProgramWithError:(NSError**)error {

    // Load the source code for the vertex and fragment shaders
```

```
NSString* vertexShaderSource =
[NSString stringWithContentsOfURL:self.vertexShaderURL
encoding:NSUTF8StringEncoding error:error];
if (vertexShaderSource == nil)
    return NO;

NSString* fragmentShaderSource =
[NSString stringWithContentsOfURL:self.fragmentShaderURL
encoding:NSUTF8StringEncoding error:error];
if (fragmentShaderSource == nil)
    return NO;

// Create and compile the vertex shader
_vertexShader = glCreateShader(GL_VERTEX_SHADER);
const char* vertexShaderSourceString =
[vertexShaderSource cStringUsingEncoding:NSUTF8StringEncoding];

glShaderSource(_vertexShader, 1, &vertexShaderSourceString, NULL);
glCompileShader(_vertexShader);

if ([self shaderIsCompiled:_vertexShader error:error] == NO)
    return NO;

// Create and compile the fragment shader
_fragmentShader = glCreateShader(GL_FRAGMENT_SHADER);
const char* fragmentShaderSourceString =
[fragmentShaderSource cStringUsingEncoding:NSUTF8StringEncoding];

glShaderSource(_fragmentShader, 1, &fragmentShaderSourceString, NULL);
glCompileShader(_fragmentShader);

if ([self shaderIsCompiled:_fragmentShader error:error] == NO)
    return NO;

// Both of the shaders are now compiled, so we can link them together and
// form a program
_shaderProgram = glCreateProgram();
glAttachShader(_shaderProgram, _vertexShader);
glAttachShader(_shaderProgram, _fragmentShader);

// First, we tell OpenGL what index numbers we want to use to refer to
// the various attributes. This allows us to tell OpenGL about where
// to find vertex attribute data.
glBindAttribLocation(_shaderProgram, MaterialAttributePosition, "position");
glBindAttribLocation(_shaderProgram, MaterialAttributeColor, "color");
glBindAttribLocation(_shaderProgram, MaterialAttributeNormal, "normal");
glBindAttribLocation(_shaderProgram, MaterialAttributeTextureCoordinates,
                     "texcoords");

// Now that we've told OpenGL how we want to refer to each attribute,
// we link the program
glLinkProgram(_shaderProgram);
```

```
        if ([self programIsLinked:_shaderProgram error:error] == NO)
            return NO;

        // Get the locations of the uniforms
        _modelViewMatrixLocation =
        glGetUniformLocation(_shaderProgram, "modelViewMatrix");
        _projectionMatrixLocation =
        glGetUniformLocation(_shaderProgram, "projectionMatrix");
        _normalMatrixLocation = glGetUniformLocation(_shaderProgram, "normalMatrix");

        _texture0Location = glGetUniformLocation(_shaderProgram, "texture0");
        _texture1Location = glGetUniformLocation(_shaderProgram, "texture1");

        _lightPositionLocation =
        glGetUniformLocation(_shaderProgram, "lightPosition");
        _lightColorLocation = glGetUniformLocation(_shaderProgram, "lightColor");
        _ambientLightColorLocation =
        glGetUniformLocation(_shaderProgram, "ambientLightColor");

        return YES;

    }
```

This method calls a pair of error-checking methods, which check to see if the shaders and program have been correctly prepared. Add them next:

```
    // Return YES if the shader compiled correctly, NO if it didn't
    // (and put an NSError in "error")
    - (BOOL)shaderIsCompiled:(GLuint)shader error:(NSError**)error {

        // Ask OpenGL if the shader compiled correctly
        int success;
        glGetShaderiv(shader, GL_COMPILE_STATUS, &success);

        // If not, find out why and send back an NSError object
        if (success == 0) {

            if (error != nil) {
                char errorLog[1024];
                glGetShaderInfoLog(shader, sizeof(errorLog), NULL, errorLog);
                NSString* errorString = [NSString stringWithCString:errorLog
                                        encoding:NSUTF8StringEncoding];

                *error = [NSError errorWithDomain:@"Material"
                code:NSFileReadCorruptFileError userInfo:@{@"Log":errorString}];
            }

            return NO;
        }

        return YES;
    }
```

```
// Return YES if the program linked successfully, NO if it didn't
// (and put an NSError in "error")
- (BOOL) programIsLinked:(GLuint)program error:(NSError**)error {

    // Ask OpenGL if the program has been successfully linked
    int success;
    glGetProgramiv(program, GL_LINK_STATUS, &success);

    // If not, find out why and send back an NSError
    if (success == 0) {
        if (error != nil) {
            char errorLog[1024];
            glGetProgramInfoLog(program, sizeof(errorLog), NULL, errorLog);
            NSString* errorString = [NSString stringWithCString:errorLog
                                    encoding:NSUTF8StringEncoding];

            *error = [NSError errorWithDomain:@"Material"
            code:NSFileReadCorruptFileError
            userInfo:@{NSUnderlyingErrorKey:errorString}];
        }
        return NO;
    }

    return YES;
}
```

The next step is to write the `prepareToDraw` method, which is called immediately before drawing takes place and tells OpenGL that the next drawing operation should use the shaders controlled by this `Material`:

```
// Called when the shader is about to be used
- (void)prepareToDraw {
    // Select the program
    glUseProgram(_shaderProgram);

    // Give the model-view matrix to the shader
    glUniformMatrix4fv(_modelViewMatrixLocation, 1, GL_FALSE,
    self.transform.modelviewMatrix.m);

    // Also give the projection matrix
    glUniformMatrix4fv(_projectionMatrixLocation, 1, GL_FALSE,
    self.transform.projectionMatrix.m);

    // Provide the normal matrix to the shader, too
    glUniformMatrix3fv(_normalMatrixLocation, 1, GL_FALSE,
    self.transform.normalMatrix.m);

    // If texture 0 is enabled, tell the shader where to find it
    if (self.texture2d0.enabled) {
        // "OpenGL, I'm now talking about texture 0."
        glActiveTexture(GL_TEXTURE0);
```

```
    // "Make texture 0 use the texture data that's referred to by
    // self.texture2d0.name."
    glBindTexture(GL_TEXTURE_2D, self.texture2d0.name);
    // "Finally, tell the shader that the uniform variable "texture0"
    // refers to texture 0.
    glUniform1i(_texture0Location, 0);
}

// Likewise with texture 1
if (self.texture2d1.enabled) {
    glActiveTexture(GL_TEXTURE1);
    glBindTexture(GL_TEXTURE_2D, self.texture2d1.name);
    glUniform1i(_texture1Location, 1);
}

// Pass light information into the shader, if it's enabled
if (self.light0.enabled) {
    glUniform3fv(_lightPositionLocation, 1, self.light0.position.v);
    glUniform4fv(_lightColorLocation, 1, self.light0.diffuseColor.v);
    glUniform4fv(_ambientLightColorLocation, 1,
                 self.lightModelAmbientColor.v);
}

// With this set, fragments with an alpha of less than 1 will be
// semitransparent
glEnable(GL_BLEND);
glBlendFunc(GL_SRC_ALPHA, GL_ONE_MINUS_SRC_ALPHA);
glBlendEquation(GL_ADD);

}
```

Finally, add the `dealloc` method, which deletes the shaders and the shader program when the `Material` object is being freed:

```
// Delete the program and shaders, to free up resources
- (void)dealloc {
    glDeleteProgram(_shaderProgram);
    glDeleteShader(_fragmentShader);
    glDeleteShader(_vertexShader);
}
```

To use a `Material` object, you first create one using the `effectWithVertexShader Named:fragmentShaderNamed:error:` method, by passing in the names of the shaders you want to use:

```
NSError* error = nil;
Material* material = [Material effectWithVertexShaderNamed:@"MyVertexShader"
fragmentShaderNamed:@"MyFragmentShader" error:&error];

if (material == nil) {
    NSLog(@"Couldn't create the material: %@", error);
    return nil;
}
```

When you're about to draw using the `Material`, you provide vertex attributes in the same way as when you're using a `GLKBaseEffect`, with a single difference—you use `MaterialAttributePosition` instead of `GLKVertexAttribPosition`, and so on for the other attributes:

```
[material prepareToDraw];

glEnableVertexAttribArray(MaterialAttributePosition);
glVertexAttribPointer(MaterialAttributePosition, 3, GL_FLOAT, GL_FALSE,
                      sizeof(Vertex), (void*)offsetof(Vertex, position));

glDrawElements(GL_TRIANGLES, self.mesh.triangleCount * 3, GL_UNSIGNED_INT, 0);
```

 "Material" is basically just a a fancy word for a collection of properties and shaders.

Discussion

A `Material` object is useful for acting as a container for your shaders. As a subclass of `GLKBaseEffect`, your `Material` class is easily able to store material information like light color and where to find transforms.

The `Material` class presented here actually has *fewer* features than `GLKBaseEffect`, but it gives you more control. `GLKBaseEffect` works by dynamically creating shaders based on the parameters you supply, which means that you can't take the base effect and add stuff on top. If you want to do more advanced rendering, you have to do it yourself—which means, among other things, writing your own shaders.

10.3. Texturing with Shaders

Problem

You want to apply textures to your objects, using shaders you've written.

Solution

Write a fragment shader that looks like this:

```
varying lowp vec4 vertex_color;
varying lowp vec2 vertex_texcoords;

uniform sampler2D texture0;

void main()
```

```
    {
        gl_FragColor = texture2D(texture0, vertex_texcoords) * vertex_color;
    }
```

Discussion

A `sampler2D` is an object that lets you get access to texture information provided by your app. When you call the `texture2D` function and pass in the sampler and the texture coordinates you want to sample, you get back a four-dimensional vector that contains the red, green, blue, and alpha components at that point in the texture.

By multiplying this color with the vertex color, you can then tint the texture.

Finally, the result is then assigned to `gl_FragColor`, which means that OpenGL uses that color for the pixel.

10.4. Lighting a Scene

Problem

You want your objects to appear lit by light sources.

Solution

In this solution, we'll cover *point lights*, which are lights that exist at a single point in space and radiate light in all directions.

To work with lights, your mesh needs to have *normals*. A normal is a vector that indicates the direction that a vertex is facing, which is necessary for calculating the angle at which light is going to bounce off the surface.

If you're using the `Mesh` class described in Recipe 9.1, you can add normals (`"nx":0, "ny":0, "nz":1` in the following example) to your mesh by adding additional info to your vertices:

```
    {
        "x":-1, "y":-1, "z":1,
        "r":1, "g":0, "b":0,
        "s":0, "t":1,
        "nx":0, "ny":0, "nz":1
    },
```

Next, use this vertex shader:

```
    uniform mediump mat4 modelViewMatrix;
    uniform mediump mat4 projectionMatrix;
    uniform mediump mat3 normalMatrix;

    attribute vec3 position;
```

```
attribute vec4 color;
attribute vec3 normal;
attribute vec2 texcoords;

varying mediump vec4 vertex_position;
varying mediump vec4 vertex_color;
varying mediump vec2 vertex_texcoords;
varying mediump vec4 vertex_normal;


void main()
{

    // "position" is in model space. We need to convert it to camera space by
    // multiplying it by the modelViewProjection matrix.
    gl_Position = (projectionMatrix* modelViewMatrix) * vec4(position,1.0);

    // Pass the color and position of the vertex in world space to the
    // fragment shader
    vertex_color = color;
    vertex_position = modelViewMatrix * vec4(position, 1.0);

    // Also pass the normal and the texture coordinates to the fragment shader
    vertex_normal = vec4(normal, 0.0);
    vertex_texcoords = texcoords;

}
```

Finally, use this fragment shader:

```
uniform mediump mat4 modelViewMatrix;
uniform mediump mat3 normalMatrix;

varying mediump vec4 vertex_color;
varying mediump vec2 vertex_texcoords;
varying mediump vec4 vertex_normal;
varying mediump vec4 vertex_position;

uniform sampler2D texture0;

uniform lowp vec3 lightPosition;
uniform lowp vec4 lightColor;
uniform lowp vec4 ambientLightColor;

void main()
{

    // Get the normal supplied by the vertex shader
    mediump vec3 normal = vec3(normalize(vertex_normal));

    // Convert the normal from object space to world space
    normal = normalMatrix * normal;
```

```
// Get the position of this fragment
mediump vec3 modelViewVertex = vec3(modelViewMatrix * vertex_position);

// Determine the direction of the fragment from the point on the surface
mediump vec3 lightVector = normalize(lightPosition - modelViewVertex);

// Calculate how much light is reflected
mediump float diffuse = clamp(dot(normal, lightVector), 0.0, 1.0);

// Combine everything together!
gl_FragColor = texture2D(texture0, vertex_texcoords) * vertex_color *
diffuse * lightColor  + ambientLightColor;

}
```

Discussion

To calculate how much light is bouncing off the surface and into the camera, you first
need to know the direction in which the surface is oriented. This is done using *normals*, which are vectors that indicate the direction of the vertices that make up the
surface.

Next, you need to know the angle from the camera to the light source. For this you need
to know where the light source is in world space, and where each point that light is
bouncing off of is in world space. You determine this by having the vertex shader convert
the position of each vertex into world space by multiplying the position by the model-
view matrix.

Once this is done, the vertex shader passes the normal information and vertex colors
to the fragment shader. The fragment shader then does the following things:

1. It ensures that the normal has length 1 by normalizing it, which is important for
   the following calculations.
2. It converts the normal into world space by multiplying it with the normal matrix,
   which has been supplied by the Material.
3. It converts the position of the fragment into world space by multiplying the vertex
   position, which was provided by the vertex shader, with the model-view matrix.
4. It then determines the vector that represents the light source's position relative to
   the fragment's position.
5. Once that's done, it takes the dot product between the normal and the light vector.
   The result is how much light is bouncing off the surface and into the camera.
6. Finally, all of the information is combined together. The texture color, vertex color,
   light color, and how much light is hitting the surface are all multiplied together, and
   the ambient light is added.

10.5. Using Normal Mapping

Problem

You want to use normal mapping to make your objects appear to have lots of detail.

Solution

First, create a normal map. They are textures that represent the bumpiness of your object. Normal maps can be made using a number of third-party tools; one that we find pretty handy is CrazyBump (*http://crazybump.com*).

Once you have your normal map, you provide a vertex shader:

```
uniform mediump mat4 modelViewMatrix;
uniform mediump mat4 projectionMatrix;
uniform mediump mat3 normalMatrix;

attribute vec3 position;
attribute vec4 color;
attribute vec3 normal;
attribute vec2 texcoords;

varying mediump vec4 vertex_color;
varying mediump vec2 vertex_texcoords;
varying mediump vec4 vertex_normal;

varying mediump vec4 vertex_position;

void main()
{

    // "position" is in model space. We need to convert it to camera space by
    // multiplying it by the modelViewProjection matrix.
    gl_Position = (projectionMatrix* modelViewMatrix) * vec4(position,1.0);

    // Next, we pass the color, position, normal, and texture coordinates
    // to the fragment shader by putting them in varying variables.
    vertex_color = color;
    vertex_position = modelViewMatrix * vec4(position, 1.0);

    vertex_normal = vec4(normal, 0.0);
    vertex_texcoords = texcoords;

}
```

and a fragment shader:

```
uniform mediump mat4 modelViewMatrix;
uniform mediump mat3 normalMatrix;
```

```
varying mediump vec4 vertex_color;
varying mediump vec2 vertex_texcoords;
varying mediump vec4 vertex_normal;
varying mediump vec4 vertex_position;

uniform sampler2D texture0; // diffuse map
uniform sampler2D texture1; // normal map

uniform lowp vec3 lightPosition;
uniform lowp vec4 lightColor;
uniform lowp vec4 ambientLightColor;

void main()
{

    // When normal mapping, normals don't come from the vertices, but rather
    // from the normal map

    mediump vec3 normal =
    normalize(texture2D(texture1, vertex_texcoords).rgb * 2.0 - 1.0);

    // Convert the normal from object space to world space.
    normal = normalMatrix * normal;

    // Get the position of this fragment.
    mediump vec3 modelViewVertex = vec3(modelViewMatrix * vertex_position);

    // Determine the direction of the fragment to the point on the surface
    mediump vec3 lightVector = normalize(lightPosition - modelViewVertex);

    // Calculate how much light is reflected
    mediump float diffuse = clamp(dot(normal, lightVector), 0.0, 1.0);

    // Combine everything together!
    gl_FragColor = texture2D(texture0, vertex_texcoords) * vertex_color *
    diffuse * lightColor + ambientLightColor;

}
```

When you create the Material using this shader, you need to provide two textures. The first is the *diffuse map*, which provides the base color of the surface. The second is the *normal map*, which is not shown to the player but is used to calculate light reflections.

Discussion

In Recipe 10.4, the normals came from the vertices. However, this generally means that there's not a lot of detail that the light can bounce off of, and the resulting surfaces look fairly flat.

When you use a normal map, the normals come from a texture, not from individual vertices. This means that you have a lot of control over how light bounces off the surface, and consequently can make the surface appear to have more detail.

The actual algorithm for lighting a normal-mapped surface is the same as that for lighting a non-normal-mapped surface. The only difference is that the normals come from the texture, instead of being passed in by the vertex shader.

Note that normal mapping doesn't actually make your object bumpier; it just reflects light *as if it were* bumpier. If you look at a normal-mapped surface side-on, it will be completely flat.

10.6. Making Objects Transparent

Problem

You want your objects to be transparent, so that objects behind them can be partly visible.

Solution

Before drawing an object, use the glBlendFunc function to control how the object you're about to draw is blended with the scene:

```
glEnable(GL_BLEND);
glBlendFunc(GL_SRC_ALPHA, GL_ONE_MINUS_SRC_ALPHA);
```

Discussion

When the fragment shader produces the color value of a pixel, that color is blended with whatever's already been drawn. By default, the output color replaces whatever was previously drawn, but this doesn't have to be the case.

When you call glEnable(GL_BLEND), OpenGL will blend the output color with the scene based on instructions that you provide. The specific way that the blending takes place is up to you, and you control it using the glBlendFunc function.

glBlendFunc takes two parameters. The first is how the source color is changed as part of the blend operation, and the second is how the destination color is changed. In this context, "source color" means the color that's emitted by the fragment shader, and "destination color" means the color that was already in the scene when the drawing took place.

By default, the blending function is this:

```
glBlendFunc(GL_ONE, GL_ZERO);
```

This means that the blending works like this:

```
      Result Color = Source Color * 1 + Destination Color * 0;
```

In this case, because the destination is being multiplied by zero, it contributes nothing to the result color, and the source color completely replaces it.

A common blending method in games is to use the alpha value of the color to determine transparency: that is, 0 alpha means invisible, and 1 alpha means completely opaque. To make this happen, use `glBlendFunc(GL_SRC_ALPHA, GL_ONE_MINUS_SRC_ALPHA)`, which has this effect:

```
      Result Color = Source Color * Source Alpha +
                     Destination Color * (1 - Source Alpha)
```

Doing this means that the higher the alpha value for the source color is, the more it will contribute to the final color.

Another common blending mode is "additive" blending, which creates a glowing appearance. You can create this effect by calling `glBlendFunc(GL_ONE, GL_ONE)`, which adds the two colors together:

```
      Result Color = Source Color * 1 + Destination Color * 1
```

 Additive blending is referred to as "linear dodge" in graphics programs like Adobe Photoshop.

10.7. Adding Specular Highlights

Problem

You want to have shiny specular highlights on your objects.

Solution

You can use the same vertex shader as seen in Recipe 10.4. However, to get specular highlights, you need a different fragment shader:

```
uniform mediump mat4 modelViewMatrix;
uniform mediump mat3 normalMatrix;

varying mediump vec4 vertex_color;
varying mediump vec2 vertex_texcoords;
varying mediump vec4 vertex_normal;
varying mediump vec4 vertex_position;

uniform sampler2D texture0; // diffuse map
uniform sampler2D texture1; // normal map
```

```
uniform lowp vec3 lightPosition;
uniform lowp vec4 lightColor;
uniform lowp vec4 ambientLightColor;

void main()
{

    mediump float shininess = 2.0;

    // When normal mapping, normals don't come from the vertices, but rather
    // from the normal map

    mediump vec3 normal =
    normalize(texture2D(texture1, vertex_texcoords).rgb * 2.0 - 1.0);

    // Convert the normal from object space to world space
    normal = normalMatrix * normal;

    // Get the position of this fragment
    mediump vec3 modelViewVertex = vec3(modelViewMatrix * vertex_position);

    // Determine the direction of the fragment to the point on the surface
    mediump vec3 lightVector = normalize(lightPosition - modelViewVertex);

    // Calculate how much light is reflected
    mediump float diffuse = clamp(dot(normal, lightVector), 0.0, 1.0);

    // Determine the specular term
    mediump float specular = max(pow(dot(normal, lightVector), shininess), 0.0);

    // Combine everything together!
    gl_FragColor = texture2D(texture0, vertex_texcoords) * vertex_color *
    (diffuse * lightColor) + (lightColor * specular) + ambientLightColor;

}
```

Discussion

Specular highlights are bright spots that appear on very shiny objects. Specular highlights get added on top of the existing diffuse and ambient light, which make them look bright.

In the real world, no object is uniformly shiny. If you want something to look slightly old and tarnished, use specular mapping: create a texture in which white is completely shiny and black is not shiny at all. In your shader, sample this texture (in the same way as when you sample a texture for color or for normals) and multiply the result by the specular term. The result will be an object that is shiny in some places and dull in others, as shown in Figure 10-1.

Figure 10-1. Using specular highlights to create shiny objects

If you want to learn more about lighting, we recommend starting with the Wikipedia article on Phong shading (*http://en.wikipedia.org/wiki/Phong_shading*).

10.8. Adding Toon Shading

Problem

You want to create a cartoon effect by making your object's lighting look flat.

Solution

Add the following code to your fragment shader:

```
diffuse = ... //  diffuse is calculated as per Recipe 10.4

// Group the lighting into three bands: one with diffuse lighting at 1.0,
// another at 0.75, and another at 0.5. Because there's no smooth
// transition between each band, hard lines will be visible between them.
```

```
if (diffuse > 0.75)
    diffuse = 1.0;
else if (diffuse > 0.5)
    diffuse = 0.75;
else
    diffuse = 0.5;

// Use diffuse in the shading process as per normal.
```

Discussion

Toon shading is an example of non-photorealistic rendering, in that the colors that are calculated by the fragment shader are not the same as those that you would see in real life.

To create a cartoon-like effect, the colors emitted should have hard edges, and fade smoothly from one area to another. This can be achieved in a fragment shader by reducing the possible values of lights to a small number. In this solution's example, the diffuse light is kept either at 0.5, 0.75, or 1.0. As a result, the final rendered color has hard, bold edges (see Figure 10-2).

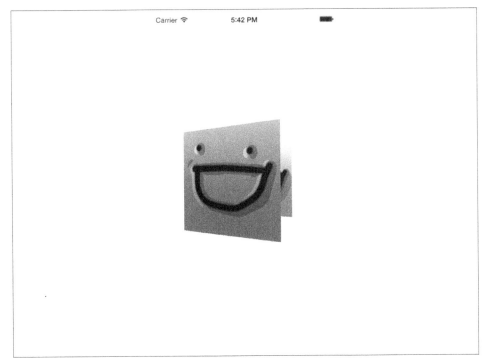

Figure 10-2. Toon shading

CHAPTER 11

Artificial Intelligence and Behavior

Games are often at their best when they're a challenge to the player. There are a number of ways for making your game challenging, including creating complex puzzles; however, one of the most satisfying challenges that a player can enjoy is defeating something that's trying to outthink or outmaneuver them.

In this chapter, you'll learn how to create movement behavior, how to pursue and flee from targets, how to find the shortest path between two locations, and how to design an AI system that thinks ahead.

11.1. Making an Object Move Toward a Position

Problem

You want an object to move toward another object.

Solution

Subtract the target position from the object's current position, normalize the result, and then multiply it by the speed at which you want to move toward the target. Then, add the result to the current position:

```
// Determine the direction to this position
GLKVector2 myPosition = ... // the location where we are right now
GLKVector2 targetPosition = ... // the location where we want to be
float movementSpeed = ... // how fast we want to move toward this target

GLKVector2 offset = GLKVector2Subtract(targetPosition, myPosition);

// Reduce this vector to be the same length as our movement speed
offset = GLKVector2Normalize(offset);
offset = GLKVector2MultiplyScalar(offset, self.movementSpeed * deltaTime);
```

```
// Add this to our current position
GLKVector2 newPosition = self.position;
newPosition.x += offset.x;
newPosition.y += offset.y;

self.position = newPosition;
```

Figure 11-1 illustrates the result.

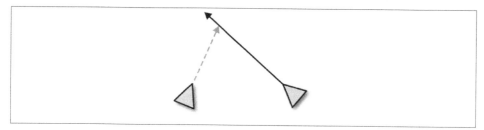

Figure 11-1. Intercepting a moving object

Discussion

To move toward an object, you need to know the direction that your destination is in. To get this, you take your destination's position minus your current position, which results in a vector.

Let's say that you're located at [0, 5], and you want to move toward [1, 8] at a rate of 1 unit per second. The destination position minus your current location is:

```
Offset = [1, 8] - [0, 5] = [1, 3]
```

However, the length (or magnitude) of this vector will vary depending on how far away the destination is. If you want to move toward the destination at a fixed speed, then you need to ensure that the length of the vector is 1, and then multiply the result by the speed you want to move at.

Remember, when you normalize a vector, you get a vector that points in the same direction but has a length of 1. If you multiply this normalized vector with another number, such as your speed, you get a vector with that length.

So, to calculate how far you need to move, you take your offset, normalize it, and multiply the result by your movement speed.

In order to get smooth movement, you're likely going to run this code every time a new frame is drawn. Every time this happens, it's useful to know how many seconds have elapsed between the last frame and the current frame (see Recipe 1.4).

To calculate how far an object should move, given a speed in units per second and an amount of time measured in seconds, you just use the time-honored equation:

```
Speed = Distance ÷ Time
```

Rearranging, we get:

```
Distance = Speed × Time
```

We can now substitute, assuming a delta time of 1/30th of a second (i.e., 0.033 seconds):

```
Movement speed = 5
Delta time     = 0.033
Distance       = Movement Speed * Delta Time
               = 5 * 0.333
               = 1.666

Normalized offset = Normalize(Offset) * Distance
                  = [0.124, 0.992]
Muliplied offset  = Normalized offset * Distance
                  = [0.206, 1.652]
```

You can then add this multiplied offset to your current position to get your new position. Then, you do the whole thing over again on the next frame.

This method of moving from a current location to another over time is fundamental to all movement behaviors, since everything else relies on being able to move.

11.2. Making Things Follow a Path

Problem

You want to make an object follow a path from point to point, turning to face the next destination.

Solution

When you have a path, keep a list of points. Move to the target (see Recipe 11.1). When you reach it, remove the first item from the list; then move to the new first item in the list.

Here's an example that uses Sprite Kit (discussed in Chapter 6):

```
- (void) moveToPath:(NSArray*)pathPoints {

    if (pathPoints.count == 0)
        return;

    CGPoint nextPoint = [[pathPoints firstObject] CGPointValue];

    GLKVector2 currentPosition =
```

```
GLKVector2Make(self.position.x, self.position.y);
GLKVector2 nextPointVector =
GLKVector2Make(nextPoint.x, nextPoint.y);

GLKVector2 toTarget = GLKVector2Subtract(nextPointVector, currentPosition);

float distance = GLKVector2Length(toTarget);

float speed = 50;
float time = distance / speed;

SKAction* moveAction = [SKAction moveTo:nextPoint duration:time];
SKAction* nextPointAction = [SKAction runBlock:^{
    NSMutableArray* nextPoints = [NSMutableArray arrayWithArray:pathPoints];
    [nextPoints removeObjectAtIndex:0];
    [self moveToPath:nextPoints];
}];

[self runAction:[SKAction sequence:@[moveAction, nextPointAction]]];
}
```

Discussion

To calculate a path from one point to another, use a path algorithm (see Recipe 11.8).

11.3. Making an Object Intercept a Moving Target

Problem

You want an object to move toward another object, intercepting it.

Solution

Calculate where the target is going to move to based on its velocity, and use the move to algorithm from Recipe 11.1 to head toward that position:

```
GLKVector2 myPosition = ... // our current position
GLKVector2 targetPosition = ... // the current position of the target
float myMovementSpeed = ... // how fast we're moving
float targetMovementSpeed = ... // how fast it's moving

GLKVector2 toTarget = GLKVector2Subtract(targetPosition, myPosition);

float lookAheadTime = GLKVector2Length(toTarget) /
(myMovementSpeed + targetMovementSpeed);

CGPoint destination = target.position;
destination.x += targetMovementSpeed * lookAheadTime;
destination.y += targetMovementSpeed * lookAheadTime;
```

```
[self moveToPosition:destination deltaTime:deltaTime];
```

Discussion

When you want to intercept a moving object, your goal should be to move to where the target is going to be, rather than where it is right now. If you just move to where the target currently is, you'll end up always chasing it.

Instead, what you want to do is calculate where the target is going to be when you arrive, by taking the target's current position and its speed, determining how fast you can get there, and then seeking toward that.

11.4. Making an Object Flee When It's in Trouble

Problem

You want an object to flee from something that's chasing it.

Solution

Use the "move to" method, but use the reverse of the force it gives you:

```
GLKVector2 myPosition = ... // our current position
GLKVector2 targetPosition = ... // the current position of the target
float myMovementSpeed = ... // how fast we're moving

GLKVector2 offset = GLKVector2Subtract(targetPosition, myPosition);

// Reduce this vector to be the same length as our movement speed
offset = GLKVector2Normalize(offset);

// Note the minus sign - we're multiplying by the inverse of
// our movement speed, which means we're moving away from it
offset = GLKVector2MultiplyScalar(offset, -myMovementSpeed * deltaTime);

// Add this to our current position
CGPoint newPosition = self.position;
newPosition.x += offset.x;
newPosition.y += offset.y;

self.position = newPosition;
```

Discussion

Moving away from a point is very similar to moving toward a point. All you need to do is use the inverse of your current movement speed. This will give you a vector that's pointing in the opposite direction of the point you want to move away from.

11.5. Making an Object Decide on a Target

Problem

You want to determine which of several targets is the best target for an object to pursue.

Solution

The general algorithm for deciding on the best target looks like this:

1. Set `bestScoreSoFar` to the worst possible score (either zero or infinity, depending on what you're looking for).

2. Set `bestTargetSoFar` to nothing.

3. Loop over each possible target:

   a. Check the score of the possible target.

   b. If the score is better than `bestScoreSoFar`:

      i. Set `bestTargetSoFar` to the possible target.

      ii. Set `bestScoreSoFar` to the possible target's score.

4. After the loop is done, `bestTargetSoFar` will either be the best target, or it will be nothing.

This algorithm is shown in code form in the following example. The `bestScoreSoFar` variable is called `nearestTargetDistance`; it stores the distance to the closest target found so far, and begins as the highest possible distance (i.e. infinity). You then loop through the array of possible targets, resetting it every time you find a new target nearer than the previous ones:

```
float nearestTargetDistance = INFINITY;
Enemy* nearestTarget = nil;

GLKVector2 myPosition = ... // the current position

NSArray* nearbyTargets = ... // an array of nearby possible targets

for (Enemy* enemy in nearbyTargets) {

    // Find the distance to this target
    GLKVector2 = enemy.position;
    GLKVector2 toTarget = GLKVector2Subtract(targetPosition, myPosition);
    float length = GLKVector2Length(toTarget);

    // If it's nearer than the current target, it's the new target
    if (length < nearestTargetDistance) {
        nearestTarget = node;
```

```
            nearestTargetDistance = length;
        }
    }
}
```

Discussion

It's worth keeping in mind that there's no general solution to this problem because it can vary a lot depending on what your definition of "best" is. You should think about what the best target is in your game. Is it:

- Closest?
- Most dangerous?
- Weakest?
- Worth the most points?

Additionally, it depends on what information you can access regarding the nearby targets. Something that's worth keeping in mind is that doing a search like this can take some time, if there are many potential targets. Try to minimize the number of loops that you end up doing.

11.6. Making an Object Steer Toward a Point

Problem

You want an object to steer toward a certain point, while maintaining a constant speed.

Solution

You can steer toward an object by figuring out the angle between the direction you're currently heading in and the direction to the destination. Once you have this, you can limit this angle to your maximum turn rate:

```
// Work out the vector from our position to the target
GLKVector2 myPosition = ... // our position
GLKVector2 targetPosition = ... // target position
float turningSpeed = ... // the maximum amount of turning we can do, in radians
                        // per second

GLKVector2 toTarget = GLKVector2Subtract(targetPosition, myPosition);

GLKVector2 forwardVector = ... // the forward vector: rotate [0,1] by whatever
                               // direction we're currently facing

// Get the angle needed to turn toward this position
float angle = GLKVector2DotProduct(toTarget, forwardVector);
angle /= acos(GLKVector2Length(toTarget) * GLKVector2Length(forwardVector));
```

```
// Clamp the angle to our turning speed
angle = fminf(angle, turningSpeed);
angle = fmaxf(angle, -turningSpeed);

// Apply the rotation
self.rotation += angle * deltaTime;
```

Discussion

You can calculate the angle between two vectors by taking the dot product of the two vectors, dividing it by the lengths of both, and then taking the arc cosine of the result.

To gradually turn over time, you then limit the result to your maximum turning rate (to stop your object from turning instantaneously), and then multiply *that* by how long you want the turning action to take, in seconds.

11.7. Making an Object Know Where to Take Cover

Problem

You want to find a location where an object can move to, where it can't be seen by another object.

Solution

First, draw up a list of nearby points that your object (the "prey") can move to.

Then, draw lines from the position of the other object (the "predator") to each of these points. Check to see if any of these lines intersect an object. If they do, this is a potential cover point.

Then, devise paths from your object to each of these potential cover points (see Recipe 11.8). Pick the point that has the shortest path, and start moving toward it (see Recipe 11.2).

If you're using Sprite Kit with physics bodies, you can use the enumerateBodiesAlon gRayStart:end:usingBlock: method to find out whether you can draw an uninterrupted line from your current position to the potential cover position:

```
CGPoint myPosition = ... // current position
CGPoint coverPosition = ... // potential cover position

SKPhysicsWorld* physicsWorld = self.scene.physicsWorld;

__block BOOL canUseCover = NO;

[physicsWorld enumerateBodiesAlongRayStart:myPosition end:coverPosition
```

```
usingBlock:^(SKPhysicsBody *body, CGPoint point, CGVector normal, BOOL *stop) {

    if (body == self.physicsBody)
        return;

    // We hit something, so there's something between us
    // and the cover point. Good!
    canUseCover = YES;

    // Stop looping
    *stop = YES;
}];

if (canUseCover) {
    // Take cover
}
```

Discussion

A useful addition to this algorithm is to make some cover "better" than others. For example, chest-high cover in a shooting game may be worth less than full cover, and cover that's closer to other, nearby cover may be worth more than an isolated piece of cover.

In these cases, your algorithm needs to take into account both the distance to the cover and the "score" for the cover.

11.8. Calculating a Path for an Object to Take

Problem

You want to determine a path from one point to another, avoiding obstacles.

Solution

There are several path-calculation algorithms for you to choose from; one of the most popular is called A* (pronounced "A star").

To use the A* algorithm, you give it the list of all of the possible waypoints that an object can be at ahead of time, and determine which points can be directly reached from other points. Later, you run the algorithm to find a path from one waypoint to another.

First, create a new class called NavigationNode:

```
@interface NavigationNode : NSObject

// The location of the node
@property (assign) CGPoint position;
```

```
// The list of nearby nodes
@property (strong) NSArray* neighbors;

// The "cost" that would be incurred if the path went through this node
@property (assign) float fScore;

// The "cost" from this point along the best known path
@property (assign) float gScore;

// Return the distance from this node to another node
- (float) distanceToNode:(NavigationNode*)node;

// Return the distance from the node's position to a point
- (float) distanceToPoint:(CGPoint)point;

@end

@implementation NavigationNode

// Return the distance from the node's position to a given point
- (float)distanceToPoint:(CGPoint)point {
    CGPoint offset;
    offset.x = point.x - self.position.x;
    offset.y = point.y - self.position.y;

    float length = sqrt(offset.x * offset.x + offset.y * offset.y);

    return length;
}

// Return the distance from the node's position to another node
- (float)distanceToNode:(NavigationNode *)node {
    return [self distanceToPoint:node.position];
}

@end
```

Next, create a second class called `NavigationGrid`:

```
@implementation NavigationGrid {
    NSMutableArray* nodes;
}

- (void)createNodesWithPoints:(NSArray *)points
maximumNeighborDistance:(float)distance {

    nodes = [NSMutableArray array];

    // Create the nodes
    for (NSValue* pointValue in points) {
        NavigationNode* node = [[NavigationNode alloc] init];

        node.position = pointValue.CGPointValue;
```

```objc
        [nodes addObject:node];
    }

    // Determine which nodes are neighbors
    for (NavigationNode* node in nodes) {

        NSMutableArray* neighbors = [NSMutableArray array];

        for (NavigationNode* otherNode in nodes) {
            if (otherNode == node)
                continue;

            // If the distance to this node is shorter than or the same
            // as the maximum allowed distance, add this as a neighbor
            if ([node distanceToNode:otherNode] <= distance) {
                [neighbors addObject:otherNode];
            }
        }

        node.neighbors = neighbors;
    }

}

// Find the nearest node to the given point
- (NavigationNode*) nearestNodeToPoint:(CGPoint)point {

    NavigationNode* nearestNode = nil;
    float closestDistance = INFINITY;

    for (NavigationNode* node in nodes) {

        float distance = [node distanceToPoint:point];

        if (distance < closestDistance) {
            closestDistance = distance;
            nearestNode = node;
        }

    }
    return nearestNode;
}

// Calculate the path from the origin to the destination
- (NSArray*) pathFromPoint:(CGPoint)origin toPoint:(CGPoint)destination {

    // First, find the nearest nodes to the origin and end point
    NavigationNode* startNode = [self nearestNodeToPoint:origin];
    NavigationNode* goalNode = [self nearestNodeToPoint:destination];

    // Reset the f-scores and g-scores for each node
```

```
for (NavigationNode* node in nodes) {
    node.fScore = 0;
    node.gScore = 0;
}

// The set of nodes that have been evaluated
NSMutableSet* closedSet = [NSMutableSet set];

// The set of nodes that should be evaluated, starting with the startNode
NSMutableSet* openSet = [NSMutableSet setWithObject:startNode];

// A weak mapping from nodes, used to reconstruct the path
NSMapTable* cameFromMap = [NSMapTable weakToWeakObjectsMapTable];

// Loop while there are still nodes to consider
while (openSet.count > 0) {

    // Find the node in the open set with the lowest f-score
    NavigationNode* currentNode =
    [[openSet sortedArrayUsingDescriptors:@[[NSSortDescriptor
    sortDescriptorWithKey:@"fScore" ascending:YES]]] firstObject];

    // If we've managed to get to the goal, reconstruct a path
    if (currentNode == goalNode) {
        NSArray* pathNodes =
        [self reconstructPath:cameFromMap currentNode:currentNode];

        // Make an array containing just points (instead of NavigationNodes)
        NSMutableArray* pathPoints = [NSMutableArray array];
        for (NavigationNode* node in pathNodes) {
            [pathPoints addObject:[NSValue valueWithCGPoint:node.position]];
        }

        return pathPoints;
    }

    // Move the current node from the open set to the closed set
    [openSet removeObject:currentNode];
    [closedSet addObject:currentNode];

    // Check each neighbor for the next best point to check
    for (NavigationNode* neighbor in currentNode.neighbors) {
        float tentativeGScore =
        currentNode.gScore + [currentNode distanceToNode:neighbor];
        float tentativeFScore =
        tentativeGScore + [currentNode distanceToNode:goalNode];

        // If this neighbor has already been checked, and using it as part
        // of the path would be worse, skip it
        if ([closedSet containsObject:neighbor] && tentativeFScore >=
        neighbor.fScore) {
            continue;
```

```
        }

        // If we haven't checked this node yet, or using it would be better,
        // add it to the current path
        if ([openSet containsObject:neighbor] ==
        NO || tentativeFScore < neighbor.fScore) {
            [cameFromMap setObject:currentNode forKey:neighbor];

            // Update the estimated costs for using this node
            neighbor.fScore = tentativeFScore;
            neighbor.gScore = tentativeGScore;

            // Add it to the open set, so we explore using it more
            [openSet addObject:neighbor];

        }
      }
    }

    return nil;

}

// Given a point, recursively determine the chain of points that link together
// to form a path from the start point to the end point
- (NSArray*) reconstructPath:(NSMapTable*)cameFromMap
currentNode:(NavigationNode*)currentNode {
    if ([cameFromMap objectForKey:currentNode]) {
        NSArray* path = [self reconstructPath:cameFromMap
        currentNode:[cameFromMap objectForKey:currentNode]];
        return [path arrayByAddingObject:currentNode];
    } else {
        return @[currentNode];
    }
}
```

Discussion

The A* algorithm is a reasonably efficient algorithm for computing a path from one
point to another. It works by incrementally building up a path; every time it looks at a
new point, it checks to see if the total distance traveled is lower than that traveled using
any of the other potential points, and if that's the case, it adds it to the path. If it ever
gets stuck, it backtracks and tries again. If it can't find *any* path from the start to the
destination, it returns an empty path.

11.9. Finding the Next Best Move for a Puzzle Game

Problem

In a turn-based game, you want to determine the next best move to make.

Solution

The exact details here will vary from game to game, so in this solution, we'll talk about the general approach to this kind of problem.

Let's assume that the entire state of your game—the location of units, the number of points, the various states of every game object—is being kept in memory.

Starting from this current state, you figure out all possible moves that the next player can make. For each possible move, create a copy of the state where this move has been made.

Next, determine a score for each of the states that you've made. The method for determining the score will vary depending on the kind of game; some examples include:

- Number of enemy units destroyed minus number of my units destroyed
- Amount of money I have minus amount of money the enemy has
- Total number of points I have, ignoring how many points the enemy has

Once you have a score for each possible next state, take the top-scoring state, and have your computer player make that next move.

Discussion

The algorithm in this solution is often referred to as a *brute force* approach. This can get very complicated for complex games. Strategy games may need to worry about economy, unit movement, and so on—if each unit has 3 possible actions, and you have 10 units, there are over 59,000 possible states that you could end up in. To address this problem, you need to reduce the number of states that you calculate.

It helps to break up the problem into simpler, less-precise states for your AI to consider. Consider a strategy game in which you can, in general terms, spend points on attacking other players, researching technologies, or building defenses. Each turn, your AI just needs to calculate an estimate for the benefit that each general strategy will bring. Once it's decided on that, you can then have dedicated attacking, researching, or defense-building AI modules take care of the details.

11.10. Determining if an Object Can See Another Object

Problem

You want to find out if an object (the *hunter*) can see another object (the *prey*), given the direction the hunter is facing, the hunter's field of view, and the positions of both the hunter and the prey.

Solution

First, you need to define how far the hunter can see, as well as the field of view of the hunter. You also need to know what direction the hunter is currently facing. Finally, you need the positions of both the hunter and the prey:

```
float distance = 30.0; // the hunter can see 30 units ahead
float fov = 90; // the hunter can see 45° to the left and right

float direction = ... // the direction the hunter is facing

GLKVector2 hunterPosition = ... // the hunter's location
GLKVector2 preyPosition = ... // the prey's location
```

Next, the first test is to calculate how far away the prey is from the hunter. If the prey is further away than distance units, then the hunter won't be able to see it at all:

```
float preyDistance = GLKVector2Length(hunterPosition, preyPosition);

if (preyDistance > distance) {
    return NO; // can't see the prey
}
```

If the prey is within seeing distance, you then need to determine if the prey is standing within the hunter's field of view:

```
float directionRadians = GLKMathDegreesToRadians(direction);
GLKVector2 hunterFacingVector =
GLKVector2Make(sin(directionRadians), cos(directionRadians));

GLKVector2 hunterToPrey = GLKVector2Subtract(preyPosition, hunterPosition);
hunterToPrey = GLKVector2Normalize(hunterToPrey);

float angleFromHunterToPrey =
acos(GLKVector2DotProduct(hunterFacingVector, hunterToPrey));

float angleFromHunterToPreyDegrees =
GLKMathDegreesToRadians(angleFromHunterToPrey);

if (fabs(angleFromHunterToPrey) < fov / 2.0) {
    return YES;
}
```

Discussion

Figuring out if one object can see another is a common problem. If you're making a stealth game, for example, where the player needs to sneak behind guards but is in trouble if she's ever seen, then you need to be able to determine what objects the guard can actually see. Objects that are within the field of view are visible, whereas those that are outside of it are not, as shown in Figure 11-2.

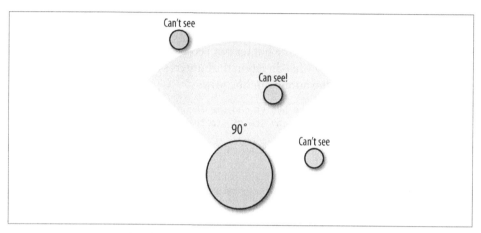

Figure 11-2. An example of how the field of view works

Calculating the distance between objects is very straightforward—you just need to have their positions, and use the GLKVector2Length function to calculate how far each point is from the other. If the prey is too far away from the hunter, then it isn't visible.

Figuring out whether or not the prey is within the angle of view of the hunter requires more math. What you need to do is to determine the angle between the direction the hunter is facing and the direction that the hunter would need to face in order to be directly facing the prey.

To do this, you create two vectors. The first is the vector representing the direction the hunter is facing, which you calculate by taking the sine and cosine of the hunter's angle:

```
float directionRadians = GLKMathDegreesToRadians(direction);
GLKVector2 hunterFacingVector = GLKVector2Make(sin(directionRadians),
                                cos(directionRadians));
```

The second vector represents the direction from the hunter to the prey, which you calculate by subtracting the hunter's position from the prey's position, and then normalizing:

```
GLKVector2 hunterToPrey = GLKVector2Subtract(preyPosition, hunterPosition);
hunterToPrey = GLKVector2Normalize(hunterToPrey);
```

Once you have these vectors, you can figure out the angle between them by first taking the dot product of the two vectors, and then taking the arc cosine of the result:

```
float angleFromHunterToPrey =
    acos(GLKVector2DotProduct(hunterFacingVector, hunterToPrey));
```

The result is measured in radians. To deal with it in degrees, which are sometimes a little easier to think about, you use the `GLKMathDegreesToRadians` function:

```
float angleFromHunterToPreyDegrees =
    GLKMathDegreesToRadians(angleFromHunterToPrey);
```

You now know the angle from the hunter to the prey. If this angle is less than half of the field of view angle, then the hunter can see the prey; otherwise, the prey is outside the hunter's field of view.

11.11. Using AI to Enhance Your Game Design

Problem

You want to make sure your game uses AI and behavior effectively to create a fun and engaging experience.

Solution

The fun in games comes from a number of places (see *http://8kindsoffun.com* for a discussion). In our opinion, one of the most important kinds of fun is challenge. Games that provoke a challenge for the player are often the most enjoyable.

Judicious and careful use of AI and behavior in your games can help them stand a cut above the rest in a sea of iOS games. You want to create an increasingly difficult series of challenges for your players, slowly getting more complex and introducing more pieces the longer they play for.

Revealing the different components of gameplay as they play is an important way to stagger the difficulty, and it's important that any AI or behavior you implement isn't using tools that the player doesn't have access to.

Reveal the pieces of your game slowly and surely, and make sure the AI is only one step, if at all, ahead of the player.

Discussion

It's hard to make a game genuinely challenging without killing the fun factor by making it too difficult. The best way to do this is to slowly peel back the layers of your game, providing individual components one by one until the player has access to the full arsenal of things he can do in your game. The AI or behavior code of your game should get access to this arsenal at approximately the same rate as the player, or it will feel too difficult and stop being fun.

CHAPTER 12

Networking and Social Media

Nobody games alone. At least, not anymore.

While single-player games remain one of the most interesting forms of interactive media, it's increasingly rare to find a game that never communicates with the outside world. *Angry Birds*, for example, is by all definitions a single-player game; however, with only a couple of taps, you can send your most recent score to Twitter and Facebook. We'll be looking at how you can implement this functionality inside your own game.

In addition to this relatively low-impact form of engaging other people with the player's game, you can also have multiple people share the same game through networking. This is a complex topic, so we're going to spend quite a bit of time looking at the various ways you can achieve it, as well as ways in which it can get challenging and how to address them.

We'll also be looking at *Game Center*, the built-in social network that Apple provides. Game Center allows you to let users share high scores and achievements, as well as challenge their friends and play turn-based games. Before we get to the recipes, we'll take a quick look at it to familiarize you with how it works.

12.1. Using Game Center

Many of the powerful networking capabilities exposed to your app come from Game Center, Apple's game-based social network. Game Center handles a number of capabilities that you often want to have as a game developer, but that it would be very tedious to develop yourself. These include:

- Player profiles
- High score tables
- Match-making

- Turn-based gameplay

You get all of these for free when you add Game Center to your game, and all you need to do is write code that hooks into the service. To get started, you first need to turn on Game Center support for your app in Xcode, and sign your player into Game Center when the game starts.

Turning on Game Center support is easy. First, you'll need to have a working iOS Developer account, since Game Center relies on it. Then:

1. In Xcode, select your project in the Project Navigator.
2. Open the Capabilities tab.
3. Open the Game Center section, and turn the switch to On (see Figure 12-1).

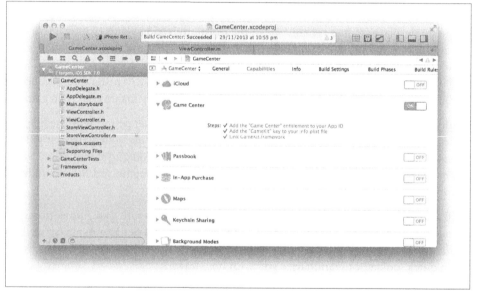

Figure 12-1. Enabling Game Center

Xcode will then walk you through the process of configuring your app to have access to Game Center.

When a player wants to use Game Center, that player needs to have a profile. This means that when you want to develop a game that uses Game Center, you also need to have a profile. When an app is running on the iOS simulator, or is running on a device and is signed with a Developer certificate, it doesn't get access to the "real" Game Center service. Instead, it gets access to the *sandbox* version of the Game Center service, which is functionally identical to but shares no data with the real one. This means that you can play around with your game without the risk of it appearing in public. It also means that you need to get a profile on the sandbox version of the Game Center service.

Here's how to get a profile on the sandbox. You'll first need to create a new, empty Apple ID by going to *http://appleid.apple.com*. Then:

1. Open the iOS simulator.
2. Open the Game Center application (Figure 12-2).

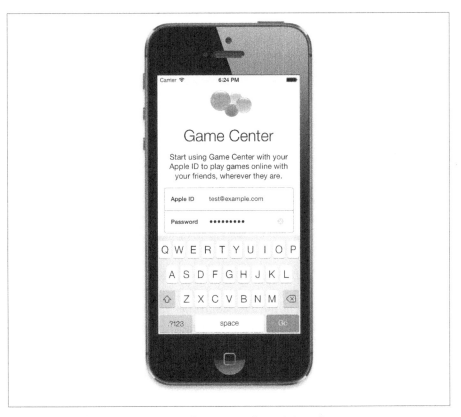

Figure 12-2. The Game center application in the iOS Simulator

3. Sign in to your new Apple ID. You'll be prompted to set up the new account.

 Don't sign in to your existing Apple ID. Existing Apple IDs are likely to have already been activated in the real, public Game Center, which means they won't work in the sandbox, and you'll get an error saying that your game is not recognized by Game Center.

Once this is done, a player profile is created in the sandbox, which you can use in your game.

To actually use Game Center, your game needs to ask Game Center if it has permission to access the player's profile. You do this by *authenticating* the player, which you do by first getting the *local player*, and providing it with an authentication handler:

```
- (void) authenticatePlayer {
    GKLocalPlayer* localPlayer = [GKLocalPlayer localPlayer];

    localPlayer.authenticateHandler = ^(UIViewController* viewController,
                                        NSError* error) {
        if (viewController != nil) {
            [self presentViewController:viewController animated:YES
            completion:nil];
        } else if (localPlayer.isAuthenticated) {
            // We're now authenticated!
        } else {
            // Game Center is unavailable, either due to the network or because
            // the player has turned it off.
        }
    };
}
```

Here's how this works. When you provide the GKLocalPlayer object with an authentication handler, Game Center immediately tries to authenticate the player so that the game can get access to the Game Center features. Whether this succeeds or not, the authentication handler is called.

The handler receives two parameters: a view controller, and an error. If Game Center needs the user to provide additional information in order to complete the authentication, your app needs to present the view controller and let the user provide whatever information Game Center needs. If the view controller parameter is nil, you check to see if the GKLocalPlayer has been authenticated. If it has, great! If not, you can find out why by looking at the provided NSError parameter.

There are many reasons why the player may not get authenticated. These include network conditions, the player not having a Game Center account, the player *declining* to sign up for one, the player being underage, or parental restrictions in place.

Regardless of the reason, your game needs to be designed to handle not being able to access Game Center. If your game displays errors or refuses to work without the user signing in, you'll have trouble getting it approved by Apple when you submit it to the store.

12.2. Getting Information About the Logged-in Player

Problem

You want to find out information about the currently logged-in player, such as the user's nickname and avatar.

Solution

Use the `GKLocalPlayer` class to get information about the player:

```
GKLocalPlayer* localPlayer = [GKLocalPlayer localPlayer];

self.playerName.text = localPlayer.alias;

[[GKLocalPlayer localPlayer] loadPhotoForSize:GKPhotoSizeNormal
withCompletionHandler:^(UIImage *photo, NSError *error) {
    self.playerPhotoView.image = photo;
}];
```

Discussion

Showing information about the player is a good way to indicate that she's a part of the game. You can get the display name and player ID from a `GKPlayer` object. `GKLocal Player` is a special object that represents the currently signed-in user.

If you want to load the player's photo, you have to do a special call. Note that not all users have a photo.

12.3. Getting Information About Other Players

Problem

You want to get information about the people that the player is friends with, such as their names and avatars.

Solution

Use the `GKLocalPlayer` class's `loadFriendsWithCompletionHandler:` method to get the list of identifiers for each friend the player has. For each identifier you receive, use the `loadPlayersForIdentifiers:withCompletionHandler:` method to load information about that friend:

```
[[GKLocalPlayer localPlayer] loadFriendsWithCompletionHandler:^
(NSArray *friendIDs, NSError *error) {

    [GKPlayer loadPlayersForIdentifiers:friendIDs withCompletionHandler:^
```

```
        (NSArray *players, NSError *error) {

            // Get info for each player

            for (GKPlayer* player in players) {
                NSLog(@"Friend: %@", player.displayName);
            }

        }];

    }];
```

Discussion

Using the `loadFriendsWithCompletionHandler:` method, you get the list of players that the local player is friends with. Note that this method just gives you an array of `NSStrings`, which are the player IDs of the local player's friends. To get more detailed information on each player, you call `loadPlayersForIdentifiers:withCompletion Handler:` and pass it the array of player ID strings.

12.4. Making Leaderboards and Challenges with Game Center

Problem

You want to show high scores and high-ranking players, and let players challenge their friends to beat their scores.

Solution

Go to iTunes Connect (*http://itunesconnect.apple.com*) and register a new app. (You'll need to provide information for a bunch of things needed for the App Store, including screenshots, but because Apple won't actually look at any of this until you submit the game to the App Store, you can just supply placeholder text and blank images.)

 This recipe assumes you're creating a new game that you want to have this functionality. However, you can easily adapt it to add a leaderboard to an existing game.

Once it's all set up, click Manage Game Center (Figure 12-3); the Manage Game Center button is on the right, at the top of the list.

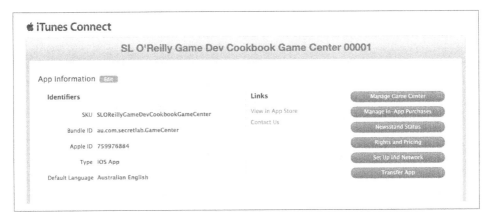

Figure 12-3. iTunes Connect

You'll be asked if you want to set up the game as a standalone game, or as a group of games. If you choose a group of games, you'll be able to share the leaderboard with other games that you make. If you're just making a single game, choose Single Game, as in Figure 12-4.

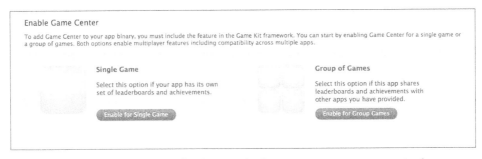

Figure 12-4. iTunes connect will ask you whether you want to set up a single game or multiple games

Next, click Add Leaderboard. You'll be prompted to provide information about the leaderboard, including:

- The name of the leaderboard (shown only to you, inside iTunes Connect, and not shown to the player)
- The ID of the leaderboard, used by your code
- How to format the leaderboard scores (whether to show them as integers, decimal numbers, currency, or times)
- Whether to sort them by best score or by most recent score
- Whether to sort them with low scores first or high scores first

- Optionally, a specified range that scores can be within (Game Center will ignore any scores outside this range)

You then need to provide at least one language that the leaderboard will be shown in. To do this, click Add Language in the Leaderboard Localization section, and choose a language (see Figure 12-5). For each language you provide, you need to provide information on how your scores are being described (see Figure 12-6).

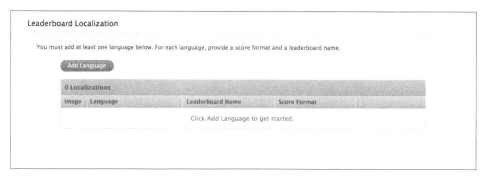

Figure 12-5. Adding a language to leaderboard

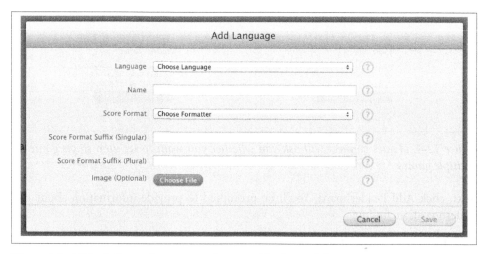

Figure 12-6. The information you need to provide for each language

To submit a high score, you need to create a GKScore object and provide it with the score information. When it's created, it's automatically filled out with other important information, such as the player ID of the player who's reporting the score, the date that the score was created, and other data.

When you create the score, you need to provide the ID of the leaderboard. This is the same ID as the one that you gave to iTunes Connect when creating the leaderboard. This tells Game Center where the score should end up.

Once that's done, you report the score to Game Center using the `reportScores:with CompletionHandler:` method. This method takes an `NSArray` of `GKScore` objects, which means you can submit multiple scores at the same time:

```
GKScore* score =
    [[GKScore alloc] initWithLeaderboardIdentifier:@"leaderboardtest1"];
    score.value = scoreValue;

[GKScore reportScores:@[score] withCompletionHandler:^(NSError *error) {
    NSLog(@"Completed; error = %@", error);
}];
```

To get the scores, you use the `GKLeaderboard` class. This class lets you get the list of leaderboards that have been defined in iTunes Connect, and from there, get the list of scores in the leaderboard:

```
// Get the list of scores defined in iTunes Connect
[GKLeaderboard loadLeaderboardsWithCompletionHandler:^(NSArray *leaderboards,
                                                       NSError *error) {

    // For each leaderboard:
    for (GKLeaderboard* leaderboard in leaderboards) {

        // Get the scores
        [leaderboard loadScoresWithCompletionHandler:^(NSArray *scores,
                                                       NSError *error) {

            NSLog(@"Leaderboard %@:", leaderboard.title);

            // Show the score
            for (GKScore* score in scores) {
                NSLog(@"%@", score.formattedValue);
            }
        }];
    }
}];
```

When you have a `GKScore`, you can issue a challenge to one or more of the player's friends. They'll receive a challenge notification, which will prompt them to try and beat the challenge. If a friend submits a score to the leaderboard that's better than this challenge, your player will receive a notification saying that the challenge has been beaten.

You issue a challenge by presenting a view controller to the players with the specified player IDs (listed in an `NSArray`):

```
NSArray* friendIDs = ... // an NSArray containing the player IDs you want
                         // to challenge
```

```
UIViewController* challengeCompose =
[score challengeComposeControllerWithPlayers:friendIDs
  message:@"Beat this!" completionHandler:^(UIViewController *composeController,
                                            BOOL didIssueChallenge,
                                            NSArray *sentPlayerIDs) {
     [self dismissViewControllerAnimated:YES completion:nil];
}];

[self presentViewController:challengeCompose animated:YES completion:nil];
```

Discussion

Leaderboards and challenges are a great way to encourage the player to try to best other players, and to keep track of their progress in your game. There's a huge degree of flexibility available to you when you create them.

If you want to quickly show a user interface that displays the scores, you can use the GKGameCenterViewController class. This is a view controller that shows Game Center information for the current player, including that player's scores and challenges.

To use it, you first need to make your view controller conform to the GKGameCenter ControllerDelegate protocol. Then, when you want to show the view controller, you create it and present it to the player:

```
GKGameCenterViewController* viewController =
    [[GKGameCenterViewController alloc] init];

viewController.gameCenterDelegate = self;

[self presentViewController:viewController animated:YES completion:nil];
```

You then implement the gameCenterViewControllerDidFinish: method, which is called when the player decides to close the Game Center view controller. All this method has to do is dismiss the view controller:

```
- (void)gameCenterViewControllerDidFinish:(GKGameCenterViewController *)vc {
    [self dismissViewControllerAnimated:YES completion:nil];
}
```

12.5. Finding People to Play with Using Game Center

Problem

You want your players to find people to play games with over the Internet.

Solution

To find people to play with, you first create a GKMatchRequest:

```
GKMatchRequest* request = [[GKMatchRequest alloc] init];

request.maxPlayers = 2;
request.minPlayers = 2;
```

You then create a GKMatchmakerViewController and give it the GKMatchRequest:

```
GKMatchmakerViewController* viewController = [[GKMatchmakerViewController alloc]
                                    initWithMatchRequest:request];

viewController.matchmakerDelegate = self;

[self presentViewController:viewController animated:YES completion:nil];
```

You also need to conform to the GKMatchmakerViewControllerDelegate protocol, and implement three important methods:

```
- (void)matchmakerViewController:(GKMatchmakerViewController *)vc
didFindMatch:(GKMatch *)match {
    // Start using the match
    [self dismissViewControllerAnimated:YES completion:nil];
}

- (void)matchmakerViewController:(GKMatchmakerViewController *)vc
didFailWithError:(NSError *)error {
    // We couldn't create a match
    [self dismissViewControllerAnimated:YES completion:nil];
}

- (void)matchmakerViewControllerWasCancelled:(GKMatchmakerViewController *)vc {
    // The user cancelled match-making
    [self dismissViewControllerAnimated:YES completion:nil];
}
```

The really important one is matchmakerViewController:didFindMatch:. This gives you a GKMatch object, which is what you use to communicate with other players.

 You'll note that in all three cases, it's up to you to dismiss the view controller.

Discussion

GKMatchRequest objects let you define what kinds of players you're looking for in a match. If you set the playerGroup property on a GKMatchRequest to any value other than 0, the player will only be matched with other people who have the same value for playerGroup.

Matches can be *peer-to-peer* or *hosted*; peer-to-peer means that players pass information between themselves directly, while hosted games go through a server that you run.

Many games work best in a client/server model, in which one player (the server) acts as the owner of the game, and all clients communicate with it. This simplifies the problem of keeping the clients in sync, since each client just needs to stay in sync with the server. However, it puts additional load on the server; this has to communicate with every client, which means that the server has to be the player with the best ability to perform these additional duties.

You can configure Game Center to automatically select the best player to act as the server, using the `chooseBestHostPlayerWithCompletionHandler:` method. This method runs checks on all players to find out which one has the best connection, and then calls a block and passes it the player ID of the player who should be host (or `nil` if the best host couldn't be found). If the player ID returned is *your* player ID, you're the server, and you should start sending updates to other player, and receiving input from them. If the player ID is not your player ID, you're the client, and you should start sending commands to the server and receiving game updates. If the player ID is `nil`, there was a problem, and each copy of the game running on the different players' devices should let its player know that network conditions probably aren't good enough to run a game.

12.6. Using Bluetooth to Detect Nearby Game Players with the Multipeer Connectivity Framework

Problem

You want to let players play with people who are physically close by, using Bluetooth.

Solution

Use the Multipeer Connectivity framework. First, add the framework to your class, and import the header file:

```
#import <MultipeerConnectivity/MultipeerConnectivity.h>
```

Multipeer connectivity works like this:

First, you make your class conform to the `MCSessionDelegate` protocol. You need to implement several methods as part of this protocol (many of which aren't used, but you'll get a compiler warning if they're not there):

+

```
- (void)session:(MCSession *)session
peer:(MCPeerID *)peerID didChangeState:(MCSessionState)state {
```

```
    // A peer has changed state—it's now either connecting, connected,
    // or disconnected
}

- (void)session:(MCSession *)session
didReceiveData:(NSData *)data fromPeer:(MCPeerID *)peerID {
    // Data has been received from a peer
}

- (void)session:(MCSession *)session
didStartReceivingResourceWithName:(NSString *)resourceName
fromPeer:(MCPeerID *)peerID withProgress:(NSProgress *)progress {
    // A file started being sent from a peer (not used in this example)
}

- (void)session:(MCSession *)session
didFinishReceivingResourceWithName:(NSString *)resourceName
fromPeer:(MCPeerID *)peerID atURL:(NSURL *)localURL
withError:(NSError *)error {

    // A file finished being sent from a peer (not used in this example)
}


- (void)session:(MCSession *)session
didReceiveStream:(NSInputStream *)stream withName:(NSString *)streamName
fromPeer:(MCPeerID *)peerID {

    // Data started being streamed from a peer (not used in this example)
}
```

Next, you create a peer ID. A peer ID is an object of type MCPeerID, and you create it by providing a display name. This should be the local player's alias, which means you should create it after the player has authenticated with Game Center:

```
MCPeerID* peerID = [[MCPeerID alloc] initWithDisplayName:
[GKLocalPlayer localPlayer].alias];
```

When you've created the MCPeerID, keep it around in an instance variable.

You don't have to use Game Center. If you prefer, you can just create an MCPeerID using a string of your choosing—consider letting the user enter his name. The advantage of using Game Center is that you save your player some typing.

Once you have the MCPeerID, you create an MCSession and provide it with the peer ID:

```
MCSession* session = [[MCSession alloc] initWithPeer:peerID];
session.delegate = self;
```

Once you have the MCSession, you can send data to it and receive data from it. What you do next depends on whether you want to host a game or join someone else's game. If you want to host a game and accept connections from others, you create an MCAdver tiserAssistant, tell it what kind of service you want to advertise, and start it up:

```
NSString* serviceType = @"mygame-v1"; // should be unique
MCAdvertiserAssistant* advertiser =
[[MCAdvertiserAssistant alloc] initWithServiceType:serviceType
                                discoveryInfo:nil session:session];
[self.advertiser start];
```

If you want to connect to someone else, you can create an MCBrowserViewController, give it your MCSession, and present it. To use this, your class needs to conform to the MCBrowserViewControllerDelegate protocol:

```
MCBrowserViewController* viewController =
[[MCBrowserViewController alloc] initWithServiceType:serviceType
                                session:self.session];

viewController.minimumNumberOfPeers = 2;
viewController.maximumNumberOfPeers = 2;

viewController.delegate = self;

[self presentViewController:viewController animated:YES completion:nil];
```

You then implement the browser delegate methods:

```
- (void)browserViewControllerDidFinish:(MCBrowserViewController *)vc {
    // The MCSession is now ready to use

    [self dismissViewControllerAnimated:YES completion:nil];
}

- (void)browserViewControllerWasCancelled:(MCBrowserViewController *)vc {
    // The user cancelled

    [self dismissViewControllerAnimated:YES completion:nil];
}
```

When a user connects to another device, the host calls the session:peer:didChangeS tate: method, indicating that a peer has joined.

Discussion

Multipeer connectivity doesn't require any WiFi or cellular access, but only works with users who are close together—for example, in the same room. This means that you can't connect to peers over the Internet in addition to nearby people—you're either relying on WiFi or cellular networks for all communication, or not using them at all.

12.7. Making Real-Time Gameplay Work with Game Kit and the Multipeer Connectivity Framework

Problem

You want to send information to other players in the game in realtime.

Solution

The specific methods you use to send and receive data from other players depend on whether you're using Game Center or Multipeer Connectivity.

If you're using Game Center, you first need to have a `GKMatch` (see Recipe 12.5). Once you have a `GKMatch`, you can send data to your fellow players by using the `sendData:toPlayers:withDataMode:error:` method:

```
NSData* data = ... // some data you want to send to other players
GKMatch* match = ... // a GKMatch
NSArray* players = ... // an NSArray of player ID strings
NSError* error = nil;

[match sendData:data toPlayers:players withDataMode:GKMatchSendDataReliable
error:&error];
```

The `sendData:toPlayers:withDataMode:error:` method takes the data you want to send, an `NSArray` of player IDs that you want to send the data to, information on whether you want to send the data *reliably* or *unreliably*, and a pointer to an `NSError` variable. If, for some reason, sending the data fails, the method will return `NO` and the error will be set to an `NSError` object.

If you're using Multipeer Connectivity, you send your `MCSession` object (see Recipe 12.6) to the `sendData:toPeers:withDataMode:error:` method. It works in much the same way:

```
NSData* data = ... // some data you want to send to other players
MCSession* session = ... // an MCSession
NSArray* peers = ... // an NSArray of MCPeerIDs
NSError* error = nil;

[session sendData:data toPeers:players withDataMode:GKMatchSendDataReliable
error:&error];
```

You receive data in a similar way. Both `MCSession` and `GKMatch` will send their delegates `NSData` objects when data arrives.

To receive information from a `GKMatch`, you conform to the `GKMatchDelegate` protocol and implement the `match:didReceiveData:fromPlayer:` method:

```
- (void)match:(GKMatch *)match didReceiveData:(NSData *)data
fromPlayer:(NSString *)playerID {
    // Do something with the received data, on the main thread
    [[NSOperationQueue mainQueue] addOperationWithBlock:^{
        // Process the data
    }];
}
```

The process is similar for receiving data from an MCSession:

```
- (void)session:(MCSession *)session didReceiveData:(NSData *)data
fromPeer:(MCPeerID *)peerID {
    // Data has been received from a peer

    // Do something with the received data, on the main thread
    [[NSOperationQueue mainQueue] addOperationWithBlock:^{
        // Process the data
    }];
}
```

 Data can come in from the network at any time, and your code could be in the middle of something important when it does. Because of this, you should always use operation queues to schedule the work of processing the received data on the main queue (see Recipe 1.12).

Discussion

When you send data, you choose whether it should be sent *reliably* or *unreliably*. If you send the data reliably, the system guarantees that the data will arrive, and that multiple packets of data will arrive in the same order as they were sent. If a packet can't be delivered, it keeps trying to resend it until it manages to go through. (If it *still* can't get through, the entire connection will drop.) If you send it unreliably, then the system makes no promises as to whether the data will be received, or in which order it will be received. As compensation, sending data unreliably is *much* faster than sending data reliably.

There are a number of things you can do to ensure that your players enjoy a great experience:

- Limit packet size to 2 KB. The bigger the packet is, the more risk there is that it will be broken into smaller packets, which can hamper performance.

- Don't send too often. Even real-time games probably only need to send data 10 to 15 times a second.

- Don't send too much. Only send updates on objects that have changed state since the last time any updates were sent over the network.

- Don't use reliable sending for data that will be redundant later. Using reliable mode consumes more resources, and it can slow down your game if used too much. If you're updating the position of an object that's moving often, use unreliable mode.

12.8. Creating, Destroying, and Synchronizing Objects on the Network

Problem

You want to create and remove objects in the game, and ensure that everyone sees when an object changes state.

Solution

To synchronize objects across the network, you need to be able to get information from them that represents what their current state is. The "current state" of an object is all of the important information that defines its situation: its position, its health, where it's facing, and more. Because all games are different, the specific information that makes up game state in your game may vary.

In any case, you need to get the information from the object wrapped in an `NSData` object. For example, if you have an object whose entire state is a vector defining its position, you can create an `NSData` object for it like this:

```
unsigned int objectID = ... // some number that uniquely identifies this object
                            // in the game
GLKVector3 position = ... // the object's position

struct {
    NSUInteger objectID;
    GLKVector3 position;
} data;

data.objectID = self.objectID;
data.position = self.position;

NSData* dataToSend = [NSData dataWithBytes:&data length:sizeof(data)];
```

You can then send this data over the network. When it's received, you then get the data, find the object that it's referring to, and apply the change. If it's an object that doesn't exist yet, you create it:

```
NSData* dataReceived = ... // data received over the network

struct {
    NSUInteger objectID;
    GLKVector3 position;
```

```
    } data;

    [dataReceived getBytes:&data length:sizeof(data)];

    GameObject* object = [self findObjectByID:data.objectID];
    if (object == nil) {
        object = ... // create the object
    }

    object.position = data.position;
```

Removing an object is similar, but instead of sending an NSData object that contains information about the object, you instead send a packet that instructs clients to remove the object from the game.

Only the server should be in charge of creating, updating, and removing objects. Clients should send instructions to the server, telling them what changes they'd like to make, but it's up to the server to actually make those changes and send back the results of the changes to clients. This prevents clients from falling out of sync with each other, since the server is continuously telling them the "official" version of the game state. (For more on the client/server model of gameplay, see Recipe 12.5.)

Discussion

It's important that all players in a game have the same approximate game state at all times. If this ever stops being the case, the players aren't able to interact in any meaningful way, since what they're all seeing will be different.

When you send data that contains instructions to create or remove objects, you want it to be reliable because it's important that all players have the same objects in their game. Updates can usually be sent as unreliably (see Recipe 12.7).

If you're using a component based model, you'll need all components to be able to provide information to be sent over the network, so that every aspect of your object can be represented.

Don't forget that not every detail of an object needs to be exactly replicated on all players. Important information, like the position of a monster, is important, while the position of sparks coming off it is not. If your game can work without that information being synchronized over the network, then don't synchronize it.

12.9. Interpolating Object State

Problem

You want to minimize the amount of network traffic in your game, but ensure that everyone has a smooth experience.

Solution

When a packet is received from the server, note the time when it arrived, and subtract that from the time the *last* packet arrived. Store this value somewhere:

```
NSTimeInterval timeOfSecondMostRecentPacket;

NSTimeInterval timeOfMostRecentPacket = [NSDate timeIntervalSinceReferenceDate];

float smoothingTime = timeOfMostRecentPacket - timeOfSecondMostRecentPacket;

timeOfSecondMostRecentPacket = timeOfMostRecentPacket;
```

When a data packet arrives that updates the position of an object, first note the *current* location of the object (i.e., its position before applying the update). Then, over the course of smoothingTime, move the object from its original position to that in the most recently received update:

```
// When a new packet comes in:
float interpolationTime = 0.0;

// For each frame:
float deltaTime = ... // the time since the last frame
interpolationTime += deltaTime;

float interpolationPoint = interpolationTime / smoothingTime;
// 0 = start of interpolation, 1 = end of interpolation

GLKVector3 position = GLKVector3Interpolate(originalPosition,
                                            destinationPosition,
                                            interpolationPoint);
```

If an update packet arrives *during* this process (which is possible), restart the process, using the object's current position and the *new* position.

Discussion

To save bandwidth, your server should send at a rate much lower than the screen refresh rate. While the screen is likely updating at 60 frames per second (at least, it should be!), the network should only be sending updatings 10 to 15 times per second.

However, if you're only sending position updates at a rate of 10 frames per second, your network game will appear jerky, because objects will be moving around the screen at a low rate of updates.

What's better is *interpolation*: when an update comes in, smoothly move the object from its current location to the location that you just received. This has the effect of always making the player be a few milliseconds behind the server, but makes the whole game-play experience feel better.

12.10. Handling When a Player Disconnects and Rejoins

Problem

You want to gracefully handle when players drop out of the game, and when they rejoin.

Solution

If you're using GKMatch, when a player's connection state changes the delegate provided to your GKMatch receives the match:player:didChangeState: message:

```
- (void)match:(GKMatch *)match player:(NSString *)playerID
didChangeState:(GKPlayerConnectionState)state {
    if (state == GKPlayerStateDisconnected) {
        // Let the player know that the connection has been dropped
    }
}
```

If a player drops from a GKMatch, the delegate gets sent the match:shouldReinvite Player: message. If this returns YES, Game Center will try to reconnect the player so that player rejoins the match:

```
- (BOOL)match:(GKMatch *)match shouldReinvitePlayer:(NSString *)playerID {
    // Attempt to reconnect; the player will rejoin the match
    return YES;
}
```

Note that this happens *only* if there are exactly two players in the match. If there are more, then the player's gone forever, and you'll have to tell the player to create a new match.

Discussion

If you're using MCSession to do local, Bluetooth-based networking, there's unfortunately no ability to reinvite players to join the game.

Players can leave the game in one of two ways: they can deliberately decide to leave the game, or they can drop out due to a crash, networking conditions, or something else outside their control. Losing a player is generally annoying to other players, but it can be even more annoying if your game doesn't indicate the distinction between a player losing her connection and a player quitting the game. If your game lets your player know the difference, it feels nicer.

Making your game send an "I'm going away" packet immediately before quitting allows other players to understand the difference between a conscious decision to leave the game and a dropout.

12.11. Making Turn-Based Gameplay Work with GameKit

Problem

You want to use Game Center to coordinate turn-based gameplay.

Solution

First, generate a match request by creating a GKMatchRequest. You create the GKMatchRequest in the exact same way as if you were making a non-turn-based game, and you can learn more about how you do that in Recipe 12.5.

Next, you should make your class conform to the GKTurnBasedMatchmakerViewCon trollerDelegate protocol, which contains some necessary methods used for determining which turn-based match the player wants to play.

Once you have your GKMatchRequest, you create a view controller, GKTurnBasedMatch makerViewController, and provide your match request to it:

```
GKMatchRequest* matchRequest = [[GKMatchRequest alloc] init];
matchRequest.minPlayers = 2;
matchRequest.maxPlayers = 2;

GKTurnBasedMatchmakerViewController* matchmaker =
[[GKTurnBasedMatchmakerViewController alloc] initWithMatchRequest:matchRequest];
matchmaker.turnBasedMatchmakerDelegate = self;

[self presentViewController:matchmaker animated:YES completion:nil];
```

Next, you need to implement methods from the GKTurnBasedMatchmakerViewControl lerDelegate protocol:

```
- (void)turnBasedMatchmakerViewController:
(GKTurnBasedMatchmakerViewController *)viewController didFindMatch:
(GKTurnBasedMatch *)match {

    // Close the matchmaker
    [self dismissViewControllerAnimated:YES completion:nil];

    // Do something with the match. For example:

    if ([match.currentParticipant.playerID
    isEqual:[GKLocalPlayer localPlayer].playerID]) {
        // We're the current player, so we can do something
    } else {
        // It's not our turn, so just show the game state
    }
}

- (void)turnBasedMatchmakerViewControllerWasCancelled:
```

```
(GKTurnBasedMatchmakerViewController *)viewController {
    // The matchmaker was closed without selecting a match
    [self dismissViewControllerAnimated:YES completion:nil];
}

- (void)turnBasedMatchmakerViewController:
(GKTurnBasedMatchmakerViewController *)viewController
didFailWithError:(NSError *)error {
    // The matchmaker failed to find a match for some reason
    [self dismissViewControllerAnimated:YES completion:nil];
}

- (void)turnBasedMatchmakerViewController:
(GKTurnBasedMatchmakerViewController *)viewController
playerQuitForMatch:(GKTurnBasedMatch *)match {
    // Tell the matchmaker view controller that we want to quit
    // a game in which they're the current player.

    [self dismissViewControllerAnimated:YES completion:nil];

    NSData* matchData = match.matchData;

    // Do something with the match data to reflect the fact that we're
    // quitting (e.g., give all of our buildings to someone else,
    // or remove them from the game)

    // Tell Game Center that we've quit
    [match participantQuitInTurnWithOutcome:GKTurnBasedMatchOutcomeQuit
    nextParticipants:nil turnTimeout:2000.0 matchData:matchData
    completionHandler:^(NSError *error) {
        // Finished telling Game Center that we quit
    }];

}
```

You should also conform to the GKLocalPlayerListener protcol, and implement methods that tell your code about when other players have changed the game state:

```
- (void)player:(GKPlayer *)player
receivedTurnEventForMatch:(GKTurnBasedMatch *)match
didBecomeActive:(BOOL)didBecomeActive {
    // The game was updated. The player might have just become the current
    // player in the game.
}

- (void)player:(GKPlayer *)player matchEnded:(GKTurnBasedMatch *)match {
    // Tell the player that the match is over
}
```

Finally, you can update the game state, if it's the current player's turn. To end the turn, you do this:

```
GKTurnBasedMatch* match = ... // the current match
NSData* matchData = ... // the current game state

NSArray* nextParticipants = ... // an NSArray

// nextParticipants is an NSArray of GKTurnBasedParticipants. You can get the
// list of participants using match.participants. Game Center will tell the
// first participant in the array that it's their turn; if they don't do it
// within 600 seconds (10 minutes), it will be the player after that's turn,
// and so on. (If the last participant in the array doesn't complete their
// turn within 10 minutes, it remains their turn.)
[match endTurnWithNextParticipants:nextParticipants turnTimeout:600
matchData:matchData completionHandler:^(NSError *error) {
    // We're done sending the match data
}];
```

You can also end the entire match by doing this:

```
// End the match. All players will receive the updated state.
[match endMatchInTurnWithMatchData:matchData
completionHandler:^(NSError *error) {
    // We're done telling Game Center that the match is done
}];
```

Additionally, the current player can update the game state *without* ending his turn. If he does this, all other players get notified of the new game state:

```
GKTurnBasedMatch* match = ... // the current match
NSData* matchData = ... // the current game state

// Tell other players about the new state of the game. It still remains
// the current player's turn.
[match saveCurrentTurnWithMatchData:matchData
completionHandler:^(NSError *error) {
    // We're done sending the match data
}];
```

This can be used if the player decides to do something that's visible to all other players; for example, if the player decides to buy a house in a game like *Monopoly*, all other players should be notified of this so that they can adjust their strategy. However, buying a house doesn't end the player's turn.

Discussion

Turn-based games are hosted by Game Center. In a turn-based game, the entire state of the game is wrapped up in an NSData object that's maintained by Game Center. When it's a given player's turn, your game retrieves the game state from the Game Center server and lets the player decide what she'd like to do with her turn. When the player's done, your game produces an NSData object that represents the *new* game state, which takes into account the decisions the player has made. It then sends it to Game Center, along with information on which player should play next.

It's possible for a player to be involved in multiple turn-based games at the same time. This means that even when it isn't the player's turn in a particular match, she can still play your game. When you present a GKTurnBasedMatchmakerViewController, the view controller that's displayed shows all *current* games that the player can play. When the player selects a match, your code receives the GKTurnBasedMatch object that represents the current state of the game.

If the player creates a new match, Game Center finds participants for the match based on the GKMatchRequest that you pass in, and tells its delegate about the GKTurnBased Match object. Alternatively, if the player selects a match that she's currently playing in, the view controller gives its delegate the appropriate GKTurnBasedMatch.

It's important to let the player know when it's her turn. When your code gets notified that it's the player's turn in any of the matches that she's playing in, your code should let the player know as soon as possible.

12.12. Sharing Text and Images to Social Media Sites

Problem

You want to allow your users to send tweets or post to Facebook from your games, so that they can share their high scores and characters.

Solution

The SLComposeViewController is available as part of Apple's Social framework. To use it, you'll need to add *Social.framework* to your project and import *Social/Social.h* in the view controller where you want to use it. You can then use code similar to the following to allow the user to send a tweet containing nothing but text:

```
SLComposeViewController *tweetSheet =
[SLComposeViewController
 composeViewControllerForServiceType:SLServiceTypeTwitter];
[tweetSheet setInitialText:@"My high score was legendary!"];
[self presentViewController:tweetSheet animated:YES completion:Nil];
```

The first line creates an SLComposeViewController (also known as a "tweet sheet") with the service type set to Twitter, and the last line displays it. The second line is where you can set a string to be sent as the tweet; the user will be able to edit or remove this text once the view is presented.

You can also attach an image or a URL to a tweet:

```
[tweetSheet addImage:[UIImage imageNamed:@"Apollo"]];
[tweetSheet addURL:[NSURL URLWithString:@"http://www.secretlab.com.au"]];
```

The addImage: method takes a UIImage as a parameter, in this case referring to an image inside an asset catalog. The addURL: method takes an NSURL as a parameter; in this case, we're creating a new URL from a string.

Allowing your users to post to Facebook is similar, but when you create the SLCompose ViewController, instead of setting the service type to Twitter you set it to Facebook:

```
SLComposeViewController *facebookSheet = [SLComposeViewController
composeViewControllerForServiceType:SLServiceTypeFacebook];
```

As with Twitter, posting to Facebook supports the addition of a URL and an image. The SLComposeViewController also supports posting to Sina Weibo. You can check if a particular social service is available using the SLComposeViewController. For example:

```
if ([SLComposeViewController isAvailableForServiceType:SLServiceTypeTwitter])
{
        // We know that Twitter is available
}
else
{
        // We know that Twitter is not available
}
```

This code checks with the SLComposeViewController for the availability of SLService TypeTwitter, allowing you to perform alternate actions if the user has not added any social accounts of the type that you are attempting to use.

Discussion

Allowing your users to push content or high scores from your game out to their social networks is a great way to spread the word about what you've built. iOS makes it easy to attach content and links to social network posts, as you can see.

12.13. Implementing iOS Networking Effectively

Problem

You want to make effective and compelling use of the networking features of iOS in your game.

Solution

There's one very simple rule you can follow to make a great iOS game with networking: use as much of the provided game-network infrastructure as possible!

By tying your game to the features that are provided by iOS, such as Game Center, you're ensuring that your game will work properly alongside future versions of iOS, and that players will already know how to work many of the network-based components of your game through their exposure to other games.

Discussion

By adhering to Apple's recommended standards and techniques for building networked games, you'll create experiences that users already know how to use and understand. Don't be tempted to deviate! Your users will suffer because of it.

12.14. Implementing Social Networks Effectively

Problem

You want to make sure that your game makes effective use of the social features of iOS.

Solution

The solution here is simple: don't go overboard with social. It's very tempting to encourage users to tweet and post status updates about your game at every turn. After all, you have near-unfettered access to their social networking accounts, so why not encourage them to post constantly?

Here's a tip: you should use these great powers only sparingly. Users don't want to spam their friends, and they probably don't want to talk about a game they're not enjoying—and you don't want them to do these things either! Offer the ability to tweet and post status updates at junctures in your game when your users are likely to be at their happiest. Did they just win a level? Offer them the ability to tweet it. Did they just lose? Don't offer them the ability to tweet it.

Discussion

While it's tempting to put links to social media everywhere, it really only works best when it's exposed to happy, fulfilled users. Users who are bored or have just lost a game are likely to tweet (at best) meaningless spam or (at worst) critical comments about your game. Don't encourage them—choose your moments carefully.

CHAPTER 13

Game Controllers and External Screens

iOS devices can interact with a wide range of other devices. Some of these devices, such as external screens and game controllers, are particularly useful when you're building games!

iOS has supported multiple screens for several versions now, but as of iOS 7 it also supports game controllers, which are handheld devices that provide physical buttons for your players to use. Game controllers have both advantages and disadvantages when compared with touchscreens. Because a game controller has physical buttons, the player's hands can feel where the controls are, which makes it a lot easier to keep attention focused on the action in the game. Additionally, game controllers can have *analog inputs*: a controller can measure how hard a button is being held down, and the game can respond accordingly. However, game controllers have fixed buttons that can't change their position, or look and feel, which means that you can't change your controls on the fly.

Game controllers that work with iOS devices must obey a specific set of design constraints specified by Apple; these constraints mean that you can rely on game controllers built by different manufacturers to all behave in a consistent way and provide the same set of controls for your games. In a move that is both as empowering for gamers as it is infuriating for developers, Apple requires that *all* iOS games must be playable without a controller at all, even if they support a controller. A controller must never be required by an iOS game. This means that you'll end up developing two user interfaces: one with touchscreen controls, and one with game-controller controls.

To make matters more complex, there are several different *profiles* of game controller. The simplest (and usually cheapest) is the *standard* game controller (Figure 13-1), which features two shoulder buttons, four face buttons, a pause button, and a d-pad. The next step up is the *extended* gamepad(Figure 13-1), which includes everything in the standard profile, and adds two thumbsticks and two triggers. Your game doesn't need to make use of every single button that's available, but it helps.

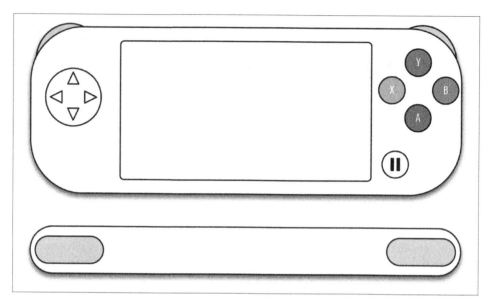

Figure 13-1. The basic game controller

Figure 13-2. The extended game controller (note the thumbsticks and additional shoulder buttons)

In addition to game controllers, iOS games can make use of external screens. These can be directly connected to your device via a cable, or they can be wirelessly connected via AirPlay. Using external screens, you can do a number of things: for example, you can make your game appear on a larger screen than the one that's built in, or even turn the iPhone into a game controller and put the game itself on a television screen (effectively turning the device into a portable games console).

Like controllers, external screens should never be required by your game. External screens are useful for displaying supplementary components of your game, or providing the main game view while using the iOS device itself as a controller and secondary view.

In this chapter, you'll learn how to connect to and use game controllers, how to use multiple screens via cables and wireless AirPlay, and how to design and build games that play well on the iPhone/iPod touch and iPad, or both.

13.1. Detecting Controllers

Problem

You want to determine whether the user is using a game controller. You also want to know when the user connects and disconnects the controller.

Solution

Game controllers are represented by instances of the `GCController` class. Each `GCController` lets you get information about the controller itself and the state all of its buttons and controls.

To get a `GCGameController`, you ask the `GCController` class for the `controllers` property, which is the list of all currently connected controllers:

```
for (GCController* controller in [GCController controllers]) {
    NSLog(@"Controller made by %@", controller.vendorName);
}
```

The `controllers` array updates whenever controllers are connected or disconnected. If the user plugs in a controller or disconnects one, the system sends a `GCController DidConnectNotification` or a `GCControllerDidDisconnectNotification`, respectively. You can register to receive these notifications like this:

```
[[NSNotificationCenter defaultCenter] addObserver:self
    selector:@selector(controllerConnected:)
    name:GCControllerDidConnectNotification object:nil];
[[NSNotificationCenter defaultCenter] addObserver:self
    selector:@selector(controllerDisconnected:)
    name:GCControllerDidDisconnectNotification object:nil];
```

```
// Elsewhere:

- (void) controllerConnected:(NSNotification*)notification {
    GCController* newController = notification.object;
    // Do something with newController
}

- (void) controllerDisconnected:(NSNotification*)notification {
    GCController* controller = notification.object;
    // Controller just got disconnected, deal with it
}
```

When a controller is connected, you can find out whether it's a standard gamepad or an extended gamepad by using the gamepad and extendedGamepad properties:

```
GCController* controller = ... // a GCController

if (controller.extendedGamepad) {
    // It's an extended gamepad
} else if (controller.gamepad) {
    // It's a standard gamepad
} else {
    // It's something else entirely, and probably can't be used by your game
}
```

Discussion

The GCController class updates automatically when a controller is plugged in to the device. However, your user might have a wireless controller that uses Bluetooth to connect to the iPhone, and it might not be connected when your game launches.

Your player can leave the game and enter the Settings application to connect the device, but you might prefer to let the player connect the controller while still in your game. To do this, you use the startWirelessControllerDiscoveryWithCompletionHandler: method. When you call this, the system starts looking for nearby game controllers, and sends you a GCControllerDidConnectNotification for each one that it finds. Once the search process is complete, regardless of whether or not any controllers were found, the method calls a completion handler block:

```
[GCController startWirelessControllerDiscoveryWithCompletionHandler:^{
    // This code is called once searching is finished
}];

// Notifications will now be sent when controllers are discovered
```

You can also manually stop the searching process with the stopWirelessController Discovery method:

```
[GCController stopWirelessControllerDiscovery];
```

It's important to note that the system won't show any built-in UI when you're searching for wireless controllers. It's up to you to show UI that indicates that you're searching for controllers.

Once a wireless controller is connected, your game treats it just like a wired one—there's no difference in the way you talk to it.

Once you have a `GCController`, you can set the `playerIndex` property. When you set this property, an LED on the controller lights up to let the player know which player he is. This property is actually remembered by the controller and is the same across *all games*, so that the player can move from game to game and not have to relearn which player number he is in multiplayer games.

13.2. Getting Input from a Game Controller

Problem

You would like people to be able to control your game using their external controllers.

Solution

Each controller provides access to its buttons through various properties:

```
GCController *controller = ... // a GCController

BOOL buttonAPressed = controller.gamePad.buttonA.pressed;

float buttonAPressAmount = controller.gamePad.buttonA.value;
```

You use the same technique to get information about the gamepad's directional pads. The d-pad and the thumbsticks are both represented as `GCControllerDirectionPad` classes, which lets you treat them as a pair of axes (i.e., the x-axis and the y-axis), or as four separate buttons (up, down, left, and right):

```
// -1 = fully left, 1 = fully right
float xAxis = controller.gamePad.dpad.xAxis;

// Alternatively:
BOOL isLeftButtonPressed = controller.gamePad.dpad.left.pressed;
```

Discussion

There are two different types of inputs available in a game controller:.

- A *button input* tells you whether a button is being pressed, as a Boolean YES or NO. Alternatively, you can find out *how much* a button is being pressed down by, as a floating-point value that goes from 0 (not pressed down at all) to 1 (completely pressed down).

- An *axis input* provides two-dimensional information on how far left, right, up, and down the d-pad or thumbstick is being pressed by the user.

The face and shoulder buttons are all represented as GCControllerButtonInput objects, which let you get their value either as a simple BOOL or as a float. The d-pad and the thumbsticks are both represented as GCControllerAxisInput objects.

Both button inputs and axis inputs also let you provide *value changed handlers*, which are blocks that the system calls when an input changes value. You can use these to make your game run code when the user interacts with the controller, as opposed to continuously polling the controller to see its current state.

For example, if you want to get a notification every time the A button on the controller is interacted with, you can do this:

```
controller.gamePad.buttonA.valueChangedHandler = ^(GCControllerButtonInput
    *button, float value, BOOL pressed) {
        // The button has changed state, do something about it
};
```

This applies to both button inputs and axis inputs, so you can attach handlers to the thumbsticks and d-pad as well. Note that the value changed handler will be called multiple times while a button is pressed, because the value property will change continuously as the button is being pressed down and released.

In addition to adding handlers to the inputs, you can also add a handler block to the controller's pause button:

```
controller.controllerPausedHandler = ^(GCController* controller) {
    // Toggle between being paused or not
}
```

The controller itself doesn't store any information about whether the game is paused or not—it's up to your game to keep track of the pause state. All the controller will do is tell you when the button is pressed.

13.3. Showing Content via AirPlay

Problem

You would like to use AirPlay to wirelessly display elements of your game on a high-definition screen via an Apple TV.

Solution

Use an `MPVolumeView` to provide a picker, which lets the user select an AirPlay device.

```
UIView* view = ... // a UIView you want to show the picker in
MPVolumeView *volumeView = [[MPVolumeView alloc] init] ;
volumeView.showsVolumeSlider = NO; // don't show the volume slider,
                                   // just the AirPlay picker
[volumeView sizeToFit];
[view addSubview:volumeView];
```

This creates a button that, when tapped, lets the user select an AirPlay device to connect to the existing device. When the user selects a screen, a `UIScreenDidConnectNotifica` `tion` is sent, and your game can use the AirPlay device using the `UIScreen` class (see Recipe 13.4.)

> The `MPVolumeView` will only show the AirPlay picker if there are Air-Play devices available. If no AirPlay device is nearby, nothing will appear.

Discussion

When the user has selected an AirPlay display, iOS treats it as if a screen is attached. You can then treat it as a `UIScreen` (there's no distinction made between wireless screens and plugged-in screens).

Just like with a plugged-in screen, the contents of the primary screen will be mirrored onto the additional screen. If you give the screen to a `UIWindow` object, mirroring will be turned off and the screen will start showing the `UIWindow`. If you remove the `UIScreen` from the `UIWindow`, the screen will return to mirroring mode.

> If there are more than two screens attached, only one screen will mirror the main display. The other screens will be blank until you give them to a `UIWindow`.

13.4. Using External Screens

Problem

You would like to display elements of your game on a screen external to the iOS device.

Solution

To get the list of available screens, you use the `UIScreen` class:

```
for (UIScreen* connectedScreen in [UIScreen screens]) {
    NSLog(@"Connected screen: %@", NSStringFromCGSize(screen.currentMode.size));
}
```

On iPhones, iPod touches, and iPads, there's always at least one `UIScreen` available—the built-in touchscreen. You can get access to it through the `UIScreen`'s `mainScreen` property:

```
UIScreen* mainScreen = [UIScreen mainScreen];
```

When you have a `UIScreen`, you can display content on it by creating a `UIWindow` and giving it to the `UIScreen`. `UIWindows` are the top-level containers for all views—in fact, they're views themselves, which means you add views to a screen using the `addSub view:` method:

```
UIScreen* screen = ... // a UIScreen from the list

UIWindow* newWindow = [[UIWindow alloc] initWithFrame:screen.bounds];

UIView* aView = [[UIView alloc] initWithFrame:CGRect(10,10,100,100)];
aView.backgroundColor = [UIColor redColor];

[newWindow addSubview:aView];

newWindow.screen = screen;
```

Discussion

You can detect when a screen is connected by subscribing to the `UIScreenDidConnect Notification` and `UIScreenDidDisconnectNotification` notifications. These are sent when a new screen becomes available to the system—either because it's been plugged in to the device, or because it's become available over AirPlay—and when a screen becomes unavailable.

If you want to test external screens on the iOS simulator, you can select one by choosing Hardware→TV Out and choosing one of the available sizes of window (see Figure 13-3). Note that selecting an external display through this menu will restart the entire simulator, which will quit your game in the process. This means that while you can test *having* a screen connected, you can't test the `UIScreenDidConnectNotifica tion` and `UIScreenDidDisconnectNotification` notifications.

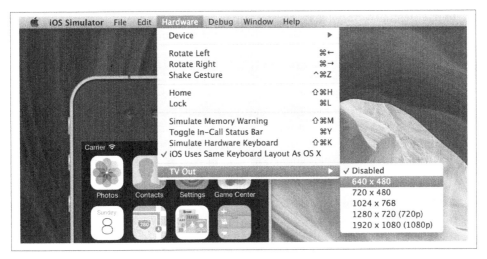

Figure 13-3. Choosing the size of the external screen in the iOS Simulator

13.5. Designing Effective Graphics for Different Screens

Problem

You want your game to play well on different kinds of screens and devices, including iPhones, iPads, and large-scale televisions.

Solution

When you design your game's interface, you need to consider several factors that differ between iPhones, iPads, and connected displays. Keep the following things in mind when considering how the player is going to interact with your game.

Designing for iPhones

An iPhone:

Is very portable
> People can whip out an iPhone in two seconds, and start playing a game within five. Because they can launch games very quickly, they won't want to wait around for your game to load.

> Additionally, the iPhone is a very light device. Users can comfortably hold it in a single hand.

Has a very small screen
> The amount of screen space available for you to put game content on is very small. Because the iPhone has a touchscreen, you can put controls on the screen. However,

to use them, players will have to cover up the screen with their big, opaque fingers and thumbs. Keep the controls small—but not too small, because fingers are very imprecise.

Will be used in various locations, and with various degrees of attention
People play games on their iPhones in a variety of places: in bed, waiting for a train, on the toilet, at the dinner table, and more. Each place varies in the amount of privacy the user has, the amount of ambient noise, and the amount of distraction. If you're making a game for the iPhone, your players will thank you if the game doesn't punish them for looking away from the screen for a moment.

Additionally, you should assume that the players can't hear a single thing coming from the speaker. They could be sitting in a quiet room, but they could just as easily be in a crowded subway station. They could also be playing in bed and trying not to wake their partners, or they could be hard of hearing or deaf.

Your game's audio should be designed so that it enhances the game but isn't necessary for the game to work. (Obviously, this won't be achievable for all games; if you've got a game based heavily on sound, that's still a totally OK thing to make!)

Designing for iPads

An iPad:

Is portable, but less spontaneous
Nobody quickly pulls out an iPad to play a 30-second puzzle game, and then puts it back in their pocket. Generally, people use iPads less frequently than smartphones but for longer periods. This means that "bigger" games tend to do very well on the iPad, beacuse the user starts playing them with an intent to play for at least a few minutes rather than (potentially) a few seconds.

Has a comparatively large screen
There are two different types of iPad screens: the one present on the iPad mini, and the one present on larger-size iPads (such as the iPad 2 and the iPad Air). The mini's screen is smaller, but still considerably larger than that on the iPhone. This gives you more room to place your controls, and gives the player a bigger view of the game's action.

However, the flipside is that the iPad is heavier than the iPhone. iPads generally need to be held in both hands, or placed on some kind of support (like a table or the player's lap). This contributes to the fact that iPads are used less often but for longer sessions: it takes a moment to get an iPad positioned just how the user wants it.

Will be used in calmer conditions
For the same reason, an iPad tends to be used when the user is sitting rather than walking around, and in less hectic and public environments. The user will also be more likely to give more of their attention to the device.

Designing for larger screens

When the player has connected a larger screen:

They're not moving around
An external screen tends to be fixed in place, and doesn't move around. If the screen is plugged directly into the iPad, this will also restrict movement. This means that the players are likely to play for a longer period of time—because they've invested the energy in setting up the device with their TV, they'll be in for the (relatively) long haul.

The player has two screens to look at
A player who's connected an external screen to his iOS device will still be holding the device in his hands, but he's more likely to not be looking at it. This means that he's not looking at where your controls are. If he's not using a controller, which is likely, he won't be able to feel where one button ends and another begins. This means that your device should show *very large* controls on the screen, so that your users can focus on their wonderfully huge televisions and not have to constantly look down at the device.

Having two devices can be a tremendous advantage for your game, for example, if you want to display secondary information to your user—*Real Racing 2* does this very well, in that it shows the game itself on the external screen, and additional info like the current speed and the map on the device.

More than one person can comfortably look at the big screen
Large displays typically have a couch in front of them, and more than one person can sit on a couch. This means that you can have multiple people playing a game, though you need to keep in mind that only one device can actually send content to the screen.

Discussion

Generally, you'll get more sales if your game works on both the iPhone and the iPad. Players have their own preferences, and many will probably have either an iPhone or an iPad—it's rare to have both, because Apple products are expensive.

When it comes to supporting large screens, it's generally a cool feature to have, but it's not very commonplace to have access to one. You probably shouldn't consider external screen support to be a critical feature of your game unless you're deliberately designing a game to be played by multiple people in the same room.

13.6. Dragging and Dropping

Problem

You want to drag and drop objects into specific locations. If an object is dropped some-where it can't go, it should return to its origin. (This is particularly useful in card games.)

Solution

Use gesture recognizers to implement the dragging itself. When the gesture recognizer ends, check to see whether the drag is over a view that you consider to be a valid *destination*. If it is, position the view over the destination; if not, move back to its original location.

The following code provides an example of how you can do this. In this example, CardSlot objects create Cards when tapped; these Card objects can be dragged and dropped only onto other CardSlots, and only if those CardSlot objects don't already have a card on them, as shown in Figure 13-4.

Figure 13-4. The Drag and Drop example in this recipe

Additionally, card slots can be configured so they delete any cards that are dropped on them.

Create a new Objective-C class called `CardSlot`, which is a subclass of `UIImageView`. Put the following code in *CardSlot.h*:

```
@class Card;

@interface CardSlot : UIImageView

// The card that's currently living in this card slot.
@property (nonatomic, weak) Card* currentCard;

// Whether cards should be deleted if they are dropped on this card
@property (assign) BOOL deleteOnDrop;

@end
```

Then, put the following code in *CardSlot.m*:

```
#import "CardSlot.h"
#import "Card.h"

@interface CardSlot ()

// The tap gesture recognizer; when the view is tapped, a new Card is created
@property (strong) UITapGestureRecognizer* tap;

@end

@implementation CardSlot

// Called when the view wakes up in the Storyboard.
- (void) awakeFromNib {

    // Create and configure the tap recognizer.
    self.tap = [[UITapGestureRecognizer alloc] initWithTarget:self
                action:@selector(tapped:)];
    [self addGestureRecognizer:self.tap];

    // UIImageViews default to userInteractionEnabled being set to NO,
    // so change that.
    self.userInteractionEnabled = YES;
}

// Called when the tap recognizer changes state.
- (void) tapped:(UITapGestureRecognizer*)tap {

    // If a tap has been recognized, create a new card
    if (tap.state == UIGestureRecognizerStateRecognized) {

        // Only card slots that aren't 'delete on drop' can create cards
        if (self.deleteOnDrop == NO) {
```

```
            Card* card = [[Card alloc] initWithCardSlot:self];

            [self.superview addSubview:card];

            self.currentCard = card;
        }
    }
}

// Called by the Card class to transfer ownership of the card.
- (void)setCurrentCard:(Card *)currentCard {

    // If we're marked as "delete on drop" then delete the card
    // and set our current card variable to nil
    if (self.deleteOnDrop) {
        [currentCard delete];
        _currentCard = nil;
        return;
    }

    // Otherwise, our current card becomes the new card
    _currentCard = currentCard;
}

@end
```

Then, create another `UIImageView` subclass called Card. Put the following code in *Card.h*:

```
@class CardSlot;

@interface Card : UIImageView

// Creates a new card, given a card slot for it to exist in.
- (id) initWithCardSlot:(CardSlot*)cardSlot;

// Deletes the card with an animation.
- (void) delete;

// The card slot that we're currently in.
@property (weak) CardSlot* currentSlot;

@end
```

And the following code in *Card.m*:

```
#import "Card.h"
#import "CardSlot.h"

@interface Card ()

@property (strong) UIPanGestureRecognizer* dragGesture;
```

```
@end

@implementation Card

// Creates a card, and
- (id)initWithCardSlot:(CardSlot *)cardSlot {

    if (cardSlot.currentCard != nil) {
        // This card slot already has a card and can't have another.
        return nil;
    }

    // All cards use the same image.
    self = [self initWithImage:[UIImage imageNamed:@"Card"]];

    if (self) {
        // Cards appear at the same position as the card slot.
        self.center = cardSlot.center;

        // We're using this slot as our current card slot
        self.currentSlot = cardSlot;

        // Create and set up the drag gesture
        self.dragGesture = [[UIPanGestureRecognizer alloc]
                            initWithTarget:self action:@selector(dragged:)];
        [self addGestureRecognizer:self.dragGesture];

        // UIImageViews default to userInteractionEnabled to NO; turn it on.
        self.userInteractionEnabled = YES;
    }

    return self;

}

// Called when the drag gesture recognizer changes state.
- (void) dragged:(UIPanGestureRecognizer*)dragGestureRecognizer {

    // If we've started dragging...
    if (dragGestureRecognizer.state == UIGestureRecognizerStateBegan) {

        // The drag has moved enough such that it's decided that a pan
        // is happening. We need to animate to the right location.
        CGPoint translation = [dragGestureRecognizer
                               translationInView:self.superview];

        translation.x += self.center.x;
        translation.y += self.center.y;

        // Animate to where the drag is at right now, and rotate
        // by a few degrees
        [UIView animateWithDuration:0.1 animations:^{
```

```
        self.center = translation;

        // Rotate by about 5 degrees
        self.transform = CGAffineTransformMakeRotation(M_PI_4 / 8.0);
    }];

    // Reset the drag
    [dragGestureRecognizer setTranslation:CGPointZero inView:self.superview];

    // Bring the card up to the front so that it appears over everything
    [self.superview bringSubviewToFront:self];

} else if (dragGestureRecognizer.state == UIGestureRecognizerStateChanged) {

    // The drag location has changed. Update the card's position.

    CGPoint translation = [dragGestureRecognizer
                            translationInView:self.superview];

    translation.x += self.center.x;
    translation.y += self.center.y;

    self.center = translation;

    [dragGestureRecognizer setTranslation:CGPointZero inView:self.superview];
} else if (dragGestureRecognizer.state == UIGestureRecognizerStateEnded) {

    // The drag has finished.

    // If the touch is over a CardSlot, and that card slot doesn't
    // already have a card, then we're now in that slot, and we should
    // move it; otherwise, return to the previous slot.

    CardSlot* destinationSlot = nil;

    // Loop over every view
    for (UIView* view in self.superview.subviews) {

        // First, check to see if the drag is inside the view;
        // if not, move on.
        if ([view pointInside:[dragGestureRecognizer locationInView:view]
            withEvent:nil] == NO)
            continue;

        // If the view the drag is inside the view, check to see if
        // the view is a CardSlot. If it is, and it's got no card,
        // then it's our destination.
        if ([view isKindOfClass:[CardSlot class]]) {
            if ([(CardSlot*)view currentCard] == nil)
                destinationSlot = (CardSlot*)view;
            break;
        }
```

```
        }

        // If we have a new destination, update the properties.
        if (destinationSlot) {
            self.currentSlot.currentCard = nil;
            self.currentSlot = destinationSlot;
            self.currentSlot.currentCard = self;
        }

        // Animate to our new destination
        [UIView animateWithDuration:0.1 animations:^{
            self.center = self.currentSlot.center;
        }];
    } else if (dragGestureRecognizer.state == UIGestureRecognizerStateCancelled) {

        // The gesture was interrupted (for example, because a phone call
        // came in). Move back to our original slot.

        [UIView animateWithDuration:0.1 animations:^{
            self.center = self.currentSlot.center;
        }];

    }

    // If the gesture ended or was cancelled, we need to return to
    // normal orientation.
    if (dragGestureRecognizer.state == UIGestureRecognizerStateEnded ||
        dragGestureRecognizer.state == UIGestureRecognizerStateCancelled) {

        // Rotate back to normal orientation.
        [UIView animateWithDuration:0.25 animations:^{
            self.transform = CGAffineTransformIdentity;
        }];
    }

}

// Removes the card from the view after fading out.
- (void) delete {
    [UIView animateWithDuration:0.1 animations:^{
        self.alpha = 0.0;
    } completion:^(BOOL finished) {
        [self removeFromSuperview];
    }];
}


@end
```

Add two images to your project: one called *CardSlot.png*, and another called *Card.png*.

Then, open your app's storyboard and drag in a `UIImageView`. Make it use the *Card-Slot.png* image, and set its class to `CardSlot`. Repeat this process a couple of times, until you have several card slots. When you run your app, you can tap on the card slots to make cards appear. Cards can be dragged and dropped between card slots; if you try to drop a card onto a card slot that already has a card, or try to drop it outside of a card slot, it will return to its original location.

You can also make a card slot delete any card that is dropped on it. To do this, select a card slot in the interface builder, go to the Identity inspector, and click the + button under the *User Defined Runtime Attributes* list. Change the newly added entry's key path to `deleteOnDrop`, and make the Type "Boolean" and the Value "true". When you re-run the app, any card that you drop on that card slot will disappear.

Discussion

Limiting where an object can be dragged and dropped provides constraints to your game's interface, which can improve the user experience of your game. If anything can be dropped anywhere, the game feels loose and without direction. If the game takes control and keeps objects tidy, the whole thing feels a lot snappier.

In this example, the *dragging* effect is enhanced by the fact that when dragging begins, the card is rotated slightly; when the drag ends or is cancelled, the card rotates back. Adding small touches like this can dramatically improve how your game feels.

CHAPTER 14

Performance and Debugging

At some point during its development, every game will have performance issues, and every game will crash. Fortunately, iOS has some of the best tools around for squeezing as much performance as possible out of your games and finding bugs and other issues.

In this chapter, you'll learn about how to use these tools, how to fix problems, and how to get information about how your game's behaving.

14.1. Improving Your Frame Rate

Problem

You need to coax a better frame rate out of your game so that it plays smoothly.

Solution

To improve your frame rate, you first need to determine where the majority of the work is being done. In Xcode:

1. From the Scheme menu, select your device, so that the application will be installed to the device when you build.

2. Open the Product menu and choose Profile (or press Command-I).

   The application will build and install onto the device, and Instruments will open and show the template picker (Figure 14-1).

Figure 14-1. Selecting the Instruments template

3. Select the Time Profiler instrument and run your game for a while. You'll start seeing information about how much CPU time your game is taking up.

4. Turn on Invert Call Tree and Show Obj-C Only, and turn off everything else in the list, as shown in Figure 14-2.

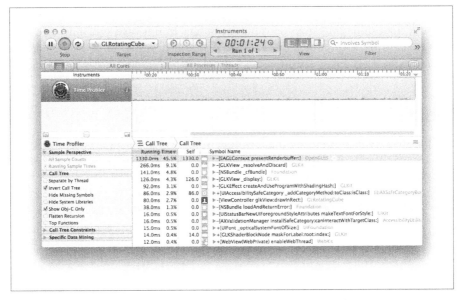

Figure 14-2. Instruments in action

5. Take note of the name of the function that's at the top of the list:

a. If the top function is [EAGLContext presentRenderbuffer:], the game is spending most of its time rendering graphics. To improve your frame rate, reduce the number of objects on the screen, and make fewer calls to glDrawEle ments and its related functions.

b. If not, the game is spending most of its time running code on the CPU. Turn on Hide System Libraries; the function at the top of the list is your code, which the game is spending most of its time processing (see Figure 14-3).

Running Time▼		Self	Symbol Name
1330.0ms	45.5%	1330.0	▶-[EAGLContext presentRenderbuffer:] OpenGLES
266.0ms	9.1%	0.0	▶-[GLKView _resolveAndDiscard] GLKit
141.0ms	4.8%	0.0	▶-[NSBundle _cfBundle] Foundation
126.0ms	4.3%	126.0	▶-[GLKView _display:] GLKit
92.0ms	3.1%	0.0	▶-[GLKEffect createAndUseProgramWithShadingHash:] GLKit
86.0ms	2.9%	86.0	▶+[UIAccessibilitySafeCategory _addCategoryMethod:toClass:isClass:] libAXSafeCategoryBur
80.0ms	2.7%	0.0	▶-[ViewController glkView:drawInRect:] GLRotatingCube

Figure 14-3. In this example, the function that's consuming the most CPU time is EAGL Context presentRenderBuffer:

If your game is spending most of its time rendering graphics, you can improve the speed by drawing fewer sprites (if you're using Sprite Kit) or drawing fewer objects (if you're using OpenGL). If most of the time is spent running code on the CPU, it's less straight-forward, since different games do different things. In this case, you'll need to look for ways to optimize your code. For example, if a long-running function is calculating a value that doesn't change very often, store the result in a variable instead of recalculating it.

Discussion

You improve frame rates by taking less time to do the work you need to do per frame. This means either reducing the total amount of work you need to do, or not making the rendering of frames wait for work to complete.

You should only profile using a real device, because the simulator performs differently to the real thing. The simulator has a faster CPU, but a slower GPU.

14.2. Making Levels Load Quickly

Problem

You want to make your levels load as quickly as possible, so that the player can get into the game immediately.

Solution

There are three main techniques for making a level load faster:

Load smaller or fewer resources
> Make the images and sounds that you load smaller. Reduce the dimensions of textures, use compressed textures, and use lower-quality audio. Alternatively, load fewer resources.

Show progress indicators
> When you begin loading resources for a new level, first count the number of resources you need to load; every time one gets loaded, show progress to the user, either using a progress indicator (such as a UILabel or UIProgressView) or a text field.

Stream textures
> When level loading begins, load very small resources, such as very small textures. Once the game has begun, begin loading full-size textures in the background; once each high-resolution texture has loaded, replace the small texture with the large one.

Discussion

Half the battle is making the game *look* like it's fast. The other half is actually *being* fast.

Loading smaller resources means that less data needs to be sent. An iOS device is really a collection of small, interconnected pieces, and it takes time to transfer data from the flash chips to the CPU and the GPU. In almost all cases, "faster loading" just means "loading less stuff."

If you can't increase the speed beyond a certain point, showing progress indicators at least means the user sees some kind of progress. If you just show a static "loading" screen, the player will get bored, and it will *feel* like it's taking longer. You can see this technique outside of games, too: when you launch an iOS application, the system first shows a placeholder image while the app launches in the background. Apple encourages developers to make this placeholder image look like part of the application, but without any text or actual data to show, and the result is that the app feels like it's launching faster.

Finally, it's often the case that you just want to get *something* on the screen so that the player can start playing, and it's OK if parts of the game don't look their best for the first few seconds. This is called *texture streaming*, and the idea is that you load a deliberately small texture during the normal loading process, let the player get into the game, and then start slowly loading a better texture in the background.

Texture streaming means that your game's loading process is faster, since there's less data that needs to be transferred before the game can start. However, it can lead to visual problems: when the larger, higher-quality texture is loaded, a visible "pop" can happen. Additionally, loading two versions of the same texture at the same time means that more memory is being consumed, which can lead to memory pressure problems on iOS devices.

14.3. Dealing with Low-Memory Issues

Problem

Your app is randomly crashing when images or other resources are loaded into memory.

Solution

There are several ways you can reduce the amount of memory that your application is using. For example:

Use fewer textures
> If you can reuse an image for more than one sprite or texture, it's better than having multiple images that vary only slightly.

Trim your textures

If you have a texture that's got some transparent area around the edges, trim them. When a texture is loaded, every pixel counts toward memory usage, including ones that are entirely transparent.

Use texture atlases

If you're using Sprite Kit, Xcode makes it pretty easy to create texture atlases. Texture atlases group multiple textures together, which is more efficient, since per-texture overhead is minimized. Xcode also automatically trims your textures for you. To create a texture atlas, create a folder with a name ending in *.atlas*, and put your images into that. Once that's done, your textures will be combined into a single image, saving a little memory.

Memory-map large files

If you need to read a large file—for example, a level file, a large collection of data, or a large sound file—you'll often load it in as an `NSData` object. However, the usual method of doing this, with `dataWithContentsOfFile:`, copies the data into memory. If you're reading from a file that you know won't change, you can instead *memory-map* it, which means instructing iOS to pretend that the entire file has been copied into memory, but to only actually read the file when parts of it are accessed. To do this, load your files using `dataWithContentsOfFile:options:error:` and use the `NSDataReadingMappedIfSafe` option:

```
NSData* data = [NSData dataWithContentsOfFile:filePath
                    options:NSDataReadingMappedIfSafe error:&error];
```

Use compressed textures

Compressed textures can dramatically reduce the amount of memory that your game's textures take up. For more information, see Recipe 14.5.

Discussion

iOS has a very limited amount of memory, compared to OS X. The main reason for this is that iOS doesn't use a *swap file*, which is a file that operating systems use to extend the amount of RAM available by using the storage medium. On OS X, if you run out of physical RAM (i.e., space to fit stuff in the RAM chips), the operating system moves some of the information in RAM to the swap file, freeing up some room. On iOS, there's no swap file for it to move information into, so when you're out of memory, you're completely out of memory.

The reason for this is that writing information to flash memory chips, such as those used in iOS devices, causes them to degrade very slightly. If the system is constantly swapping information out of RAM and into flash memory, the flash memory gradually gets slower and slower. From Apple's perspective, it's a better deal for the user to have a faster device and for developers to deal with memory constraints.

Because there's a fixed amount of memory available, iOS terminates applications when they run out of memory. When the system runs low on memory, all applications are sent a low memory warning, which is their one and only notification that they're running low.

The amount of memory available to apps depends on the device; however, as of iOS 7, there's a hard limit of 600 MB per app. If an app ever goes above this limit, it will be immediately terminated by the operating system.

14.4. Tracking Down a Crash

Problem

You want to understand why an application is crashing, and how to fix it.

Solution

First, determine what kind of crash it is. The most common kinds of crashes are:

Exceptions
> These occur when your code does something that Apple's code doesn't expect, such as trying to insert nil into an array. When an exception occurs, you'll see a backtrace appear in the debugging console.

Memory pressure terminations
> As we saw in the previous recipe, iOS will terminate any application that exceeds its memory limit. This isn't strictly a crash, but from the user's perspective, it looks identical to one. When a memory pressure termination occurs, Xcode displays a notification.

Once you know what kind of crash you're looking at, you can take steps to fix it.

Discussion

The approach you take will depend on the kind of issue you're experiencing.

Fixing exceptions

To fix an exception, you need to know where the exception is being thrown from. The easiest way to do this is to add a breakpoint on Objective-C exceptions, which will stop the program at the moment the exception is thrown (instead of the moment that the exception causes the app to crash).

To add this breakpoint:

1. Open the Breakpoints navigator, and click the + button at the bottom left of the window (Figure 14-4).

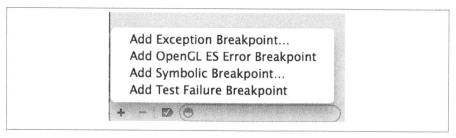

Figure 14-4. The breakpoints menu

2. Click Add Exception Breakpoint.
3. Run the application again; when the exception is thrown, Xcode will stop inside your code.

Fixing memory pressure issues

There are lots of different approaches you can take to reduce the amount of memory being consumed by your application; see Recipe 14.3 for some pointers.

14.5. Working with Compressed Textures

Problem

You want to use compressed textures, to save memory and loading time.

Solution

To work with compressed textures, you need to have compressed textures to load. Xcode comes with a texture compression tool, but it's sometimes tricky to use. It's better to write a simple script that handles many of the details of using the compression tool for you:

1. Create a new, empty file called *compress.sh*. Place this file anywhere you like.

2. Put the following text in it (note that the path must all appear on one line; it's broken here only to fit the page margins):

```
PARAMS="-e PVRTC --channel-weighting-perceptual --bits-per-pixel-4"

/Applications/Xcode.app/Contents/Developer/Platforms/iPhoneOS.platform/
    Developer/usr/bin/texturetool $PARAMS -o "$1.pvrtc" -p "$1-Preview.png" "$1"
```

3. Open the Terminal, and navigate to the folder where you put *compress.sh*.

4. Type the following commands:

```
chmod +x ./compress.sh
./compress.sh MyImage.png
```

After a moment, you'll have two new images: *MyImage.png.pvrtc* and *MyImage.png-Preview.png*. The preview PNG file shows you what the compressed version of your image looks like, and the PVRTC file is the file that you should copy into your project.

Once you have your compressed texture, you load it like any other texture. If you're using Sprite Kit, you load a texture using the `textureWithImageNamed:` method, providing it with the name of your PVRTC file:

```
SKTexture* texture = [SKTexture textureWithImageNamed:
                        @"MyCompressedTexture.pvrtc"];
```

With GLKit, it's much the same process, though you have to get the full path of the image file using `NSBundle`'s `pathForResource:ofType:` method. Once you have that, you use `GLKTextureLoader`'s `textureWithContentsOfFile:options:error:` method to load the texture:

```
NSString* textureLocation = [[NSBundle mainBundle] pathForResource:
                        @"MyCompressedTexture" ofType:@"pvrtc"];
NSError* error = nil;
GLKTextureInfo* texture = [GLKTextureLoader textureWithContentsOfFile:
                        textureLocation options:nil error:&error];
```

 Unfortunately, it's not possible to load a *.pvrtc* file using the `UIImage` class's methods. This means that you can't use compressed textures in `UIImageViews`, which is annoying. The only places you can use compressed textures are in OpenGL or when using Sprite Kit.

Discussion

Compressed textures use much less memory, and take less time to load (because there's less data to transfer to the graphics chip), but they look worse. How much "worse" depends on the type of image you want to compress:

- Photos and similar-looking textures do quite well with compression.

- Line art tends to get fuzzy fringes around the edges of lines.

- Images with transparent areas look particularly bad, because the transparent edges of the image get fuzzy.

On iOS, compressed textures are available as 2 bits per pixel (not bytes, *bits*) and 4 bits per pixel. Whereas a full-color 512 x 512 image would take up 1 MB of graphics memory, a 4 bpp version of the same image would take up only 128 kb of graphics memory.

The compression system used is called PVRTC, which stands for PowerVR Texture Compression (PowerVR provides the graphics architecture for iOS devices).

An image can only be compressed when it fits all of the following requirements:

- The image is square (i.e., the width is the same as the height).

- The image is at least 8 pixels high and wide.

- The image's width and height are a power of 2 (i.e., 8, 16, 32, 64, 128, 512, 1024, 2048, 4096).

Use compressed textures with care. While they can dramatically improve performance, reduce memory usage, and speed up loading times, if they're used without care they can make your game look very ugly, as in the zoomed-in Figure 14-5. The image on the left is the compressed version; PVRTC introduces compression artifacts, which creates a slight "noisy" pattern along the edge of the circle. There's also a subtle color difference between the image on the left and on the right, which is an additional consequence of compression. Experiment, and see what looks best in your game.

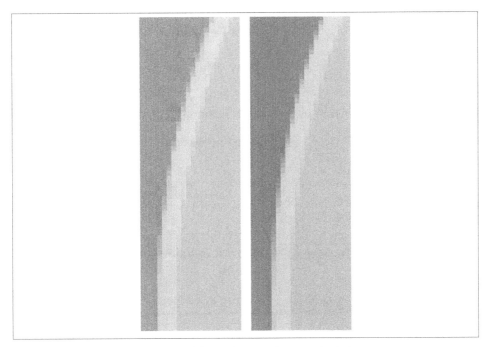

Figure 14-5. Compressed image (left) and original image (right)

14.6. Working with Watchpoints

Problem

You want to know when a specific variable changes.

Solution

To make Xcode stop your program when a variable changes from one value to another, you use a watchpoint. To set a watchpoint on a variable:

1. First, stop your program using a breakpoint.

   When the program stops, the list of visible variables appears in the debugging console.

2. Add the watchpoint for the variable you want to watch.

   Find the variable you want to watch, right-click it, and choose "Watch *name of your variable*," as shown in Figure 14-6.

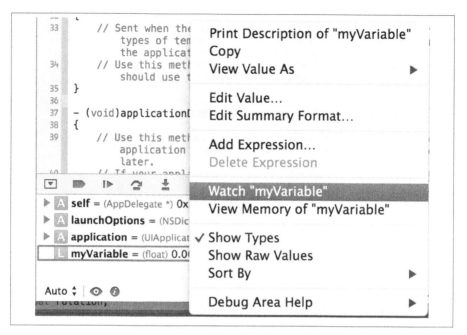

Figure 14-6. Creating a watchpoint

3. Continue the application.

   The application will stop when the variable you've watched changes value.

Discussion

Watchpoints are breakpoints that "watch" a location in memory and stop the program the moment the value stored in that location changes. Watchpoints can't be added to properties—they only watch regions of memory. If you want to watch a property, you need to locate the instance variable that that property uses, and watch it.

Keep in mind that when you stop and relaunch a program, the locations of the variables you were watching last time will have changed, and you'll need to add the watchpoints again.

14.7. Logging Effectively

Problem

You want to log additional information about what your application is doing when information is logged to the console.

Solution

You can make NSLog show additional information by overriding it:

1. Open your project's precompiled header. It's the file ending in *.pch*, and is usually in the "Supporting Files" group.

2. Add the following line before the final #endif line:

```
#define NSLog(text, ...) NSLog((@"%s [%@:%d] " text), __PRETTY_FUNCTION__,
    [@__FILE__ lastPathComponent], __LINE__, ##__VA_ARGS__)
```

Now when you use NSLog, the debugging console will show the names of the class and the method that the line is in, as well as the file name and line number of the logging statement:

```
NSLog(@"Yes");
```

logs:

```
2013-11-08 16:14:46.922 Logging[66492:70b] -[AppDelegate
    application:didFinishLaunchingWithOptions:] [AppDelegate.m:20] Yes
```

Discussion

The compiler provides several "magic" variables that change based on where they're used in your code.

For example, the LINE variable always contains the current line number in the file that's currently being compiled, and the FILE variable contains the full path to the source code file that's being compiled. The PRETTY_FUNCTION variable contains a nicely formatted version of the name of the current function, and includes information like the class that the method belongs to and whether it's an instance method or a class method.

By defining a macro that replaces the NSLog method with one that adds more information, you can make all the existing NSLog calls in your project include a lot more information.

In the solution given in this recipe, we've done a little bit of extra coding to make the logs easier to read. We mentioned that the FILE variable contains the full path to the file that's being compiled, but that's often way too long—most of the time, you just want the filename. To get just the filename, you can turn the FILE variable into an NSString, and then send that string to the lastPathComponent method, which returns the last part of the path.

14.8. Creating Breakpoints That Use Speech

Problem

You want to receive audio notifications when something happens in your game.

Solution

Add a spoken breakpoint that doesn't stop the game:

1. Add a breakpoint where you want a notification to happen.
2. Right-click the breakpoint, and choose Edit Breakpoint.
3. Turn on "Automatically continue after evaluating."
4. Click Add Action.
5. Change the action type from Debugger Command to Log Message.
6. Type the text you want to speak.
7. Click Speak Message.

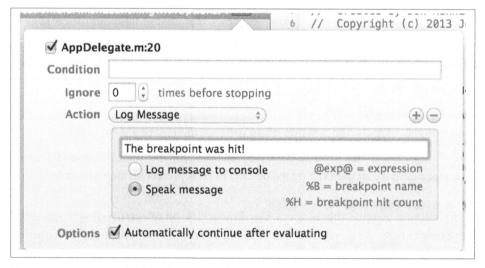

Figure 14-7. Making the breakpoint speak

When the breakpoint is hit, Xcode will speak the log message.

Discussion

Using spoken breakpoints is a really useful way to get notifications on what the game's doing without having to switch away from the game. Breakpoints are spoken by your computer, not by the device, which means that they won't interfere with your game's audio (don't forget to unmute your computer's speakers).

Index

We'd like to hear your suggestions for improving our indexes. Send email to index@oreilly.com.

crashes, tracking down, 351
CrazyBump, 275
CREATE TABLE statement, 137
cross-fade transition, creating, 161
cross-fading between tracks, 112
current time, 8
    NSDate object, 14

D

Dafont, 160
data storage, 125–144
    deciding whether to use files or a database, 136
    game design and, 144
    loading structured information, 134
    managing collection of assets, 139
    saving state of your game, 125
    storing high scores locally, 128
    using iCloud key/value store, 132
    using iCloud to save games, 129
    using NSUserDefaults, 142
    using SQLite, 137
database, using for data storage, 136
    SQLite, 137
dataWithContentsOfFile:options:error:, 350
dealloc method, 246
    deleting shaders and shader program when Material obect is freed, 270
debugging, 345
    fixing exceptions, 352
    fixing memory presure issues, 352
    logging additional information, 356
    tracking down a crash, 351
    using spoken breakpoints, 358
    working with watchpoints, 355
decoding, 127
degrees, converting to and from radians, 88
delta, 149
delta times, calculating, 7, 209
density, 199
dependencies, adding to operations, 27
depth buffers, 237
destinationViewController, 53
device orientation, 101
    using to control gravity, 211
devices, syncing documents and information across, 131
diffuse map texture, 276
direction pads, information about, 331

dismissViewControllerAnimated:completion: method, 121
dispatch groups, 28
dispatch queues, 21
    priorities of background queues, 29
dispatch sources, 25
dispatch_after function, 21
dispatch_group_create function, 29
dispatch_queue_t, 25
dispatch_resume function, 26
dispatch_source_t, 25
dispatch_time_t, 21, 114
distanceFromLocation: method, 95
dot product, 151
DownUpGestureRecognizer (example), 80–83
drag gestures, 75
drag: (recipe) method, 75
dragging objects around the screen, 212
draw calls, batching, 255
duration property, CADisplayLink, 8
dynamic bodies, 194
dynamic property, SKPhysicsBody, 194

E

EAGLContext, 224
    setCurrentContext method, 237
easing equations, 254
edge chains, 200
edge colliders, 193, 199
    shapes of, 200
edge loops, 200
effects (GLKit), 230
Emitter editor, 171
encodeObject:forKey: method, 127
encodeWithCoder: method, 125, 126
encoding methods, NSCoder, 126
endGeneratingPlaybackNotifications method, 118
exceptions, 351
    fixing, 352
exit segues, 53
explosion offset, 210
explosions, creating, 209
extended game controllers, 327
extendedGamepad property, GCController, 330

F

Facebook, allowing game players to post to, 325

fading in and fading out, AVAudioPlayer, 113
Failed state, UIGestureRecognizer, 83
far clipping plane, 222
field of view, 222
files, using for data storage, 136
fill color, 167
filteredArrayUsingPredicate method, 27
first responder, 85
fixed joints, 207
folder reference, 141
folders, asset collection in, 139
font families, 159
fonts
    custom, including in your game, 160
    determining availability for your game, 159
    for text sprites, 158
forces
    applyiing to objects, 208
    defined, 192
    working with, 207
foreground, application in, 10
fragment shaders, 261, 277
    creating, 262
    creating for normal mapping, 275
    for specular highlights, 278
    for toon shading, 280
    using to texture objects, 273
    writing to use in texturing objects, 271
frame rate, improving, 345
frames per second (fps), 154
frames, time between, 8
free function, 247
friction, 192

G

Game Center, 129, 301–304
    authenticating the player, 304
    capabilities of, 301
    getting player profile on sandbox, 303
    making leaderboards and challenges with, 306
    selecting best player to act as server, 312
    sending and receiving data from other players, 315
    turn-based games, 323
    using to find people to play with, 310
game controllers, 327
    connecting and disconnecting, notification of, 329

detecting, 329
    determining if standard or extended gamepad, 330
    getting input from, 331
    iOS games playable without, 327
    player connecting to while in the game, 330
GameKit, making turn-based gameplay work, 321
GameObject class, 2, 4
    subclassing, 3
gamepad property, GCController, 330
GCController, 329
GCControllerAxisInput, 332
GCControllerButtonInput, 332
GCControllerDidConnectNotification, 329
GCControllerDidDisconnectNotification, 329
GCControllerDirectionPad classes, 331
GCD (Grand Central Dispatch), 21
    scheduling volume changes in AVAudio-Player, 114
GCGameController, 329
geocoding, 99
    reverse geocoding, 100
gesture recognizers, 74
gestures, 73
    (see also input)
    custom, creating, 79–83
    giving direct control over games, 104
GKGameCenterViewController, 310
GKLeaderboard, 309
GKLocalPlayer, 304
    getting information about logged-in player, 305
    loadFriendsWithCompletionHandler: method, 305
    loadPlayersForIdentifiers:withCompletion-Handler: method, 305
GKLocalPlayerListener, 322
GKMatch
    changes in player's connection state, 320
    receiving data from, 315
    sendData:toPlayers:withDataMode:error: method, 315
GKMatchmakerViewController, 311
GKMatchRequest, 310
    playerGroup property, 311
    turn-based games, 321
GKPlayer, 305
GKScore, 308

NSFileManager, 110, 129
    getting ubiquityIdentityToken from, 132
NSJSONSerialization, 134
    isValidJSONObject method, 135
NSKeyedArchiver, 126
NSKeyedUnarchiver, 126
    decoding methods, 127
NSLog, 357
NSMetadataQuery, 130
    results showing conflicts in file versions, 131
    stopQuery method, 131
NSMetadataUbiquitousItemHasUnresolved-
    ConflictsKey, 131
NSMutableDictionary, 142
NSMutableSet object, 6
NSNotificationCenter, 9
NSObject, blocks stored as properties in, 22
NSOperationQueue, 19, 88
    mainQueue method, 20
    wrapper around GCD features, 21
NSPredicate, 28
NSSet, 73
NSString, as block parameter, 16
NSTimeInterval, 14
NSTimer, 10
    repeats, 11
    timeInterval, 11
NSUbiquitousKeyValueStore, 132
NSURL, 108, 129
NSUserDefaults, 142
    dictionary of keys and values to use, 143
    kinds of objects stored in, 142
    synchronize method, 142
    users modifying data in, 143

O

Objective-C
    blocks, 15
    creating a new subclass, 43
objects
    blocks referencing, 17
    interpolating object state, 318
    provided to encodeObject:forKey:, 127
    removing from the game, 318
    retain cycles, 23
    storing blocks in, 22
    synchronizing on the network, 317
OpenGL
    camera, 240

displaying a texture on a surface, 233
drawing a 3D cube with texture on its faces,
    235–238
drawing a square on screen using, 225–232
drawing fewer object, 348
OpenGL ES API, 219, 224
OpenType (.otf font files), 160
operation queues, 19
    running a block on at a future time, 21
    use by motion manager, 88
orientation, 101
origin, 148
orthographic projection transform matrix, 221
orthographic projection, creating, 222
outlets, 49

P

Painter's Algorithm, 238
pan gesture recognizers, 75
parent object, 252
particle effects, 171
pathForResource:ofType: method, NSBundle,
    234
paths, 167, 196
    calculating path for object to take, 291
    from object to cover points, 290
    making objects follow a path, 285
    using to create edge collider shapes, 200
pauseSpeakingAtBoundary: method, 115
pausing, 10
    handler for game controller's pause button,
    332
    parts of game paused while other parts run,
    13
peer IDs, 313
peer-to-peer matches, 312
performance, 345
    dealing with low-memory issues, 349
    improving frame rate, 345
    making levels load quickly, 348
    using spoken breakpoints, 358
    working with compressed textures, 352
performSegueWithIdentifier:sender: method, 52
perspective and orthographic matrices, creating,
    223
perspective projection transform matrix, 221
physics, 191–217
    adding thrusters to objects, 208
    adding to sprites, 193

Sprite Kit, 153
   theming with UIAppearance, 65
   UIWindow, 334
   using constraints to position, 53
viewWillAppear: method, 49
   animated image, 61
viewWillDisappear: method, 49
visual effects
   creating smoke, fire, and other particle ef-
     fects, 171
   using image effects on sprites, 169

W

watchpoints, 355
Wavefront OBJ, 247
weak references, 17, 24
weight, 198
wireless controllers, discovering and connecting
   to, 330

world, 192, 201
world space, 259

X

x coordinate, 148
Xcode
   Emitter editor, 171
   enabling Game Center, 302
   folder reference, 141
   Texture Atlas Generation, 166
XCTestAssertions, 31
XCTestCase, 30

Y

y coordinate, 148
yaw, 87, 90

About the Authors

Jon Manning is a Core Animation demigod, and frequently finds himself gesticulating wildly in front of classes full of eager to learn iOS developers. Jon used to be the world's biggest Horse ebooks (*https://twitter.com/Horse_ebooks*) fan, but has since come to accept their betrayal. He will soon have a PhD, and can be found on Twitter as @desplesda (*https://twitter.com/desplesda*).

Paris Buttfield-Addison has coded for everything from 6502 assembly, to Qt, to iOS, and still thinks digital watches are a pretty neat idea. Paris speaks constantly at conferences and enjoys the company of greyhounds. He too will soon have a PhD. He can be found on Twitter as @parisba (*http://twitter.com/parisba*).

Jon Manning and Paris Buttfield-Addison are both the cofounders of Secret Lab, an independent game development studio based in Hobart, Tasmania, Australia. Through Secret Lab, they've worked on award-winning apps of all sorts, ranging from iPad games for children, to instant messaging clients, to math games about frogs. Together they've written numerous books on game development, iOS software development, and Mac software development. Secret Lab can be found online (*http://www.secretlab.com.au*) and on Twitter at @thesecretlab (*http://www.twitter.com/thesecretlab*).

Colophon

The animal on the cover of *iOS Game Development Cookbook* is a queen triggerfish (*Balistes vetula*), a reef-dwelling triggerfish from the Atlantic Ocean. They can reach up to 24 in (60 cm), though on average, they measure about half that measurement. Typically, the queen triggerfish is blue, purple, turquoise, and green with a yellow throat, with light blue lines on its head and fins. When stressed, the triggerfish can change color to match its surroundings.

Queen triggerfish can be found at depths of 9.8–98.4 ft (3–30 m) around coral or rocky reefs ranging from Canada to southern Brazil in the West Atlantic; they've also been found as deep as 902 ft (275 m) and in areas with sand or seagrass. In the East Atlantic, queen triggerfish can be found at Cape Verde, Azores, Ascension, and Angola. Commonly found along the shores of Florida, the Bahamas, and the Caribbean, the queen triggerfish preys on invertebrates such as sea urchins.

The queen triggerfish is one of the largest and most aggressive of the triggerfish, and therefore isn't a good choice for marine aquariums. An ideal aquarium for this species is a 500 gallon aquarium, with food sources of shrimp, squid, clams, octopus, scallops, and crab.

The cover image is from origin unknown. The cover fonts are URW Typewriter and Guardian Sans. The text font is Adobe Minion Pro; the heading font is Adobe Myriad Condensed; and the code font is Dalton Maag's Ubuntu Mono.

Have it your way.

Get even more for your money.

Join the O'Reilly Community, and register the O'Reilly books you own. It's free, and you'll get:

- $4.99 ebook upgrade offer
- 40% upgrade offer on O'Reilly print books
- Membership discounts on books and events
- Free lifetime updates to ebooks and videos
- Multiple ebook formats, DRM FREE
- Participation in the O'Reilly community
- Newsletters
- Account management
- 100% Satisfaction Guarantee

Signing up is easy:

1. Go to: oreilly.com/go/register
2. Create an O'Reilly login.
3. Provide your address.
4. Register your books.

Note: English-language books only

To order books online:
oreilly.com/store

For questions about products or an order:
orders@oreilly.com

To sign up to get topic-specific email announcements and/or news about upcoming books, conferences, special offers, and new technologies:
elists@oreilly.com

For technical questions about book content:
booktech@oreilly.com

To submit new book proposals to our editors:
proposals@oreilly.com

O'Reilly books are available in multiple DRM-free ebook formats. For more information:
oreilly.com/ebooks

Spreading the knowledge of innovators   oreilly.com

CPSIA information can be obtained at www.ICGtesting.com
Printed in the USA
BVOW10s0352160414

350697BV00001B/1/P

9 781449 368760